Study Guide

for

Fabes and Martin
Exploring Child Development
Transactions and Transformations

prepared by

Denise Ann Bodman
Arizona State University

Allyn and Bacon
Boston   London   Toronto   Sydney   Tokyo   Singapore

Copyright © 2000 by Allyn & Bacon
A Pearson Education Company
160 Gould Street
Needham Heights, Massachusetts 02494-2130

Internet: www.abacon.com

All rights reserved. No part of the material protected by this copyright notice
may be reproduced or utilized in any form or by any means, electronic or
mechanical, including photocopying, recording, or by any information
storage and retrieval system, without the written permission of the copyright owner.

ISBN 0-205-30771-X

Printed in the United States of America

10 9 8 7 6 5 4 3 2 1   03 02 01 00 99

TABLE OF CONTENTS

Preface v

How to Pass An Exam vii

Chapter 1 Introduction to the Study of Children's Development 1

Chapter 2 Understanding Development 13

Chapter 3 Genetics and Prenatal Development 33

Chapter 4 Birth and Neonatal Development 52

Chapter 5 Physical and Cognitive Development in Infancy and Toddlerhood 75

Chapter 6 Social and Emotional Development in Infancy and Toddlerhood 96

Chapter 7 Physical, Cognitive, and Language Development in Early Childhood 116

Chapter 8 Social and Emotional Development in Early Childhood 134

Chapter 9 Physical, Cognitive, and Language Development in Late Childhood 157

Chapter 10 Social and Emotional Development in Late Childhood 179

Chapter 11 Social and Emotional Development in Early Adolescence 198

Chapter 12 Social and Emotional Development in Early Adolescence 212

Chapter 13 Physical and Cognitive Development in Late Adolescence 231

Chapter 14 Social and Emotional Development in Late Adolescence 247

Appendix 1: Crossword Puzzles 265

Appendix 2: Careers in Child Development 295

Preface

My daughter once wrote an essay on the many uses of books. She stated that a book could be used as a booster seat, flower press, doorstop, and lap tray. She also wrote that the cover of a book makes a fine straight edge when a ruler is lacking, and the pages can be used for doodling, paper mache, and stuffing a pinata (for which she recommended *A Tale of Two Cities*). For amusement, she said that books could be set up around the room like dominoes and then knocked over. Finally, she wrote, "I have also heard that some people even read books. I guess that is a good use for them, too!" What an idea!

As a senior lecturer and advisor, I am amazed by the number of students who have come to my office at the end of the semester wondering what they can do to improve their flagging grade. Usually, these students admit that they have not given their best efforts. Perhaps they did not attend class, or perhaps they had not read the book (I have even had students who didn't buy the book until they were failing). I have also found that many students have tried hard, but for some reason, were not making the grade. These students have, indeed, spent as much (if not more) time studying, but they had not yet developed the study skills of the "A" student. They had not learned how to pick out the information most teachers find important, how to commit that information to memory, or how to effectively take an exam. When these students finally do acquire these skills, it is frequently in their last few semesters, when they must work twice as hard to bring up their lower GPAs.

This study guide is designed to help **all** students pick out the important concepts of the text and gain a deeper understanding and appreciation for that information. It is designed to go beyond simple rote memorization of facts and into application of knowledge learned. It is structured to help students create links of newly learned material with life experience. These are skills that will help you not only in this class but in other classes as well.

Sprinkled throughout the study guide are helpful tips from my former students who want to share with you their success in college. These students have already charted the way - why not follow them and heed their advice? Also sprinkled throughout the study guide are interesting facts, humorous anecdotes, and occasional jokes just to keep things interesting. I certainly do <u>not</u> agree with Aristotle when he wrote, "Education ought not to be made a means of amusement. Young people are not playing when they are learning because all learning is painful" (although some of you may agree with the "all learning is painful" part).

To use this study guide effectively, you should read each chapter in *Exploring Child Development* as you would a good book, highlighting important information and making notes in the text margin. After you have read the chapter, complete the items in this study guide, including the study questions. Completing the items will take less time than you think. When it's test time, use your study guide to review. I caution you against waiting until the night before the exam, reading the chapter summaries, and then looking up the answers to the sample test questions in the study guide. If you do this, you will probably bomb the test. To understand the subtleties of child development, you must read the entire chapter and then use the study guide to actually *guide your studying*.

I believe that the information you learn from *Exploring Child Development: Transactions and Transformations* will have more application in your life than most books. Why? One reason is that we were all children once and can draw on our own experiences growing up. Another reason is that if you don't have children now, you are likely to have children in the not-so-distant future. And even if you don't raise children of your own, most of you will have family members or colleagues who do. Don't be surprised when they seek advice or information from you once they learn you're taking this course! Many students have found that they want to keep their textbook as a reference book for the future.

Now, back to my daughter's advice. You paid for these books…read them! I guarantee putting the book under your pillow at night will not transfer information into your brain through osmosis. You have got to put in the effort, and remind yourself that learning is an active process. The publishers at Allyn and Bacon and I hope this study guide will help you reach your academic potential.

Acknowledgements

If you find particular aspects of this study guide helpful (or tedious), please let me know. I am always looking for a way to build a better mousetrap, and your ideas could end up in a "new and improved" version of a study guide. I thank you in advance. I also want to thank all my students, past and present, who have motivated me to become a better teacher. They have also provided me with ideas, as well as several of the humorous stories and other materials in the study guide. Material for "How to Pass an Exam" was gleaned from personal experience, as well as numerous sources on the Internet, for which I am grateful. Thanks go to Richard Fabes and Carol Martin, who allowed me the opportunity to write this study guide as a companion to their excellent text, and to Jodi Devine, whose editorial guidance was certainly "divine." And, of course, special thanks go to my husband, Rudy, and my children, Bethany and Christopher. When my children looked through this study guide, they learned that their lives are an open book (literally!). Enjoy.

How to Pass an Exam

Before the Test
1. Attend class and read the text.
2. Organize your studying. How much time will you need for this class? Where can you study without distractions? Can you find a study group to work with?
3. Test yourself. When studying, remember the SQ3R method: Survey (get an overall picture of what you're going to study); Question (ask yourself questions as you read and study); Read (pay close attention to highlighted words and summarizing statements); Recite (recall information out loud and try to make that information meaningful to you); Review.
4. Live healthy! Eat your vegetables, get plenty of rest, and keep a positive attitude.
5. Don't cram or pull an all-nighter (see #4 above). It won't work.
6. Put everything you will need together in one place, including pencils, test booklets, pens, and paper, ready to go for the next day.

At the Test
1. Arrive to the test setting ON TIME and prepared. Avoid talking to other students and comparing last minute notes. Their nervousness can be contagious.
2. Sit in an area where there are the fewest distractions, and don't focus on anything other than the test.
3. Before starting the exam, take three deep breaths and exhale slowly. Remember, some tension is good and works in your favor. Too much tension is counterproductive.
4. Read and/or listen to the test instructions.
5. Look over the entire exam and make a mental note as to the time, questions that may require extra time, type of questions, worth of questions, etc.
6. Begin the exam.

Multiple Choice
- Read the entire question and all of the answers. Don't choose "a" without reading "b" ,"c", and "d."
- Cover the answer portion of a question, read the question, and then see if you can recall the answer before looking at the alternatives.
- When choosing an answer, write "true" or "false" next to each alternative (if you are allowed to write on the exam).
- Circle key words in the question, such as NOT or TRUE (if you are allowed to write on the exam).
- If a question or answer seems ambiguous, ask the instructor or test proctor for clarification.
- Watch out for qualifying words, such as "always" or "never" (which are usually incorrect statements) and "sometimes" or "often" (which are usually correct statements).
- Answer the easiest questions first, then go back and answer the harder questions.
- If you're unsure about a question, eliminate the answers you know are wrong, then choose what you think is the best answer.
- If you are totally clueless, remember: (a) "b" and "c" are more likely to be the answer than "a" or "d"; (b) "All of the above" is more likely to be the answer; (c) extra long answers with a lot of jargon tend to be decoys; and (d) pay attention to grammar and tense, choosing the answer that is grammatically consistent.
- DO NOT GO BACK AND CHANGE YOUR ANSWERS, unless you KNOW that you marked the wrong answer.

Essay
- Write your answer VERY legibly.
- Read the question carefully, paying attention to words such as "describe," "compare," and "explain." Jot down some notes, then organize your answer. Start with a thesis statement that generally answers the question, with points you will discuss in detail. Write a concluding sentence that sums up the answer.
- Leave extra room in case you have time and want to add to your answer
- Allow time to proofread and then proofread.
- Number the parts of the question so the instructor knows exactly what you are answering.

After the Test
1. Don't simply look at your score. Figure out what you did wrong and what can you do better.
2. Did you miss most questions from the lectures? Compare your notes with a classmate's; you may find that you need to improve your note-taking skills.
3. Did you miss more questions from your text? Remember to read the entire chapter, ask yourself questions as you read, and use available study guides to study from.
4. Did you tend to choose incorrect answers that seemed logical? A test is supposed to test you. This means you must have the knowledge of the subject and not simply rely on what seems logical.
5. Did you choose an answer that was "correct" but correct for another question? Make sure you read the question. Often students will overlook the "NOT" in a test item asking, "Which of the following is NOT true?"
6. Did you have problems applying facts? Being able to apply what you learn is a skill that takes practice. When reading or studying your notes, ask yourself, "What does this mean?"
7. Did you read into the question? Sometimes questions are so straightforward, you may think, "This is too easy…my answer must be wrong."

REMEMBER: NO T-I-P CAN SUBSTITUTE FOR R-A-P…Read – Attend Class – Prepare for the exam!

Chapter 1
Introduction to the Study of Children's Development

My mother taught me LOGIC...
"If you fall off that swing and break your neck, you can't go to the store with me!"
                                                              -Things My Mother Taught Me

Objectives
When you have completed this chapter, you will be able to
- state 3 developmental domains;
- identify 2 major influences on child development;
- discuss the nature-nurture controversy and give examples of biological/genetic influences and environmental influences, as well as interactions of these influences;
- explain how twin studies are used to determine genetic and environmental influences;
- define continuity and discontinuity and give an example of each;
- compare and contrast critical periods and sensitive periods;
- discuss the historical roots of the study of child development, including the influence of Plato, John Locke, Jean-Jacques Rousseau, Charles Darwin, and G. Stanley Hall;
- identify changes that have occurred in contemporary American life that influence the study of child development;
- explain the transactional perspective; and
- define the key terms and concepts listed on page 27 of your text.

☑ Study Check List

☐ Read Chapter 1 Introduction to the Study of Children's Development

☐ Re-read the Chapter 1 Summary to refresh your memory.

☐ Read the Chapter 1 Objectives listed above.

☐ Complete the following items:

What is Child Development? (pp. 5 - 6)

Three developmental domains focused on in this text are:
(a) _____; (b) _____;
and (c) _____ (1).

2 Study Guide for Exploring Child Development

_____(2) involves growth and change in a person's body and body functions.

_____(3) involves mental processes used to process information, become aware, solve problems, and gain knowledge.

_____(4) involves processes related to one's interactions with others and includes the study of relationships.

Match the specific example to the developmental domain:

Language development ____
(5)
Growth spurt in adolescence ____
(6)
Development of empathy ____
(7)
Memory strategies ____
(8)
Learning to walk ____
(9)

a. Physical Development

b. Cognitive Development

c. Social-emotional Development

What are Some Critical Issues in the Study of Child Development? (pp. 6 - 13)

Developmental changes happen because of a variety of influences. Some development changes mainly result from a series of preprogrammed transformations in the form, structure, or function of an individual. These changes are referred to as ma_____(10). Other developmental changes mainly are influenced by the en_____(11). These influences can begin even before a child is _____(12). The environment can also influence behavior through le_____(13). The process that helps children learn to become members of a social group, family, or community is referred to as so_____(14). When children are well socialized, they have adopted the values, beliefs, customs, and expectations of their group or society.

1 Minute Quiz

1. Name 3 domains of development.

   a._____

   b._____

   c._____

2. How are maturational changes different from environmental changes?

   _____

   _____

   _____

Like other scientific disciplines, child developmentalists have debated several issues. One issue is whether development is mostly influenced by biological and genetic factors or whether it is mostly influenced by the environment. This debate is often referred to as the _____ _____(15). Other terms used in this controversy are maturation vs. environment or inborn vs. learned.

⇒ **MEMORY JOG:** Mother <u>Nature</u> (i.e., inborn) vs. Mother's <u>Nurture</u> (i.e., learned)

Some people believe that the Wild Boy of Averyon was severely intellectually and socially retarded because he was born with a genetic defect, such as autism. These people are likely to fall on the **nature/nurture** *(circle one)* (16) side of the debate. Other people believe the Wild Boy of Averyon was severely intellectually and socially retarded because he did not have access to adults who could teach him. These people are likely to fall on the **nature/nurture** *(circle one)* (17) side of the debate.

4 Study Guide for Exploring Child Development

Identify whether the following characteristics are a result of mostly nature, mostly nurture, or an interaction between the two:

blue eyes _____ (18)

naturally curly hair _____ (19)

yellowed teeth due to taking antibiotics _____ (20)

athletic skill _____ (21)

In the study of twins, MZ stands for _____(22). This means that the twins are _____(23). DZ stands for _____(24). This means that the twins are _____(25). Scientists use twins to study the influence of genetics and environment. George and Michael are monozygotic or identical twins who are both very "high strung." Sam and Dan are dizygotic or fraternal twins. Sam is laid back and Dan is high strung. If scientists found that monozygotic twins were more similar in personality than dizygotic twins, they are likely to conclude that personality is strongly influenced by **genes/environment** *(circle one)* (26).

⇒ **MEMORY JOG** - "mono" means one and "zygotic" means fertilized egg cell
"di" means two and "zygotic" means fertilized egg cells.

Another major controversy in child development is whether development occurs smoothly and gradually or in a series of steps and stages. This controversy is co_____ vs. dis_____(27).

Ana studies how children learn language. She counts words that children learn and can tell you the average vocabulary of a 1-year-old, a 2-year-old, and a 3-year-old. She is likely to view development of language as **continuous/discontinuous** *(circle one)* (28). Pete also studies how children learn language.

He notes that children go through several stages of language development, from cooing to babbling to speaking words. Pete is likely to view the development of language as **continuous/ discontinuous** *(circle one)* (29).

Finally, developmentalists are concerned with whether there are critical periods for development of certain behaviors or abilities. A critical period is a time period when an organism MUST be stimulated to learn a certain behavior; if the time period passes without stimulation, then the organism will never be able to learn that behavior. The strongest evidence for critical periods in children's development is in the area of _____(30).

A sensitive period is different from a critical period. A sensitive period is _____
_____
_____(31).
In other words, just because the sensitive period has passed does not mean that the organism cannot still learn the behavior. It may be more difficult or the behavior may not be learned as well, but the behavior is not completely lost.

---

1 Minute Quiz

1. **Believing development is mostly influenced by biology refers to** _____.

2. **Believing development occurs in stages refers to** _____.

3. **Believing an organism must be stimulated at a certain time or will never acquire the behavior refers to** _____.

6 Study Guide for Exploring Child Development

What are Some Historical Roots of the Study of Child Development? (pp. 13 - 16)

Match the following:

____Plato (32)

____Locke (33)

____Rousseau (34)

____Darwin (35)

____Hall (36)

1. Child's mind is a blank slate (tabula rasa)
2. Human behavior and development evolves slowly
3. Believed children should be separated from parents and reared by the state
4. Pioneered scientific procedures to study children; first to study adolescents
5. Grandfather of permissive parenting

What Changes In Contemporary American Life Influence the Study of Child Development? (pp. 16 - 23)

Use these words to complete the following paragraphs:

race; blended; multiracial; single-parent; similar; ethnicity; extended; particular group; nuclear

The "traditional" family of biological mother, father, and child is called the _____(37) family. However, the fastest growing family type in the United States today is the _____ _____ (38) family. Widowed or divorced people who remarry form _____ (39) families; and families that include additional relatives, such as grandmothers, aunts, or cousins are _____(40) families.

Aside from changing family structures, researchers are aware of other family diversity, including racial and ethnic diversity, as well as diversity in sexual orientation. _____(41) refers to a group whose members share a genetic heritage. _____(42) refers to a group whose members share a common cultural heritage and a sense of belonging. It is very difficult to classify people by _____(43), especially because many people are _____(44), being more than one race. Researchers today have only begun to recognize the diversity that exists in our society. Although many developmental processes probably

Chapter 1 Introduction 7

emerge in a _____(45) fashion regardless of race/ethnicity/sexual orientation, researchers still must consider factors and situations that may be unique to a _____(46).

What is the Conceptual Basis for this Book? (pp. 23 - 26)

Use these words to complete the following paragraph:

characteristics	dynamic	interdependent
divergent	relate	environment
diversity	unique	

The transactional model emphasizes the _____(47) nature of development and the _____(48) aspects of the transactions between the child and the child's environment. The impact of different environments depends on the _____(49) characteristics of the child. Some are vulnerable, others are not. There is considerable _____(50) of individual _____(51) and _____(52) that influence development and _____(53) to one another. Thus, the transactional perspective emphasizes the diverse and _____(54) nature of development.

---

1 Minute Quiz

1. This philosopher believed that children are innately good. _____

2. This scholar was first to study adolescence. _____

3. A family that includes mother, father, grandmother, and children is referred to as _____.

4. The authors of your text follow a _____ model of development.

8 Study Guide for Exploring Child Development

☐ Complete "Chapter 1 – Introduction" crossword puzzle in Appendix 1 – Crossword Puzzles.

☐ Go to the beginning of this chapter, and on a separate sheet of paper, write out the answers to the lesson objectives.

> **SAGE Advice**
>
> "Get a study partner and try to teach concepts to them - you always learn (understand) better when you try to teach it to someone else."

STUDY QUESTIONS

Multiple Choice (The following questions are identified as being "A," *applied questions* that require the application of knowledge learned or "F," *factual questions* that rely on the recall of facts).

1. Piaget is interested in how children acquire knowledge. His developmental domain of study is: (p. 5; A)
    a. physical.   b. social-emotional.   c. cognitive.   d. psychometric.

2. Maturation refers to: (p. 6; F)
    a. changes that occur largely from the unfolding of one's genetic code.
    b. changes that occur with age.
    c. changes that are influenced by the environment.
    d. changes that are the result of appropriate learning and socialization.

3. The nature side of the nature vs. nurture debate: (p. 7; F)
    a. emphasizes the role of biological/genetic factors.
    b. emphasizes the role of the environment.
    c. has received more support for its role in development than nurture.
    d. has received less support for its role in development than nurture.

4. The cases of "wild children" (such as the Wild Boy of Averyon) provide: (p. 7-8; F)
    a. limited evidence about the roles of nature and nurture in influencing development.
    b. conclusive evidence about the role of nature in influencing development.
    c. conclusive evidence about the role of nurture in influencing development.
    d. no evidence of anything, but they make really great movies!

5. Monozygotic (MZ) twins are: (p. 10; F)
   a. called identical twins.
   b. called fraternal twins.
   c. genetically different.
   d. not used in research as often as DZ twins.

6. If a characteristic has a strong genetic component, then: (p. 10; F)
   a. DZ twins would be more alike than MZ twins.
   b. MZ twins would be more alike than DZ twins.
   c. MZ twins would be no more likely than DZ twins to have that characteristic.
   d. it is impossible to tell if MZ twins or DZ twins would be more likely to have that characteristic.

7. Mary and Sherry are monozygotic twins. They are both 5'3" tall. Karen and Sharon are dizygotic twins. Karen is 5'2" tall and Sharon is 5'6" tall. The differences in height are probably because: (pp. 10-11; A)
   a. height is largely genetically determined.
   b. Mary and Sherry probably had more similar diets when they were growing, compared to Karen and Sharon.
   c. Karen probably had a metabolic disorder or illness resulting in her shorter height, because DZ twins are more likely to have similar heights than MZ twins.
   d. Sharon always wanted to be a model so her wishful thinking probably impacted her physical growth.

8. Shared environments appear to play a greater role in the development of: (p. 10; A)
   a. personality.   b. height.   c. body type.   d. intelligence.

9. Jean Piaget identified 4 stages of mental development in children (sensorimotor, preoperational, concrete operational, and formal operational). Thus, Piaget's view of cognitive development is: (p. 11; A)
   a. continuous.
   b. discontinuous.
   c. primarily affected by nature.
   d. primarily affected by nurture.

10. If a duckling does not see its mother when it first hatches and imprints on another moving object, it will never follow its mother in a normal manner. This is because, for ducks, the period immediately following hatching is: (p. 12; A)
    a. a critical period.
    b. a sensitive period.
    c. the functional exposure period.
    d. reflexive.

11. The idea that a child's mind is like a blank slate (tabula rasa) is attributed to: (p. 14; F)
    a. Plato.   b. Hall.   c. Rousseau.   d. Locke.

12. Jamal and Teri have a 3-year-old child that they let get away with everything. They believe that children are basically good and should be allowed to grow and develop with little outside pressure from them (they don't want to hurt the child's self-esteem). Jamal and Teri's ideas are very similar to: (p. 15; A)
    a. Plato.   b. Hall.   c. Rousseau.   d. Locke.

10 Study Guide for Exploring Child Development

13. G. Stanley Hall: (pp. 15-16; F)
    a. was the first scientist to focus on adolescent development.
    b. pioneered the application of scientific procedures to the study of child development.
    c. wrote one of the first developmental textbooks.
    d. All of the above.

14. Erika lives with her half-brother, step-sister, step-mother, and biological father. This type of family structure is known as a/n: (p. 16; A)
    a. nuclear family.   b. blended family.   c. extended family.   d. dysfunctional family.

15. The fastest growing family type in the United States in recent years is the: (p. 16; F)
    a. nuclear family.   b. blended family.   c. single parent family   d. extended family.

16. The authors of your textbook view development from a/n: (p. 23; F)
    a. nature perspective.   c. transactional perspective.
    b. nurture perspective.   d. humanistic perspective.

17. Which of the following words does NOT apply to the transactional perspective? (pp. 23-27; A)
    a. dynamic   b. complex   c. independent   d. divergent

True/False Questions (If a statement is FALSE, correct it).

1. Cognitive development involves processes related to one's interactions with others and includes the study of relationships, emotions, personality, and moral development. (p. 5) True/False.

2. Children learn values, beliefs, customs and expectations of their society through a process called socialization. (p. 6) True/False.

3. The nurture side of the nature/nurture debate emphasizes the role of biological or genetic factors. (p. 7) True/False.

4. Dizygotic twins can be as similar genetically as monozygotic twins. (p. 10) True/False.

5. Many human characteristics are the result of a complex interaction of genetic and environmental forces. (p. 10-11) True/False.

6. Scientists who focus on the acquisition of qualitatively new patterns of behavior view development as discontinuous. (p. 11) True/False.

7. Development in human children (especially infants) is marked by a number of critical periods for acquiring certain behaviors, such as bonding. (p. 12) True/False.

8. The science of child development is centuries old. (p. 13) True/False.

9. Today's ideas about children are rooted in relatively recent philosophies. (p. 13-16) True/False.

10. Charles Darwin has had a large impact on the study of child development. (p. 15) True/False.

11. More U.S. children today live in traditional nuclear families than in single-parent or blended families combined. (p. 16) True/False.

12. Race primarily refers to a group whose members share a common cultural heritage and a sense of belonging. (p. 21) True/False.

13. Research on children from gay or lesbian homes suggests that they are no different from children reared by heterosexual parents. (p. 23) True/False.

14. The impact of different environments often depends on the unique characteristics of the child. (p. 25) True/False.

15. Researchers tend not to observe, interpret, and respond to developmental processes according to their own values and goals. (p. 25-26) True/False.

☐ **REWARD YOURSELF! Go for a walk, call a friend, or eat a piece of chocolate!**

12 Study Guide for Exploring Child Development

ANSWERS - Chapter 1 Introduction to the Study of Children's Development

What is Child Development? (pp. 5-6)
(1) Physical, cognitive, and social-emotional; (2) physical; (3) cognitive; (4) social-emotional; (5) b; (6) a; (7) c; (8) b; (9) a

What are Some Critical Issues in the Study of Child Development? (pp. 6 - 13)
(10) maturation; (11) environment; (12) born; (13) learning; (14) socialization
1 Minute Quiz: 1. physical; cognitive; social-emotional
              2. Maturational changes are biological and environmental changes are influenced by the environment.

(15) nature vs nurture; (16) nature; (17) nurture; (18) blue eyes – nature; (19) naturally curly hair –nature; (20) yellowed teeth due to taking antibiotics – nurture; (21) athletic skill - interaction of nature (height, flexibility; spatial orientation) and nurture (practice; coaches)
(22) monozygotic twins; (23) identical; (24) dizygotic twins; (25) fraternal; (26) genes
(27) continuity vs discontinuity; (28) continuous; (29) discontinuous; (30) language development; (31) a time that is optimal for development of certain functions, but is not necessary
1 Minute Quiz: 1. Nature   2. Discontinuity   3. A critical period

What are the Historical Roots of the Study of Child Development? (pp. 13-16)
(32) 3; (33) 1; (34) 5; (35) 2; (36) 4

What Changes in Contemporary American Life Influence the Study of Child Development? (pp. 16-23)
(37) nuclear; (38) single-parent; (39) blended; (40) extended; (41) race; (42) ethnicity; (43) race; (44) multiracial; (45) similar; (46) particular group

What is the Conceptual Basis for this Book? (pp. 23-26)
(47) divergent; (48) dynamic; (49) unique; (50) diversity; (51) characteristics; (52) environment; (53) relate; (54) interdependent

1 Minute Quiz: 1. Rousseau   2. Hall   3. extended family   4. Transactional

STUDY QUESTIONS
Multiple Choice: 1. c   2. a   3. a   4. a   5. b   6. a   7. d   8. b   9. a   10. d   11. c   12. d
13. b   14. c   15. c   16. c   17. a

True/False Questions:
1. False; social-emotional
1. True
2. False; nature
3. False; cannot
4. True
5. True
6. False; is not
7. False; relatively recent
8. False; old
9. True
10. False; Fewer
11. False; Ethnicity
12. True
13. True
14. False; tend to

Chapter 2
Understanding Development

My mother taught me MEDICINE...
"If you don't stop crossing your eyes, they're going to freeze that way."
                                            -Things My Mother Taught Me

Objectives
When you have completed this chapter, you will be able to
- state how theories and facts interrelate;
- list the characteristics of a good theory;
- describe the important assumptions, features, and concepts of major theories of human development;
- categorize theories of human development as biological, psychoanalytic, environmental, cognitive, or contextual;
- identify the theoretical perspective used in real-life problems and solutions;
- state the four steps of the scientific method;
- compare and contrast basic and applied developmental research;
- summarize various research methodologies, including case studies, clinical interviews, surveys, naturalistic studies, correlational studies, and experimental studies;
- summarize developmental research methodologies, including cross-sectional, longitudinal, and cohort-sequential designs, identifying strengths and weaknesses;
- identify the research methodology used, given real-life examples;
- state four broad categories of measures used by social scientists; and
- define the key terms and concepts listed on pages 57 to 58 of your text.

☑ Study Check List

☐ Read Chapter 2 Understanding Development.

☐ Re-read the Chapter 2 Summary to refresh your memory.

☐ Read the Chapter 2 Objectives listed above.

☐ Complete the following items:

How Do Theories Explain Child Development? (pp. 29 - 30)
Define the following:

A scientific theory is an _____(1).

A fact is _____(2).

14 Study Guide for Exploring Child Development

Identify whether the following statements are FACTS or THEORIES:

1. Preschool boys often prefer their mother's company to their father's company and may even tell the father to "Go away! Don't kiss my Mommy!" _____(3)

2. Preschool boys prefer their mothers to their fathers because mothers give them more attention and children like attention. _____(4)

3. Preschool boys prefer their mothers to their fathers because they have unconscious desires for their mother. _____(5)

4. The United States has comparatively high teenage pregnancy rates. _____(6)

5. Teenagers get pregnant because they identify with the female role of being a mother. _____(7)

6. Teenagers get pregnant because they can get welfare money to live on and move out of the house. _____(8)

7. Teenagers get pregnant because they do not have the cognitive development to understand the long-term consequences of raising children. _____(9)

Consider the above statements. If you were a researcher, and you believed the theory in statement #5, what do you think you would study? _____

_____(10)

What type of intervention programs do you think might come from people who believe in the theory stated in statement #6? _____

_____(11)

Statement #7? _____

_____(12)

In short, facts are what we actually see, theories are what we make up to try to explain those facts, and the theories we hold affect the type of intervention strategies we use!

Chapter 2 Understanding Development 15

What are the Major Biology-Based Theories of Child Development? (pp. 30 - 33)

Biology-based theories assume that _____(13) influence behavior.

Use these words to complete the following paragraph:

| attachment | Ethological | Bowlby | |
| Darwin | neurodevelopmental | survival | adaptive |

_____'s (14) theory of evolution is based on the idea that individuals who have characteristics that promote _____(15) and reproduction are more likely to pass these characteristics on to future generations. _____(16) theory came from Darwin's ideas and focuses on the causes and _____(17) value of behavior. An influential ethological theory is _____(18) theory, developed by John _____(19). According to this theory, all children become emotionally connected to their caregivers. The quality of this emotional tie influences later development in children and adults.

The relationship of brain development to behavior and thinking is the focus of _____(20) approaches to the study of development. It appears that early experiences may have a crucial role in determining how the brain wires itself, and in turn, one's neurological "wiring" will influence how a person responds to stimuli.

---

1 Minute Quiz

1. **Name 4 biologically based theories.**
   a. _____   c. _____
   b. _____   d. _____

2. **Biologically based theories emphasize _____ biological factors and processes.**
   a. learned   b. interactive   c. inherited   d. external

16 Study Guide for Exploring Child Development

What are Major Psychoanalytic Theories of Child Development (pp. 33 - 35)

Scholars who support psychoanalytic theories of development believe that the most important causes of behavior are rooted in un_____(21) drives and forces within the individual. The father of psychoanalytic theory is Si_____ _____(22).

Match the following:

_____ libido (23)   a. source of reason; balances internal demands with social rules

_____ ego (24)   b. "I want it, and I want it NOW!"; survival instinct

_____ id (25)   c. one's conscience, morals, social conventions

_____ superego (26)   d. internal sexual energy that is a source of most action and behavior

List 3 criticisms of Freud's theory: (27)

1. _____

2. _____

3. _____

Is Freud's theory still influential today? You bet! Although you may not realize it, Freud's theory is a common part of our way of thinking about behavior and development. Have you ever used the term "ego" or called someone "anal retentive?" Have you wondered what happened in someone's childhood that made them the way they are? Have you made a "Freudian slip" or interpreted a person's dream? Then you, too, have been touched by Freud!

The theorist who took Freud's theory and extended it was Erik E_____(28). According to Erikson, each person goes through a series of eight psy_____(29) stages of development. Each stage is marked by a cr_____(30) that is critical in one's personality development. These stages are invariant (fixed), but the crises are resolved differently for each person depending on individual circumstances and experiences.

Erikson's stages are different from Freud because Erikson's stages go beyond ad_____(31), recognize the importance of cul_____(32), and focus on hea_____(33) development rather than maladaptive development. Although Erikson was a master at description, however, his theory provides little explanation as to the "hows" of development and is difficult to t_____(34).

Fun Facts

Theories do not grow out of vacuums. Often, when we study the background of a theorist, it is easy to see how his or her theory developed. It also can help in matching the theorist to the theory.

For example, did you know that Erik Erikson's birth name was not Erik Erikson? Erik's biological father left Erik's mother before he was even born. His mother married the physician who treated her, and Eric was raised as Erik Homburger.

When Erik was older, he learned that the man he thought was his father was not. As a result of this crisis, he changed his name from Erik Homburger to Erik Erikson (son of Eric)! Erik also had difficulty because of his Jewish background. His non-Jewish peers rejected him because he was Jewish and his Jewish peers rejected him because the tall Nordic young man didn't look Jewish! It is not difficult to see why each of Erikson's developmental stages are marked by different crises and why identity is at the center of his theory.

---

1 Minute Quiz

Freud or Erikson? Match the name to the concept:

1. psychosocial crises _____
2. defense mechanisms _____
3. id _____
4. identity _____
5. development beyond adolescence _____
6. psychoanalysis_____
7. early development most important for personality _____

What are the Major Environment-based Theories of Child Development (pp. 35 - 39)

Place the following words and concepts in the appropriate "Theory" column:

negative reinforcement, observation, Pavlov, shaping, salivating dogs, punishment, unconditioned stimulus, extinction, conditioned stimulus, Bandura, systematic desensitization, Skinner, vicarious reinforcement, positive reinforcement, modeling, unconditioned response

Classical Conditioning (35)	Operant Conditioning (36)	Social Learning Theory (37)

LESSONS IN REAL LIFE - LESSONS IN REAL LIFE - LESSONS IN REAL LIFE - LESSONS IN REAL LIFE

I. Aaron and Maria have a 12-month-old son. They took him to the pediatrician to get his immunizations. The nurse who gave the shot to their son was wearing a white coat. Now, whenever their son sees an adult in a white coat, he begins to cry and tries to get away from the person as fast as possible. The baby being frightened by white coats as a result of his experience at the doctor's office is an example of (circle one) **classical conditioning/ operant conditioning/ social learning.** (38)

II. Hector is having a problem with his 8-year-old son, who is not keeping his room clean. Hector is not sure what he should do, so he asks those closest to him. Hector's mother believes that Hector should spank his son when the son does not clean his room. Hector's sister tells him that he should pay his son $1 for every week that the room is clean. Hector's neighbor says that he should tell his son if he doesn't clean his room, then the son will have to do something he really hates (like washing the dishes); if he keeps his room clean, then he won't have to do these things. Match the piece of advice to its conditioning principle:

_____ Spanking his son when the room is dirty   a. negative reinforcement
(39)

_____ Getting a dollar a week for a clean room   b. punishment
(40)

_____ Keeping the room clean to avoid washing dishes   c. positive reinforcement
(41)

The concepts applied in Hector's situation come from **classical conditioning/ operant conditioning/ social learning** *(circle one)*. (42)

Chapter 2 Understanding Development 19

III. Jimmy loves watching the Power Rangers on television. On one program, he sees the Power Rangers kick and hit an evil being who tries to steal a person's magic necklace. The Power Rangers destroy the evil being and return the magic necklace to its owner, to the cheers of the spectators. At school, Jimmy sees another child take a toy away from a younger child, who begins crying. Jimmy walks up to the perpetrator, kicks him in the stomach, and gives the toy back to the younger child. According to **classical conditioning/ operant conditioning/ social learning theory** *(circle one)* (43), Jimmy learned this behavior through the process of vi_____ re_____(44).

What are the Major Cognition-based Theories of Child Development (pp. 39 - 43)

Unscramble the following words/concepts from **Piaget**'s *theory, using the definitions and hints provided:*

_ _ _ _ _ _ - A cognitive guide or blueprint (45)
ecehsm

_ _ _ _ _ _ _ _ _ _ _ _ _ _ _ _ _ _ - Stage of abstract thinking (46)
moalfr peraintaloo

_ _ _ _ _ _ _ _ _ _ _ _ _ - Changing a scheme to fit the information (47)
dancmiomoatoc

_ _ _ _ _ _ _ _ _ _ _ _ _ - A child at this stage is egocentric (48)
relipperaoonat

_ _ _ _ _ _ _ _ _ _ _ _ - Fitting information into an existing scheme (49)
stosnilaaimi

_ _ _ _ _ _ _ _ _ _ _ _ _ _ _ _ _ _ _ - Logic develops at this stage (50)
teencroc laponieator

⇒ **MEMORY JOG:** as**simi**lation (information is **simi**lar so it fits into existing scheme)
ac commodation (**a com**pletely new scheme is being formed)

Vygotsky believed that children use psychological tools, such as lan_____(51) to develop higher levels of thinking. When children are young, they talk out loud to themselves, and Vygotsky believed this helps children learn and organize their behavior. As children get older, they do not talk out loud but use a silent in_____(52) speech to guide behavior. Vygotsky also believed that social interactions with skilled helpers aided learning. The distance between what a child can learn by himself and what a child could learn with a helper is called the zo_____(53).

20 Study Guide for Exploring Child Development

Theories that focus on how people take in, remember, and use information are referred to as

inf _____ pr _____ (54) theories.

Label the following diagram, using the terms provided: (55)

long term memory, sensory register, input, short-term memory, output, infinite duration, limited duration, infinite capacity, limited capacity, working memory, permanent memory

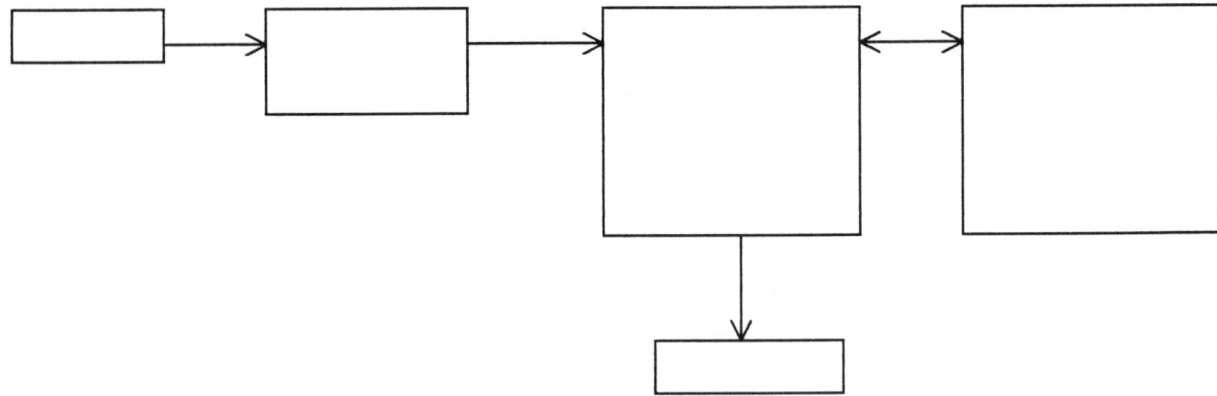

---

1 Minute Quiz

1. **Punishment and negative reinforcement are essentially the same things. True/False.**

2. **Learning through observation is an idea taken from:**
   a. social learning theory.   c. information processing.
   b. operant conditioning.   d. classical conditioning.

3. **A baby has a sucking scheme and sucks everything put in her hand. One day, she grabs a hot pepper and begins to suck it. She spits it out and learns that not everything is suckable. This baby has adapted to this new information through the process of assimilation/ accommodation *(circle one)*.**

4. **To help her 3rd grade students learn math, Mrs. Smith pairs up each student with a 4th grade helper. The person most likely to support this teaching method is:**
   a. Piaget   b. Skinner   c. Vygotsky   d. Pavlov

Chapter 2 Understanding Development 21

What are the Major Contextual Theories of Child Development (pp. 43 - 46)

Using **Bronfenbrenner's Ecological Theory** *of development, place the following aspects of Christopher's life in the appropriate column:*

Christopher's sister, Bethany   Mom's relationship with Chris' teacher   Dad likes his job
Mom and Dad's relationship   Dad's work on the police department   Local TV station
Christopher's school system   The local newspaper   Judeo-Christian culture
Christopher's friend, Matt   Christopher's teacher, Mr. Holland   Strong economy

Christopher

Microsystem (56)	Mesosystem (57)	Exosystem (58)	Macrosystem (59)

⇒ **MEMORY JOG:** "micro" means small; "meso" means middle; "exo" means outside of; and "macro" means big.

Use these words to complete the following paragraph:

rate-limiting component; complex; context; control parameters; dynamic systems theory; level; master; system; basic

One of the newest theories in child development is _____(60). Dynamic systems theorists assume that _____(61) systems form from _____(62) and simple conditions without requiring a _____(63) plan. Individual parts of a system are called _____ _____(64) and interact in ways that lead to change and a new _____(65). The slowest part of a system is called the _____

_____ (66). When this component develops,

the _____ (67) evolves into a new form. Dynamic systems theory emphasizes

the role of _____ (68) in development.

How is Child Development Studied? (pp. 46 - 56)

The four steps of the scientific method are: (69)

1. _____

2. _____

3. _____

4. _____

In one sentence, state how basic and applied research differ: (70)

_____

_____

_____

Research methods vary in terms of control, determination of causality, generalizability, and ability to apply findings to real life. *Circle the only research design that can determine cause and effect:* (71)

| case study | clinical interview | survey study |
| naturalistic study | correlational study | experimental study |

Circle the only research design that allows scientists to control variables that might influence behavior: (72)

| case study | clinical interview | survey study |
| naturalistic study | correlational study | experimental study |

Chapter 2 Understanding Development 23

Circle the research design that involves collecting information about most aspects of a person's life: (73)

case study	**clinical interview**	**survey study**
naturalistic study	**correlational study**	**experimental study**

What is one strength and one weakness of **clinical interviews**? (74)

Strength _____

Weakness _____

What is one strength and one weakness of **survey studies**? (75)

Strength _____

Weakness _____

What is one strength and one weakness of **naturalistic studies**? (76)

Strength _____

Weakness _____

C_____(77) studies compare children on two variables to determine if the variables relate to one another. For example, a researcher might want to determine if the number of hours an adolescent studies (one variable) relates to the grades that the adolescent gets in school (another variable). If the researcher finds that the more hours an adolescent studies the higher grades the adolescent gets, then the correlation is said to be p_____(78). If it doesn't matter how much the adolescent studies in terms of the grades the adolescent gets, then there appears to be _____ (79) relationship between study hours and grades. If, by some chance, the researcher finds that the more the adolescent studies, the lower the grades are, then there would be a n_____(80) correlation between study hours and grades. Suppose a researcher found a negative correlation, and those students who studied the most got the worst grades. Does this mean that studying more *causes* students to do worse??? No! Correlational designs *do not* determine causation; they simply show a relationship. It could be that the students with the lowest ability studied more in an effort to bring up their grades.

24 Study Guide for Exploring Child Development

To determine the strength of the correlation (in other words, how strongly the two variables are related to each other), researchers use **correlation coefficients**. A perfect positive relationship is +1.0 and a perfect negative relationship is -1.0. If the relationship between studying and grades is .22, it would appear that there is a **strong-moderate-weak** *(circle one)* **positive-negative** *(circle one)* (81) relationship between studying and grades. A correlation coefficient of -.87 would indicate a **strong-moderate-weak** *(circle one)* **positive-negative** *(circle one)* (82) relationship.

Cause and effect relationships are determined through the use of ex_____(83) studies. Experimental methods allow scientists to control events and variables that might influence the findings. Because scientists can't control all variables, especially those related to people, they are careful about how they choose their participants. To minimize the influence of the uncontrollable factors, scientists select participants and then assign them at r_____(84).

How does a control group differ from an experimental group? _____

_____

_____(85)

In an experimental design, the scientist manipulates some variable (the in_____(86) variable or IV); the behavior affected by the independent variable is referred to as the de_____(87) variable (or DV).

⇒ **MEMORY JOG:** Independent Variable (IV) - "The I-V is what I Vary," explained the Scientist. "The dependent variable is what I observe!"

Three methods for measuring changes over time are: (88)

1. _____
2. _____
3. _____

Three researchers are interested in children's emotional development from age 1 to 5. *Match the developmental research designs to the examples below:*

(a) longitudinal; (b) cross-sectional; (c) cohort-sequential

_____ Dr. A administers a test to a group of 1-, 3-, and 5-year-olds at a daycare center.
(89)

_____ Dr. B administers a test to a group of 1-year-olds, then comes back every two years and
(90) administers the same test to the same children.

_____ Dr. C administers a test to a group of 1-, 3-, and 5-year olds, then comes back in two
(91) years and administers the same test to the same children (now 3-, 5-, and 7-year-olds), and adds a new group of 1-year-olds.

List 4 types of measures used by developmental scientists: (92)

1. _____

2. _____

3. _____

4. _____

---

1 Minute Quiz

1. **A strength of correlational designs is the ability to determine cause and effect. True/False.**

2. **Which of the following research designs is NOT considered a developmental design?**
   a. longitudinal   b. experimental   c. cross-sectional

3. **A projective measure involves direct assessment of behavior through observation. True/False.**

4. **Basic research is designed to answer _____ questions about development.**

26 Study Guide for Exploring Child Development

☐ Complete the crossword puzzle in Appendix 1 – Crossword Puzzles.

☐ Go to the beginning of this chapter, and on a separate sheet of paper, write out the answers to the lesson objectives.

"Keep up with the reading so you have time to review it and your notes before the test."

STUDY QUESTIONS

Multiple Choice (The following questions are identified as being "A," *applied questions* that require the application of knowledge learned or "F," *factual questions* that rely on the recall of facts).

1. Which of the following statements about theories is NOT true? (p. 30; F)
   a. A theory is an organized set of ideas that attempts to organize and explain facts.
   b. A theory is a statement based on an observation with which many people agree.
   c. Theories guide future research by suggesting areas scientists should pursue.
   d. The same facts can be interpreted differently by different theories.

2. A good theory: (p. 30; F)
   a. is understandable.
   b. predicts future events.
   c. stimulates new knowledge and is testable.
   d. All of the above.

3. Which of the following theories is NOT biologically-based? (pp. 30-33; F)
   a. Evolutionary   b. Attachment   c. Classical Conditioning   d. Ethological

4. Jana believes that children should not be allowed to crawl into bed with their parents when the children are frightened because of sexual overtones that could possibly harm the children as adults. The theorist most likely to agree with Jana is: (p. 33; A)
   a. Freud.   b. Bowlby.   c. Piaget.   d. Bandura.

5. The concept most closely identified with Erikson is: (p. 35; F)
   a. attachment.
   b. conditioned response.
   c. identity.
   d. assimilation.

6. Rudy gave his 8-month-old daughter a balloon, which popped as soon as she grabbed it. To calm down his crying daughter, he quickly gave her another balloon, which also popped. Now, at 3 years of age, the daughter cries whenever she goes to a birthday party and sees balloons. The daughter's fear of balloons is best explained through the process of: (pp. 36-37; A)
   a. negative reinforcement.
   b. operant conditioning.
   c. vicarious learning.
   d. classical conditioning.

7. The likelihood of a behavior re-occurring increases with: (p. 38; F)
   a. positive reinforcement.
   b. negative reinforcement.
   c. positive and negative reinforcement
   d. positive and negative reinforcement, as well as punishment.

8. Lacey has noticed that her 4-year-old started sharing more after watching "Barney" on television. When Lacey watched "Barney" with her daughter, she saw many examples of sharing and other prosocial behaviors on the program. The theory that addresses this situation is: (pp. 38-39; A)
   a. cognitive development.
   b. operant conditioning.
   c. ecological.
   d. social learning.

9. Which of the following concepts does NOT relate to Piaget's theory of cognitive development? (pp. 39-41; F)
   a. scheme
   b. zone of proximal development
   c. sensorimotor
   d. accommodation

10. One-year-old Tommy has just learned to talk. Whenever he sees an adult male, Tommy says, "DaDa!", the word he initially used for his father. This is a good example of: (p. 41; A)
    a. assimilation.
    b. accommodation.
    c. sensorimotor thought.
    d. cognitive dissimilitude.

11. Juan is 13 years old and has begun to talk about subjects he never talked about before. For example, he recently engaged his parents in a conversation about equality and social justice, stating that he was going to be President someday so that all people will be equally served under the law. According to Piaget, it appears that Juan has entered into the stage of: (p. 41; A)
    a. assimilative thinking.
    b. formal operational thinking.
    c. preoperational thinking.
    d. concrete operational thinking.

12. Jack and Jill are very concerned about their children's education. As a result, Jill is a member of the school board and Jack has forged excellent relationships with the children's teachers and school principals. It appears, in terms of education, Jack and Jill have created a very rich _____ for their children. (pp. 43-45; A)
    a. microsystem
    b. mesosystem
    c. exosystem
    d. macrosystem

13. Which of the following would NOT be considered part of a child's microsystem? (pp. 43-44; A)
    a. a sister
    b. the playmate who lives next door
    c. the movie "Godzilla!"
    d. All of the above are considered part of a child's microsystem.

14. In dynamic systems theory, (pp. 45-46; F)
    a. complex systems develop from basic conditions without requiring a master plan.
    b. development involves self-organization in which systems change as a result of their interactions.
    c. the last developing part of a system is called the rate-limiting component.
    d. All of the above.

15. The first step of the scientific method is: (p. 46; F)
    a. collecting evidence.
    b. formulating a hypothesis.
    c. designing a study.
    d. interpreting evidence.

16. Dr. Jones is a researcher who is trying to find out why some children are born mentally retarded. This type of research is referred to as: (p. 48; A)
    a. basic.
    b. applied.
    c. complex.
    d. interpretive.

17. One of the advantages of naturalistic studies is: (pp. 50-51; F)
    a. the ability to determine cause and effect.
    b. the ability to generalize the findings.
    c. the opportunity to observe children in "real life" settings.
    d. All of the above.

18. Dr. Dooley observed how many hours 4th graders watched television and how often the children engaged in violent playground interactions. She found a correlation of .97 for hours watched and number of violent interactions. When the teachers learned of her findings, they sent home a letter reporting the findings and recommending to the parents that they limit their children's television watching to ensure a safer playground. Based on the information learned in your text, you know that: (pp. 49-53; A):
    a. the teachers' recommendations were correct. The high correlation indicates that too much television leads to violent behavior.
    b. the teachers' recommendations were incorrect. Correlational studies cannot show cause and effect, therefore, it is unknown if television led to violence on the playground.
    c. this study could be classified as an experimental study.
    d. this study could be classified as a survey study.

19. Dr. Doolittle is interested in the effects of color on infants. He attaches the infant's foot to a string attached to a brightly-colored mobile hanging over the crib. He varies the color of the mobile and determines that infants kick more with a bright red mobile. The independent variable in this case is: (pp. 53-54; A):
    a. the mobile.
    b. the color of the mobile.
    c. the amount of kicking.

20. Suppose Dr. Doolittle conducts the same study above (see question #19) but is interested in perception of color over time. He then measures the amount of kicking in 3-month-old, 5-month-old, and 7-month-old infants at an infant-care center. This type of research design is considered: (p. 54-55; A):
    a. cross-sectional.
    b. longitudinal.
    c. cohort-sequential.

True/False Questions (If a statement is FALSE, correct it).

1. No single theory will be able to explain all human behavior. (p. 30) True/False.

2. Fact or theory? Children typically speak their first word by age one. This statement is a fact. (p. 30) True/False.

3. Psychoanalytic theories propose that there are critical and sensitive periods in development. (p. 31) True/False.

4. The superego represents one's conscience, morals, and social conventions. (p. 34) True/False.

5. Erikson expanded Freud's theory by adding stages beyond adolescence and emphasizing healthy development. (p. 35) True/False.

6. Operant conditioning emphasizes the role of observation and imitation. (p. 38) True/False.

7. Making a child stand in a corner when he has done something wrong is an example of negative reinforcement. (p. 38) True/False.

8. Piaget's first stage of cognitive development is preoperational. (p. 41) True/False.

9. Vygotsky would probably agree with this statement: "Language reflects cognitive development; it does not enhance it." (p. 42) True/False.

10. The zone of proximal development refers to the distance between what the child knows and what the child can teach herself. (p. 42) True/False.

11. Television is considered part of a child's exosystem. (p. 44) True/False.

12. The goals of scientific research are to produce findings that are subjective, reliable and valid. (p. 46) True/False.

13. Experimental studies involve investigating cause and effect. (pp. 51-52) True/False.

14. A group of 10-year-olds, 12-year-olds, and 14-year-olds come into a laboratory setting and are asked to play a game. They are then return in a week and given a test related to what they remember about the game they played the week before. The researchers determine that the 14-year-olds are better able to recall details of the game. This study is considered a longitudinal design. (pp. 54-55) True/False.

15. Behavioral measures involve asking people to answer questions about their behavior or attitudes. (p. 56) True/False.

☐ **REWARD YOURSELF!** Send an e-mail message to a friend, listen to your favorite CD, or take a nap!

ANSWERS - Chapter 2 Understanding Development

How Do Theories Explain Child Development? (pp. 29-30)
(1) A scientific theory is an organized set of ideas that attempts to organize and explain facts; (2) a fact is a statement based on observation with which many people would agree.
(3) Fact; (4) Theory; (5) Theory; (6) Fact; (7) Theory; (8) Theory; (9) Theory
(10) I would study the development of roles and how to change definition of roles.
(11) An intervention program might cut down on paying money to welfare mothers who have more than a certain number of kids.
(12) An intervention program might focus on teaching teens to think about the future and make long range plans.

What are the Major Biology-based Theories of Child Development? (pp. 30-33)
(13) organic or inherited forces
(14) Darwin; (15) survival; (16) Ethological; (17) adaptive; (18) attachment; (19) Bowlby; (20) neurodevelopmental
1 Minute Quiz: 1. evolutionary; ethological; attachment; neurodevelopmental; 2. inherited

What are the Major Psychoanalytic Theories of Child Development? (pp. 33-35)
(21) unconscious; (22) Sigmund Freud
(23) libido - d; (24) ego - a; (25) id - b; (26) superego - c
(27) 1. Not based on solid scientific evidence; 2. many aspects are unmeasurable/untestable; 3. cultural bias
(28) Erikson; (29) psychosocial; (30) crisis; (31) adolescence; (32) culture; (33) healthy; (34) test
1 Minute Quiz: 1. Erikson; 2. Freud; 3. Freud; 4. Erikson; 5. Erikson; 6. Freud; 7. Freud

What are the Major Environment-based Theories of Child Development? (pp. 35-39)
(35) Classical Conditioning: Pavlov, salivating dogs, unconditioned stimulus, conditioned stimulus, systematic desensitization, unconditioned response
(36) Operant Conditioning: negative reinforcement, shaping, punishment, extinction, Skinner, positive reinforcement
(37) Social Learning Theory: observation, Bandura, vicarious reinforcement, modeling
(38) classical conditioning; (39) Spanking - b; (40) dollar - c; (41) avoid - a; (42) operant conditioning; (43) Social learning;
(44) vicarious reinforcement.

What are the Major Cognition-based Theories of Child Development? (pp. 39-42)
(45) scheme, (46) formal operational, (47) accommodation, (48) preoperational, (49) assimilation, (50) concrete operational
(51) language; (52) inner; (53) zone of proximal development; (54) information processing

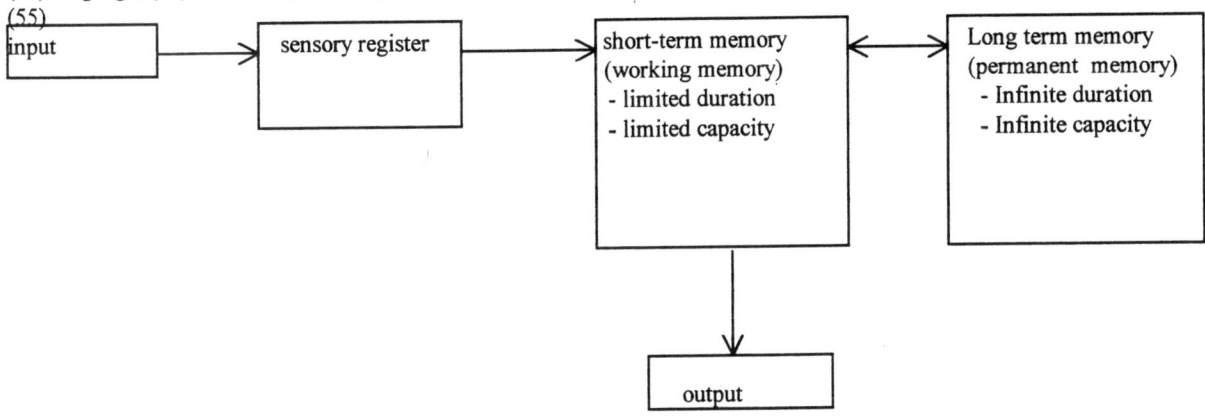

(55)
input → sensory register → short-term memory (working memory) - limited duration - limited capacity ↔ Long term memory (permanent memory) - Infinite duration - Infinite capacity
short-term memory → output

1 Minute Quiz: 1. False; 2. a; 3. accommodation; 4. c

What are the Major Contextual Theories of Child Development? (pp. 43-46)
(56) Microsystem: Christopher's sister, Bethany; Christopher's friend, Matt; Christopher's teacher, Mr. Holland
(57) Mesosystem: Mom's relationship with Chris' teacher; Dad likes his job; Mom and Dad's relationship

32 Study Guide for Exploring Child Development

(58) Exosystem: Dad's work on the police department; local television station; Christopher's school system; the local newspaper
(59) Macrosystem: Judeo-Christian culture; Strong economy
(60) dynamic systems; (61) complex; (62) basic; (63) master; (64) control parameters; (65) level; (66) rate-limiting component; (67) system; (68) context

How is Child Development Studied? (pp. 46-56)
(69) 1. formulating a hypothesis; 2. designing a study; 3. collecting evidence; 4. interpreting and reporting the evidence
(70) Basic research looks at broad, core developmental issues; applied research is designed to solve practical problems.
(71) experimental study; (72) experimental study; (73) case study
(74) Strength – flexibility; gain insight into thoughts; weakness – not useful with young children or people with language problems; data may be biased
(75) Strength – can easily obtain data from many people; weakness – people may not tell truth; may not ask right questions
(76) Strength – researcher can see how people behave normally; weakness – difficulty to generalize from settings; researcher has no control, so can't determine cause and effect
(77) Correlational; (78) positive; (79) no or zero; (80) negative; (81) weak positive; (82) strong negative; (83) experimental; (84) random
(85) A control group does not receive the experimental treatment; the experimental group does.
(86) Independent; (87) dependent
(88) 1. cross-sectional; 2. longitudinal; 3. cohort-sequential; (89) Dr. A - b; (90) Dr. B - a; (91) Dr. C - c
(92) physiological; behavioral; self-reports; projective
1 Minute Quiz: 1. False; 2. b; 3. False; 4. broad, fundamental

STUDY QUESTIONS
Multiple Choice: 1 - b; 2 - d; 3 - c; 4 - a; 5 - c; 6 - d; 7 - d; 8 - d; 9 - b; 10 - a; 11 - b; 12 - b; 13 - c; 14 - d; 15 - b; 16 - a; 17 - c; 18 - b; 19 - b; 20 - a

True/False Questions:
1. True
2. True
3. False, Ethological theories
4. True
5. True
6. Social learning theory
7. punishment
8. Sensorimotor
9. False; Vygotsky would NOT agree
10. False; what child knows and what child could learn with a helper
11. True
12. True
13. False, objective
14. False, cross-sectional
15. False, Self-reports

Chapter 3
Genetics and Prenatal Development

My mother taught me to THINK AHEAD...
"If you don't pass your spelling test, you'll never get a good job!"
- Things My Mother Taught Me

Objectives
When you have completed this chapter, you will be able to
- describe various genetic transmission patterns;
- identify common chromosomal abnormalities;
- describe common tests for prenatal detection of genetic diseases;
- state conditions for which genetic counseling is recommended;
- describe the process of fertilization;
- summarize the stages of prenatal development;
- discuss ectopic and multiple pregnancies;
- identify various teratogens and state common affects of these teratogens on the developing baby;
- describe maternal conditions that could negatively or positively affect the unborn child;
- describe the influence of culture on pregnancy; and
- define the key terms and concepts listed on page 97 of your text.

☑ Study Check List

☐ Read Chapter 3 Genetics and Prenatal Development.

☐ Re-read the Chapter 3 Summary to refresh your memory.

☐ Read the Chapter 3 Objectives listed above.

☐ Complete the following items:

How Do Genes Influence Development? (pp. 65 - 71)

Every human cell carries a blueprint for development that is coded by g_____(1). Genes can be thought of as addresses that lie on thin strands of ch_____(2). Human beings have _____(3) pairs of chromosomes, totaling _____(4) chromosomes altogether. Half of each pair of chromosomes comes from the m_____(5) and the other half comes from the f_____(6).

34 Study Guide for Exploring Child Development

Almost every cell in the body divides and duplicates itself. When a cell divides and duplicates itself, forming two cells with the exact same number of chromosomes in each, the process is called m_____(7). Ova and sperm cells, however, only have 23 chromosomes in each cell. That is because they were formed through a special called m_____(8). When the ova (with _____(9) chromosomes) meets up with the sperm (with _____(10) chromosomes), the two cells combine to form one fertilized egg cell that has a total of _____(11) chromosomes.

⇒ **MEMORY JOG:** "Mitosis" is "mighty," so it results in cells with 46 chromosomes; meiosis results in only 23 chromosomes.

Geneticists examine chromosomes by creating a k_____(12) matching the chromosomal pairs by s_____(13) and st_____(14). The first _____(15) pairs are called a_____(16); and the 23rd pair is called the s____ c_____(17). This last pair determines the s_____(18) of the child. If the last pair consists of two X chromosomes, then the child will be a f_____(19). If the last pair consists of an X and a Y chromosome, then the child will be a m_____(20). Only males carry the Y chromosome.

Fun Facts

Throughout history people have tried to choose the sex of their babies. Believing that all good things come from the right (and males are better than females), Hippocrates recommended that Greek men, who wanted sons, tie up their left testicle during intercourse. This action would result in only "good" sperm (i.e., male sperm) from the right testicle being used for fertilization. He also suggested that Greek women lie on their right side during intercourse so that the sperm could be deposited with the right ovary.

Chapter 3 Genetics and Prenatal Development 35

A person's genetic code is called their g_____(21); however, just because a person carries certain genes, doesn't mean they are evident. What you actually see is called the ph_____(22). For example, a person may carry a gene for adult-onset diabetes (**genotype**), but because of good diet and exercise, this gene might not express itself, and the person may not show signs of diabetes (**phenotype**).

⇒ **MEMORY JOG:** **Geno**type is in the **genes**; phenotype is what you actually see.

Remember that genes work in pairs, and some genes are more likely to be expressed than others. When both parents contribute the exact same copy of a gene to their child, the child is said to be h_____(23) for that trait; however, if each parent contributes a different copy of the gene, the child is said to be h_____(24) for that trait.

⇒ **MEMORY JOG:** **"Homo" means same; "hetero" means different. Thus, homozygous means the same copy of the gene, and heterozygous means different copies of the gene.**

Sometimes, in heterozygous situations, one gene expresses itself over the other. In this case, the gene that expresses itself is said to be d_____(25) and the gene that doesn't express itself is said to be r_____(26). The recessive gene will express itself only if it is paired up with another r_____(27) gene.

Sometimes people carry a recessive gene that causes a certain disease; but, because they carry the dominant gene that *doesn't* cause the disease, they are healthy. In other words, their g_____(28) is made up of a dominant gene that does not cause a disease and a recessive gene that does. Their ph_____(29) is that they appear healthy and show not signs of the disease. These people are referred to as c_____(30) of the disease. If two people are carriers, then it is possible for each to pass on their recessive gene to a child, who will then have the d_____(31).

Figure it Out! *Suppose a mother has a genotype of Cc, with the lowercase c representing the recessive gene for cystic fibrosis. Suppose the father has a genotype of CC (no recessive gene for cystic fibrosis). Fill in the table below:*

```
                  Father's genes
                    C       C
              C  ┌──────┬──────┐
Mother's genes   │      │      │
              c  ├──────┼──────┤
                 │      │      │
                 └──────┴──────┘
```

Each box represents a potential genetic combination for a child.

What is the mother's phenotype for cystic fibrosis? _____(32)

What is the father's phenotype for cystic fibrosis? _____(33)

What are the chances of having a child with cystic fibrosis? _____(34)

Suppose both the mother and father have a genotype of Cc, with the lowercase c representing the recessive gene for cystic fibrosis. Fill in the table below:

```
                  Father's genes
                    C       c
              C  ┌──────┬──────┐
Mother's genes   │      │      │
              c  ├──────┼──────┤
                 │      │      │
                 └──────┴──────┘
```

What is the mother's phenotype for cystic fibrosis? _____(35)

What is the mother's genotype for cystic fibrosis? _____(36)

Is the mother's genotype for cystic fibrosis heterozygous or homozygous? _____(37)

What is the father's phenotype for cystic fibrosis? _____(38)

What is the father's genotype for cystic fibrosis? _____(39)

Is the father's genotype for cystic fibrosis heterozygous or homozygous? _____(40)

What are the chances of having a child with cystic fibrosis? _____(41)

If the child has cystic fibrosis, is the child's genotype heterozygous or homozygous? _____(42)

****

Another pattern of genetic transmission is through the 23rd pair, or the s_____ c_____(43). This type of transmission is referred to as s_____ l_____(44) (sometimes referred to as X-linked). A woman may be a carrier for a sex-linked disorder. If she is a carrier, then on the 23rd pair of chromosomes, one of the X chromosomes has a normal gene and the other chromosome has the abnormal matching gene. Because she has the normal gene, the disease will not show itself. However, if she passes the diseased X gene on to a male offspring, the smaller Y chromosome will not have the matching normal gene and the son will have the disease. This is why females are **more likely/ less likely** *(circle one)* (45) to carry the disease and males are **more likely/ less likely** *(circle one)* (46) to have the disease. Name four characteristics that are sex-linked: (1) _____; (2) _____; (3) _____; and (4) _____ (47).

Dominant, recessive, and sex-linked patterns are three ways of passing on genetic information. However, most human characteristics require more than one gene. Characteristics that require more than one gene are referred to as p_____(48) traits. In addition, most complex human characteristics require a combination of genes interacting with environmental factors. These traits are referred to as multifactorial.

⇒ **MEMORY JOG:** "Poly" means many, thus polygenic means "many genes."

---

1 Minute Quiz

1. **Cells multiply and duplicate themselves through the process of _____.**

2. **Each human body cell contains _____ chromosomes or _____ pairs.**

3. **A child has a cleft chin (a dominant characteristic), although her father has no cleft chin. What is the child's genotype? _____ What is her phenotype? _____ Is she heterozygous or homozygous for this trait? _____**

4. **Most human characteristics require more than one gene. This form of genetic transmission is referred to as _____.**

38 Study Guide for Exploring Child Development

What are Common Chromosomal Abnormalities (pp. 71 - 72)

Most babies are born healthy. However, some babies may have a genetic disorder, that is, a problem with a gene, such as those described above. Other babies may have a chromosomal disorder. When a child has a chromosomal disorder it means that he or she was born with the wrong number of chromosomes. Too many chromosomes or too few chromosomes lead to ch_____(49) abnormalities.

Chromosomal Abnormalities - Match the following names with the characteristics below and write the letter in the space provided; then, write the chromosomal pattern (that is, XXY, XYY, XO, extra 21st chromosome) in the space provided.

Characteristics		Chromosomal Pattern
(50) _____	1. Down Syndrome	_____
(51) _____	2. Turner's Syndrome	_____
(52) _____	3. Klinefelter's Syndrome	_____
(53) _____	4. XYY (Supermale Syndrome)	_____

A. Normal verbal skills, poor spatial skills; webbed neck, short stature, immature external genitalia
B. Sterile; fail to develop masculine characteristics at puberty; language deficits.
C. Appear normal; tall; more Y's lower intelligence; impulsive.
D. Affects 1 in 900 births; wide-spaced eyes; protruding tongue; heart problems; risk increases with age of mother.

How are Genetic Diseases Detected? (pp. 72 - 75)

LESSONS IN REAL LIFE - LESSONS IN REAL LIFE - LESSONS IN REAL LIFE - LESSONS IN REAL LIFE

I. Marge just got back from the doctor's office. She is so excited because she got her "first baby pictures" and her baby is not even born yet! She said it didn't hurt at all, and the doctor was able to tell if there might be any heart conditions or physical deformities in the fetus. Marge just had a procedure known as a/n _____. (54)

II. MacKenzie is only 9 weeks pregnant. She is very worried about her pregnancy because she and her husband carry a recessive gene that if passed on to a child would be fatal. The doctor has told her that he can perform a test through her cervix that involves little risk to the developing baby. If the baby has the disorder, MacKenzie and her husband will know early if they want to continue the pregnancy or not. The procedure the doctor wants to use is _____. (55)

III. Saralyn is 42 years old and has just learned she is about 16 weeks pregnant. Her doctor has recommended that she undergo a procedure that will involve inserting a long needle through her abdominal wall. After several weeks, she will know not only the sex of her child, but if her child has Down Syndrome. This procedure is _____. (56)

IV. Candace never stops talking about her pregnancy. Today, she told you that she had a blood test done that can show if her baby has a problem, such as spinal bifida (a neural tube defect). She can't understand how a blood test can give that kind of information, but you know that she had test measuring her level of _____. (57)

List six situations in which **genetic counseling** is recommended: (58)

1. _____
2. _____
3. _____
4. _____
5. _____
6. _____

---

1 Minute Quiz

1. **Down Syndrome is an example of a (circle one) genetic disorder/ chromosomal abnormality.**

2. **The medical procedure that will give the most accurate genetic information at the earliest point in a pregnancy is:**
   a. alphafetoprotein screening.   c. amniocentesis.
   b. ultrasound.   d. chorionic villus sampling (CVS).

3. **Genetic counseling would be recommended to a person who had repeated miscarriages. True/False.**

40 Study Guide for Exploring Child Development

How does Prenatal Development Proceed? (pp. 75 - 85)

The human egg is called an o_____(59). A woman ovulates about _____(60) ova per year, or one ova every ____(61) days. For fertilization to occur, an ovum must be penetrated by a sperm cell within _____(62) hours after ovulation. A fertilized ovum is called a z_____(63). The menstrual cycle is divided into 3 phases (*list and describe*):

1. _____:_____(64)

2. _____:_____(65)

3. _____:_____(66)

Sperm are developed in a process called sp_____(67). It takes about _____(68) days to produce a mature sperm. Approximately _____(69) sperm are released at each ejaculation. A man is considered fertile if he has _____(70) sperm in a normal ejaculation. The sperm can survive in the woman's reproductive tract for up to ___(71) days. Each sperm carries an _____(72) or a _____(73) sex chromosome; each ovum only carries an _____(74) sex chromosome.

What are the 3 stages of prenatal development and how long is each stage? (75)

1. _____

2. _____

3. _____

Match the following terms and definitions:

_____ ectopic pregnancy   a. first fetal movements are felt
(76)

_____ amnion   b. agents that can cause malformations in unborn child
(77)

_____ chorion   c. from conception to implantation
(78)

_____ placenta   d. becomes the muscles, bones, and circulatory system
(79)

_____ umbilical cord   e. age at which a child could survive if born
(80)

___ cephalocaudal development (81)
___ proximodistal development (82)
___ quickening (83)
___ mesoderm (84)
___ teratogens (85)
___ embryonic stage (86)
___ fetal stage (87)
___ germinal stage (88)
___ age of viability (89)
___ ectoderm (90)

f. implantation in the fallopian tube
g. implantation to first 8 weeks
h. membrane that fills with fluid to protect baby
i. organ that allows exchange of nutrients and oxygen
j. growth from head to foot
k. 8 weeks to birth
l. connects embryo to placenta
m. growth from center of body to hands and feet
n. becomes the skin and nervous system
o. membrane that helps form placenta

⇒ **MEMORY JOG:** "Cephalo" means head and "caudal" means tail; "proximo" means near and "distal" means far.

Turn to Tables 3.5 and 3.6 (pp. 83-84) in your textbook and answer the following questions:

1. How many days does it take for implantation to occur? _____ (91)

2. How many days after fertilization is the first missed period? _____ (92)

3. At what age does the heart form and start to beat? _____ (93)

4. When do the arms and legs become distinct? _____ (94)

5. When do the external genitalia develop, as well as fingernails and toenails? _____ (95)

6. When does the face look human? _____ (96)

7. When does hair form on the head and body? _____ (97)

8. What is the age of viability? _____ (98)

9. When do the teeth form? _____ (99)

10. When does the baby change position for birth? _____ (100)

42 Study Guide for Exploring Child Development

---

1 Minute Quiz

1. A fertilized egg is called a/n:
   a. ovum.   b. chorion.   c. zygote.

2. The ovum contains ____ chromosomes, and the sperm contains _____ chromosomes.
   a. 23, 23   b. 46, 23   c. 23, 46   d. 46, 46

3. Fetal growth occurs from the center of the body out. True/False.

4. The age of viability is around the _____ month.
   a. 5th   b. 7th   c. 9th

What Conditions Influence Pregnancy and Prenatal Development? (pp. 86 - 96)

The effects of teratogens depend on these three factors: (101)

1. _____

2. _____

3. _____

Use these words to complete the following paragraphs:

radiation	AIDS	drugs	teratogens	environmental
diseases	thalidomide	alcoholic	fetal alcohol syndrome	syphilis
rubella	chemicals	cocaine	heroin	cigarettes

Several agents can cross the placental barrier and affect the developing baby. These agents are called _____(102). Teratogens can be categorized into 3 major categories: _____, _____, and _____(103).

Diseases account for about 3 to 5 percent of birth defects. One disease that can cause deafness and blindness in the unborn child, especially if the mother has it early in pregnancy, but can be prevented through immunization, is _____(104). A disease that's more dangerous later in prenatal development is _____(105). It can lead to blindness, retarded growth, and liver damage. Finally, a disease that can be transmitted through the placental barrier as well as during delivery is _____(106). HIV-infected fetuses are more likely to have impaired brain growth, infections, cognitive deficits, and muscle weakness.

Drugs also can affect the developing baby. One of the most powerful teratogenic drugs used to control morning sickness but later found to affect the development of the baby's arms and legs, was _____(107). Women who use illegal drugs, such as _____(108) or _____(109) are putting their developing babies as risk. However, legal drugs, such as alcohol and _____(110) can also affect the fetus. For example, women who drink alcoholic beverages may have a child with _____(111). Characteristics of FAS include flat faces and noses, narrow heads, mental retardation, and hyperactivity. Drinking only 1 to 2 _____(112) beverages a day may result in a child with fetal alcohol effects (FAE). Smoking poses dangers not only to the parents, but the child as well. Infants born to smokers are smaller and less likely to survive. Some studies have found that, compared to children of nonsmokers, children of smokers have more problems in motor coordination, physical growth, reading, and learning.

Expectant parents often overlook environmental hazards. A very powerful teratogenic agent is _____(113). The most common effects of radiation are microencephaly and mental retardation. Mercury, lead, insecticides, and food preservatives are common _____(114) that affect the developing child. Such chemicals can lead to mental retardation, as well as irreversible physical and neurological impairments.

List 3 maternal conditions that increase the risk of abnormal development to the unborn child: (115)

1. _____
2. _____
3. _____

What 3 things can a couple do to increase their chances of having a healthy baby? (116)

1. _____
2. _____
3. _____

A couple's experience with pregnancy can vary a lot depending on their c_____(117). West Africans view pregnancy as a divine gift. On the island of Yap in Micronesia, the largeness of a pregnant woman is a symbol of her ability to produce children. And in India, Brahman men stop chewing betel palm leaves until their wives give birth.

Summarize the meaning of pregnancy for men and women in Western cultures. Consider the meaning of pregnancy itself, weight gain, anticipation of the unborn child, and couvade: (118)

_____
_____
_____
_____
_____
_____

1 Minute Quiz

1. The effect of a particular teratogen (such as rubella, alcohol, or lead) can be lessened if the mother watches her diet for the remainder of her pregnancy. True/False.

2. Maternal smoking may affect the child after it is born, but has little affect when the child is in utero. True/False.

3. Labor and delivery are quicker and less demanding for:
   a. first born children.   b. twins.   c. later-born children.

4. Couvade refers to:
   a. the mother's experience with weight gain during pregnancy.
   b. the father's sympathetic experience of his partner's pregnancy.
   c. the cultural differences in pregnancy experience.

☐ Complete the crossword puzzle in Appendix 1 – Crossword Puzzles.

☐ Go to the beginning of this chapter, and on a separate sheet of paper, write out the answers to the lesson objectives.

sAGEdvice

"Read the assigned chapters BEFORE the professor gives the lecture."

STUDY QUESTIONS

Multiple Choice (The following questions are identified as being "F," *factual questions* that rely on the recall of facts or "A," *applied questions* that are based on real life).

1. The process of meiosis results in cells with _____ chromosomes; the process of mitosis results in cells with _____? (p.66; F)
   a. 23, 23   b. 23, 46   c. 46, 23   d. 46, 46

2. Autosomes refer to the: (p. 66; F)
   a. first 22 pairs of chromosomes in a karyotype.
   b. 23 pairs of chromosomes in a karyotype.
   c. chromosomes that are without a matching chromosome.
   d. genes that kick in when a 16-year-old gets his driver's license.

3. Assume that curly hair is a dominant characteristic. Chella (whose father had straight hair) has curly hair and Carlos (whose mother had curly hair) has straight hair. What are the chances that their baby will have curly hair? (pp. 67-70; A)
   a. 100 percent
   b. 75 percent
   c. 50 percent
   d. 25 percent

4. Regarding question #3, Chella is _____ for curly hair and Carlos is _____ for straight hair. (p.67; A)
   a. homozygous; heterozygous   c. homozygous; homozygous
   b. heterozygous; homozygous   d. heterozygous; heterozygous

5. Zita carries a gene for color blindness, a sex-linked characteristic. Her husband is colorblind. They have a newborn baby boy. What are the chances that he is colorblind? (p. 70; A)
   a. 25 percent   b. 50 percent   c. 75 percent   d. 100 percent

6. Regarding question #5, Zita's phenotype is: (p.67; A)
   a. one X chromosome with the diseased gene.   c. colorblind.
   b. two X chromosomes with the diseased gene.   d. color vision.

7. Down Syndrome is an example of a/n: (p. 71; F)
   a. sex-linked abnormality.   c. autosomal abnormality.
   b. genetic abnormality.   d. chromosomal abnormality.

8. Which abnormality involving the sex chromosomes can only be attributed to the father? (p. 72; A)
   a. Turner's Syndrome (XO)
   b. Klinefelter's Syndrome (XXY)
   c. Supermale Syndrome (XYY)
   d. No abnormality is solely attributable to the father.

9. The prenatal testing procedure that can give the earliest information about a genetic or chromosomal defect? (p. 73; F)
   a. Chorionic Villus Sampling (CVS)
   b. Amniocentesis
   c. ultrasound
   d. alpha-fetoprotein testing

10. Which of the following couples is least likely in need of genetic counseling? (p. 74; A)
    a. Lucy, who is 40 years old, and Ricky who is 42 years old.
    b. Niles and Maris who are cousins.
    c. Lauren, who is 23 and has had 2 miscarriages, and Humphrey, who is 24.
    d. Anthony, who is from Rome, and Cleopatra, who is from Egypt.

11. Women are most likely to get pregnant during the: (p. 76; F)
    a. menstrual phase.
    b. follicular phase.
    c. luteal phase.
    d. lunar phase.

12. The embryonic stage begins at: (p. 78; F)
    a. conception and lasts until the fertilized egg is implanted.
    b. implantation and lasts until about 8 weeks.
    c. 8 weeks and lasts until birth.
    d. conception and lasts until birth.

13. The main cause of ectopic pregnancies is: (p. 80; F)
    a. damaged fallopian tubes.
    b. age.
    c. use of teratogenic substances.
    d. intercourse late in the menstrual cycle.

14. Boys' and girls' sex organs: (p. 81; F)
    a. develop from the same origins but develop differently depending on the presence or absence of testosterone.
    b. develop from the same origins but develop differently depending on the presence or absence of estrogen.
    c. develop from the same origins but girls' organs develop based on estrogen and boys' organs develop based on testosterone.
    d. develop from different origins, as a result of the presence of different sex hormones.

15. Most teratogens are likely to cause the most severe birth defects during the _____ period. (p. 82; F)
    a. germinal period
    b. embryonic period
    c. fetal period
    d. lunar

16. Which of the following factors does NOT influence the affects of teratogens? (p. 86; F)
    a. when the unborn child was exposed to the teratogen
    b. how much of the teratogen the unborn child was exposed to
    c. how the individual fetus or embryo responded to the teratogen
    d. All of the above are factors that influence the affects of teratogens

17. Your friend just found out she is pregnant. She tells you that she is going to follow her grandmother's advice and drink one or two glasses of wine a day to relax and sleep. Based on the information you learned from the text, you tell her, (p. 89; A)
    a. "Yes, that is a good idea. Pregnant women need to relax and get enough sleep. This amount of alcohol will have no affect on your baby."
    b. "I don't think this is a good idea. You are putting your child at risk for fetal alcohol effects (FAE)."
    c. "I don't think this is a good idea. You are putting your child at risk for fetal alcohol syndrome (FAS)."
    d. "I'm pregnant too! Let's toast!"

18. Later-born children are: (p. 93; F)
    a. more likely to have birth defects and complications than first-born children.
    b. just as likely to have birth defects and complications than first-born children.
    c. less likely to have birth defects and complications than first-born children.

19. Your sister tells you that she is pregnant with her first child and wants to do all she can to make sure it is healthy. You tell her, (pp. 93-94; A)
    a. "Make sure you eat right. Don't forget you're eating for two now!"
    b. "Pay attention to your special nutritional needs. You should make sure you cut down on folic acid, but increase your calcium."
    c. "Make an appointment right away with your obstetrician. You need regular prenatal check-ups!"
    d. All of the above.

20. Grant and Janelle are expecting their first baby. Grant confides in you that he has a strange desire for pickles and ice cream. It appears that Grant is experiencing: (p. 95; A)
    a. parity with his wife.
    b. couvade.
    c. quickening.
    d. a midlife crisis.

True/False Questions (If a statement is FALSE, correct it).

1. Ova and sperm undergo the process of meiosis. (p. 66) True/False.

2. The 23rd pair of chromosomes are referred to as autosomes. (p. 66) True/False.

3. A child whose genotype is Bb is said to be homozygous for that trait. (p. 67) True/False.

4. A carrier is a person who carries both recessive genes for a characteristic. (p. 70) True/False.

5. Down Syndrome is also referred to as Trisomy-23 because it has three 23rd chromosomes. (p. 71) True/False.

6. The ovum can carry either the X or the Y chromosome. (p. 76) True/False.

7. Major organ development occurs during the fetal stage. (p.78) True/False.

8. Multiple pregnancies have increased since 1970 due to improved nutrition. (p. 80) True/False.

9. The endoderm develops into the muscles, bones, and circulatory system. (p. 82) True/False.

10. Cephalocaudal development refers to growth from the center of the body outward. (p. 82) True/False.

11. Quickening occurs around the 6th week of prenatal development. (p. 83) True/False.

12. Rubella is more dangerous in later prenatal development. (pp. 87-88) True/False.

13. Fathers who smoke may decrease their fertility. (p. 90) True/False.

14. Older mothers are at an increased risk of miscarrying their babies. (p. 93) True/False.

15. Pregnancy is perceived similarly the world over. (p. 95) True/False.

☐ REWARD YOURSELF! Play a video game or ride your bike!

ANSWERS - Chapter 3 Genetics and Prenatal Development

How Do Genes Influence Development? (pp. 65-71)
(1)genes; (2)chromosomes; (3)23; (4)46; (5)male; (6)female; (7)mitosis; (8)meiosis; (9)23; (10)23; (11)46; (12)karyotype; (13)size; (14)structure; (15)22; (16)autosomes; (17)sex chromosome; (18)sex; (19)female; (20)male; (21)genotype; (22)phenotype; (23)homozygous; (24)heterozygous; (25)dominant; (26)recessive; (27)recessive; (28)genotype; (29)phenotype; (30)carriers; (31)disease

	Father's genes	
	C	C
Mother's genes C	CC	CC
c	Cc	Cc

(32, 33) mo's and fa's phenotype - no cystic fibrosis
(34) 0 % chance child will have cystic fibrosis

	Father's genes	
	C	c
Mother's genes C	CC	Cc
c	Cc	cc

(35, 38) mo's/fa's phenotype: no cystic fibrosis
(36, 39) mo's/fa's genotype: Cc
(37, 40) mother and father are heterozygous
(41) ¼ (25%) chance child will have cystic fibrosis
(42) homozygous

(43)sex chromosomes; (44)sex-linked; (45)more likely; (46)more likely; (47)hemophilia, color-blindness, fragile X, baldness; (48)polygenic

1 Minute Quiz: 1. Mitosis 2. 46; 23 3. Cc; cleft chin; heterozygous 4. polygenic

What are Common Chromosomal Abnormalities? (pp. 71-72)
(49) chromosomal

	Characteristics			Chromosomal Pattern
(50)	d	1.	Down Syndrome	Extra 21st chromosome
(51)	a	2.	Turner's Syndrome	XO
(52)	b	3.	Klinefelter's Syndrome	XXY
(53)	c	4.	XYY (Supermale Syndrome)	XYY

How are Genetic Diseases Detected? (pp. 71-75)
(54) ultrasound; (55) CVS; (56) Amniocentesis; (57) Alpha-fetoprotein
(58) 1. Family has children with a genetic disorder; 2. Couple has known genetic disorder and wants family; 3. woman has had repeated miscarriages; 4. Older pregnant women; 5. At risk because of ethnicity, ancestry; 6. Couple related to each other

1 Minute Quiz: 1. Chromosomal; 2. C; 3. True

How does Prenatal Development Proceed? (pp. 75-85)
(59) ovum; (60) 13; (61) 28; (62) 24-48; (63) zygote; (64) menstrual phase, (65) follicular phase, (66) luteal phase; (67) spermatogenesis; (68) 72; (69) 200-500 million; (70) 60 million; (71) 6; (72) X; (73) Y; (74) X
(75) germinal stage (1st two weeks); embryonic stage (2 to 8 weeks); fetal stage (8 weeks to birth)

(76)Ectopic-f, (77)amnion-h, (78)chorion-o, (79)placenta-i, (80)umbilical-l, (81)cephalocaudal-j, (82)proximodistal-m, (83)quickening-a, (84)mesoderm-d, (85)teratogens-b, (86)embroyonic-g, (87)fetal-k, (88)germinal-c, (89)viability-e, (90)ectoderm-n

(91) 7-10; (92) 15; (93) 1 month; (94) 2 months; (95) 3 months; (96) 4 months; (97) 5 months; (98) 7 months; (99) 7 months; (100) 9 months

1 Minute Quiz: 1. C; 2. A; 3. True; 4. B

What Conditions Influence Pregnancy and Prenatal Development? (pp. 86-96)
(101)When exposure occurs; amount of teratogenic exposure; fetal characteristics
(102) teratogens; (103) diseases, drugs, environmental, (104) rubella; (105) syphilis; (106) AIDS; (107) thalidomide; (108) cocaine; (109) heroin; (110)cigarettes; (111)fetal alcohol syndrome; (112)alcoholic; (113)radiation; (114)chemicals

(115) 1. maternal age; 2. maternal stress; 3. parity
(116) 1. Good nutrition; 2. Appropriate weight gain; 3. Prenatal care
(117) culture
(118) In Western culture, pregnancy takes on several meanings. For both men and women, it means a major transition into adulthood. Women in Western culture worry about weight gain and physical appearance because of the cultural focus on these characteristics. Men are less concerned about the pregnancy and do not report as much pleasure about it as the mother. During the partner's pregnancy, some men may have symptoms (couvade), such as change in appetite, headaches, etc., that go away after childbirth. In Western cultures, this is seen as an expression of anxiety, ambivalence, or envy.
1 Minute Quiz: 1. False; 2. False; 3. C; 4. B

STUDY QUESTIONS

Multiple Choice: 1. B; 2. A; 3. C; 4. B; 5. B; 6. D; 7. D; 8. C; 9. A; 10. D; 11. B; 12. B; 13. A; 14. B; 15. A; 16. D; 17. B; 18. C; 19. C; 20. B

True/False Questions:
1. True
2. False; sex chromosomes
3. False; heterozygous
4. False; one dominant and one recessive
5. False; Trisomy-21, 21st
6. False; sperm
7. False; embryonic
8. False; fertility drugs
9. False; mesoderm
10. False; proximodistal
11. False; 16th week
12. False; early
13. True
14. True
15. False; differently

True Story! A pair of Michigan robbers entered a record shop nervously waving revolvers. The first one shouted, "NOBODY MOVE!" When his partner moved, the startled first bandit shot him!

52 Study Guide for Exploring Child Development

Chapter 4
Birth and Neonatal Development

My mother taught me ESP...
"Put your sweater on! Don't you think I know when you're cold?"
- Things My Mother Taught Me

Objectives
When you have completed this chapter, you will be able to
- detail the birth process, including the three stages of labor and pain reduction techniques;
- describe various birthing methods available in the U.S.;
- discuss birth complications, including Cesarean sections, induced labor, and breech and transverse presentations;
- describe the childbirth experience from the mother's, father's, and newborn's perspective;
- state research findings regarding parent-infant bonding;
- summarize some cultural differences in the childbirth experience;
- describe characteristics of the newborn, as well as the newborn's functions and capacities;
- describe problems experienced by neonates, such as prematurity and low birth weight;
- state consequences for the infant, as well as the family, of prematurity, low birth weight, and other risks;
- compare and contrast infant mortality rates both within and outside the U. S.; and
- define the key terms and concepts listed on page 133 of your text.

☑ Study Check List

☐ Read Chapter 4 Birth and Neonatal Development.

☐ Re-read the Chapter 4 Summary to refresh your memory.

☐ Read the Chapter 4 Objectives listed above.

☐ Complete the following items:

How is a Baby Born? (pp. 99 - 106)

To determine a baby's due date, the doctor will count _____ (1) days from the _____ (2) day of the woman's l_____ p_____ (3). Three percent of women give birth _____ (4) their due date and over 45 percent give birth give birth _____ (5) week before or after their due date.

Chapter 4 Birth and Neonatal Development 53

Most children are delivered between _____ and _____(6) weeks' gestation, but many children are preterm or delayed. Interestingly, **boys/ girls** *(circle one)* (7) tend to be born a few days earlier than **boys/girls** *(circle one)* (8), and women with shorter menstrual cycles tend to have **shorter/ longer** *(circle one)* (9) pregnancies. It is unknown what causes labor to begin, although ho_____(10), such as ox_____(11), do appear to be a factor.

About 2 to 3 weeks before birth, many women report that they feel more comfortable and can breathe easier. Such relief is referred to as li_____(12), and occurs because the fetus has dropped down into the p_____ c_____(13), relieving internal pressure on the mom. A woman who is giving birth to her first child is referred to as pr_____(14). She will probably be in labor **longer/ shorter** *(circle one)* (15) than a woman who is m_____, (16) or has had a baby before. Throughout pregnancy, women will have mild, irregular muscular contractions of the uterus. These contractions are called B_____(17). During late pregnancy, women may even have f_____ l_____(18); these contractions decrease in time, especially when women ex_____(19).

There are three stages of labor. These are: (20)

1. _____

2. _____

3. _____

Match the following:

_____episiotomy (21)   a. head elongates to allow easier passage through birth canal

_____crowning (22)   b. last part of dilation; contractions most severe

_____epidural block (23)   c. small incision to allow passage of baby's head

_____transition (24)   d. mucous plug dislodges

_____bloody show (25)   e. top of baby's head becomes visible

_____molding (26)   f. local anesthetic resulting in no pain from waist down

Stages of Labor - Place the following characteristics and experiences in the appropriate column: expulsion of placenta; dilation of cervix; mother relatively passive; expulsion of fetus; begins with cervix fully dilated, ends with baby's birth; 30-60 second contractions at 5-20 minute intervals; occurs 15-30 minutes after delivery; cervix dilates from .3 cm to 10 cm; contractions about 60 seconds, 1-3 minutes apart; water breaks; crowning; episiotomy; 5 minutes or less for multiparous woman, 1-2 hours for primiparous woman; lasts 12 to 24 hours in primiparous woman, 4-6 hours in multiparous woman; contractions continue to move placenta through canal; mucous plug dislodged; mother begins intense physical effort; transition; contractions most severe at end

Stage 1 (27)	Stage 2 (28)	Stage 3 (29)

Chapter 4 Birth and Neonatal Development 55

Women experience and respond to labor and delivery differently. For those women who experience a lot of pain, various me_____(30) have been used to alleviate it. In the past, sedatives and even general anesthesia have been used to help women sleep, rest, and manage labor pain. Unfortunately, it has been found that these medications cross the pl_____(31) and can af_____(32) the baby. For example, large dosages of sedatives or anesthetics may make a baby re_____(33) and wi_____(34) for days following birth. Some drugs are related to l_____ g d_____ (35) among school children. However, most evidence indicates that l_____(36) levels of medications used during birth do not significantly affect healthy babies. Mothers must weight the b_____(37) of pain relief with the potential af_____(38) of drugs on the newborn.

LESSONS IN REAL LIFE - LESSONS IN REAL LIFE - LESSONS IN REAL LIFE - LESSONS IN REAL LIFE

I. Sandy is pregnant and due to deliver in the next couple of months. She is going to special classes provided by a nurse at her local hospital. These classes have taught her about what to expect in delivery and how to prepare for labor. In fact, she talks about "taking cleansing breaths" and focus on a special picture she's chosen to help her relax and control pain. She also has chosen a coach to help her during the delivery. Her coach will be with her during labor and delivery. Apparently, Sandy is taking L_____(39) classes.

II. Terrance and his wife have chosen an obstetrician who believes that infants may experience trauma during the typical birthing procedure. The obstetrician uses a birthing room that is warm, with dim lighting. After the delivery, the obstetrician places the naked infant on the mother's bare belly, even before she cuts the umbilical cord. The infant is then given a warm bath. This obstetrician is following the birthing method pioneered by L_____(40).

III. Jayce has decided not to go to a hospital to have her baby. Instead, she is going to a place that allows her to eat, drink, get into any position that is comfortable for labor and delivery, and has nurse-midwives providing most of the care. These places are referred to as b_____ g c_____(41).

LESSONS IN REAL LIFE - LESSONS IN REAL LIFE - LESSONS IN REAL LIFE - LESSONS IN REAL LIFE

Women most at risk for complications during delivery are a_____(42), o_____(43) women (especially if it's a first child), women with certain di_____(44), and women carrying mu_____(45) babies.

56 Study Guide for Exploring Child Development

> ## Fun Facts
> It has been reported that Mrs. Fyodor Vassilyer (1707-1782) of Russia gave birth to 16 sets of twins, 7 sets of triplets, and 4 sets of quadruplets. Of her 69 children, 67 survived infancy!

Use these words to complete the following paragraphs:

breech	**induce**	**5**	**expensive**	**transverse**
infection	**increased**	**pitocin**	**cesarean section**	**longer**
abdomen	**repeat**	**malpractice**	**longer**	**21**

The most common type of major surgery performed in the U. S. today is the _____(46), in which the baby is delivered through an incision in the mother's _____(47). The number of these surgeries has _____(48) dramatically since the 1970s, from _____ (49) percent of all deliveries in 1970 to about _____ (50) percent today. Many reasons account for the increase in cesarean sections, including the ability of women to have _____(51) cesarean sections and concerns about _____(52) suits. Though sometimes necessary, cesarean sections have several drawbacks: They are _____(53), result in a _____(54) recovery period, and increase the risk of _____(55) to both mother and baby.

Sometimes, physicians are face with problems during pregnancy. For example, they may need to give the expectant mother _____(56) in an effort to _____(57) labor and delivery when it is determined that the pregnancy should not be prolonged. In addition, the fetus is not always positioned correctly in the uterus. Occasionally, the baby is positioned sideways in the uterus; such a position is known as a _____(58) presentation. More often, a baby is positioned so that it is born feet-first or butt-first. This position is referred to as _____(59) and usually involves _____(60) periods of labor. Some breech presentations may require a cesarean delivery.

---

1 Minute Quiz

1. The third stage of labor is marked by:
   a. contractions 5 to 10 seconds apart.
   b. the water breaking.
   c. expulsion of the fetus.
   d. expulsion of the placenta.

2. Irregular muscle contractions are referred to as false labor. True/False

Match (letters may be used more than once):
3. _____ Leboyer Method
4. _____ Transverse Presentation
5. _____ Cesarean Section
6. _____ Pitocin

   a. Major abdominal surgery
   b. Used to induce labor
   c. Feet first
   d. Teaches breathing, relaxation
   e. There is not match for this term.

How is Childbirth Experienced? (pp. 106 - 110)

List factors that contribute to the "baby blues:" (61)

1. _____
2. _____
3. _____
4. _____
5. _____
6. _____

How do the "baby blues" differ from postpartum depression? (62) _____

_____

_____

_____

58 Study Guide for Exploring Child Development

Fathers can play an important role in the birth process. They often serve as co_____(63) during labor and delivery. The more involved fathers are, the cl_____(64) they feel to their spouses and newborns. Father's involvement also affects the m_____(65) birth experience. When fathers are involved, mothers are less an_____(66) and not as likely to need me_____(67).

During the birth process, newborns produce extremely high levels of st_____(68) hormones, called ca_____(69). These stress hormones appear to help the newborn survive outside the womb, by clearing the l_____(70), promoting normal br_____(71), increasing the met_____(72) (resulting in heightened al_____) (73), and promoting parent-infant b_____(74).

Klaus and Kennell believe that there is a s_____(75) period immediately following birth in which mothers and infants b_____(76) through close physical contact. If this bonding is interrupted, parenting failures are **more/ less** *(circle one)* (77) likely, and the child is at **greater/ lesser** *(circle one)* (78) risk for abuse, neglect, and poorer parenting. However, research has not supported their original findings. It appears that there is *no* cr_____(79) period for parent-infant bonding. The ties that develop between caregivers and children develop over a l_____(80) period of time and over the course of multiple interactions. Therefore, newborns who are hospitalized at birth or are adopted can still develop healthy parent-child ties.

Who is most likely to attend a birth in the United States? _____(81)

Who is most likely to attend a birth among the Jahara of South America? _____(82)

What is meant by the statement "Birth is a social as well as a physical event?" Give an example. (83)

_____

_____

_____

_____

Chapter 4 Birth and Neonatal Development 59

---

1 Minute Quiz

1. The majority of women experience <u>baby blues/postpartum depression</u> *(circle one)* following birth.

2. Postpartum depression appears to be related to the following factor/s:
   a. biology.
   b. stressful life events.
   c. delivery complications.
   d. All of the above.

3. Fathers who are supportive during birth and labor have partners who are less anxious and distressed. True/False.

4. Stress hormones in the newborn appear to be <u>helpful/ harmful</u> *(circle one)*.

5. There is no evidence of a _____ period for human bonding.

What are the Characteristics of a Newborn (pp. 110 - 118)

List four major tasks newborns must accomplish: (84)

1. _____
2. _____
3. _____
4. _____

When a baby is born, it doesn't look like the Gerber baby. In fact, it is more likely to resemble Rocky Balboa after the 10th round of boxing! Its face is swollen, nose is flattened, and head is pointed. The newborn is covered with a waxy substance called <u>v_____</u>(85). The baby's coloring is uneven, and the genitalia is <u>en_____</u>(86). The average, healthy newborn is from _____ to _____(87) inches in length, and weighs about _____ to _____(88) pounds.

60 Study Guide for Exploring Child Development

To determine if the baby is healthy, medical personnel perform a quick screening test developed by Dr. Virginia Agar. It is referred to as the _____ (89) Scale. The baby is given a score of zero, one, or two on five different dimensions. These five dimensions are: (90)

1. _____
2. _____
3. _____
4. _____
5. _____

Memory Jog ⇒ "**M**y **C**olor **R**eflects **H**er **R**oses" - Muscles, Color, Reflexes, Heart rate, Respiration

Figure it Out! *Using Table 4.2, on page 111, determine the Apgar score for the following infants:*

Baby A's fingers and toes are blue, but her chest area is pink. Her heart rate is 125 beats per minute, and her breathing is slow and irregular. She makes active movements of her arms and legs. She cries vigorously during reflex testing. Baby A's Apgar score is _____. (91)

Baby B appears quite limp and only grimaces in response to reflexes. His respiration in slow and irregular and his heart rate is 79. Although his trunk is pink, his extremities are blue. Baby B's Apgar score is _____. (92)

Baby C enters the world crying lustily. His heart rate is 160 and he is pink all over. He actively moves his arms, legs, and head, and cries vigorously as the nurses attempt to test his reflexes. Baby C's Apgar score is _____. (93)

Match the reflex to the description and indicate its developmental course (see Table 4.3 on page 112):

a. _____ rooting (94)
b. _____ sucking (95)
c. _____ moro (96)
d. _____ babinski (97)
e. _____ palmar grasp (98)

1. Sucks rhythmically
2. Toes spread out and curl, foot turns inward when bottom of foot stroked
3. Grasps finger placed in palm of hand
4. Turns head toward finger or nipple brushed on side of cheek
5. Arches back, throws arms out then draws them in, in response to loud noise

1. Disappears in 5 to 6 mo's
2. Declines after 3 to 4 months
3. Disappears around 3 to 4 months
4. Changes to voluntary movement by 2 months
5. Changes at 12 months

Chapter 4 Birth and Neonatal Development 61

Babies are on a continuum of arousal from quiet sleep to active crying. These states will vary depending on the quality of the caregiving the infant receives. It is important to understand infant states because: (99)

1. _____
2. _____
3. _____

In terms of sleep, a newborn averages _____ (100) hours of sleep a day; however, they don't sleep in one long stretch. In fact, newborns typically sleep at _____ to _____ (101) hour intervals throughout the day. After about two weeks, newborns will sleep **longer/ shorter** *(circle one)* (102) during the night than during the day. As the infant gets older, the infant will sleep **more/ less** *(circle one)* (103). The amount of time an infant sleeps may be an indicator of br_____ dev_____(104).

One of the most surprising capabilities of newborns is their ability to i_____(105) facial expressions, such as pursed lips or stuck-out tongue. Babies as young as o_____(106) day old can imitate simple expressions and head movements. By s_____(107) weeks of age, infants not only imitate others in their presence, but can i_____(108) behaviors that have occurred in the past. This ability is known as d_____ i_____(109).

The most widely used instrument to test newborn behavior is the Brazelton N_____l B_____ A_____ S_____(110), which was developed to measure a newborn's response to the environment. Using simple equipment, the examiner assesses the newborn's r_____(111), m_____(112) capabilities, abilities to control a_____(113) and behavior, and responses to int_____(114) with others. By identifying problems in newborns early on, appropriate inter_____(115) can be developed.

62 Study Guide for Exploring Child Development

---

1 Minute Quiz

1. Neonate is another word for _____.

2. A screening test designed to determine whether emergency intervention is needed with newborns is the _____; a perfect score on this scale is _____.

3. The rooting reflex is an example of a (circle one) survival/ protective reflex.

4. Infants learn better in the _____ state.
   a. nonalert waking   c. fussing/crying
   b. quiet alert   d. sleep/wake transition

5. Infants are not capable of imitation until about 4 months of age. True/False.

How Does Early Brain Development Proceed? (pp. 118 - 121)

Match the following terms and definitions:

_____ neurons (116)   a. flexibility; aids in recovery from damage

_____ dendrites (117)   b. cells involved in the communication system of the brain

_____ axon (118)   c. normal decrease of neurons/connections due to genes and environment

_____ synapses (119)   d. outside covering of neurons; speeds electrical impulses.

_____ myelination (120)   e. at base of neuronal cell body, used for sending messages

_____ plasticity (121)   f. small gaps or spaces between cells

_____ pruning (122)   g. used for receiving messages

The chief architect of the brain is experience. What does this statement mean? (123)

_____
_____
_____
_____
_____

Chapter 4 Birth and Neonatal Development 63

List 4 serious outcomes of disruptions in growth and development during the brain's growth spurt: (124)

1. _____

2. _____

3. _____

4. _____

A serious source of disruption for infants is receiving inadequate st_____(125) during sensitive periods.

How Do Neonates Perceive Their Worlds? (pp. 121 - 124)

Compare the newborn and the adult in terms of sensory capabilities.

Newborn	Adult
Vision (126)	
Hearing (127)	
Taste (128)	
Smell (129)	
Touch (130)	

64 Study Guide for Exploring Child Development

What is meant by the "Dance of Perception?" (131)

_____

_____

---

1 Minute Quiz

1. Electrical impulses travel 3 times faster along _____.
   a. axons   b. dendrites   c. myelinated pathways.

2. Infant brains recover better from serious assaults because they are more:
   a. plastic than adult brains.
   b. protected than adult brains.
   c. immature than adult brains.

3. Caregivers who do not adequately stimulate their infants may cause their children to have poor brain development. True/False.

4. The least developed sense at birth is:
   a. vision   b. smell   c. taste   d. hearing.

Why are Some Newborns at Risk? (pp. 125 - 132)

What is meant by "preterm" or "premature" infants and "low birth weight" infants? (132)

_____

_____

Give an example of how prematurity and low birth weight interact with cultural and social variations in caregiving environments to influence a child's developmental outcome. (133)

_____

_____

_____

_____

Chapter 4 Birth and Neonatal Development 65

MOST PREMATURE OR LOW BIRTH WEIGHT BABIES DEVELOP NORMALLY. Some infants have negative outcomes. List 9 physical, social, and intellectual difficulties premature or low birth weight babies might have. (134)

1. _____

2. _____

3. _____

4. _____

5. _____

6. _____

7. _____

8. _____

9. _____

Describe the environment of a modern neonatal intensive care unit. (135)

_____

_____

_____

Cross out all of the following statements related to parenting a high-risk infant that are FALSE? (136)

1. The baby may need to be monitored for sleep apnea or require a ventilator.

2. Family life may deteriorate as parents spend less time with each other or with other children to care for the infant.

3. Families may experience financial difficulties.

4. Preterm infants tend to be more responsive, alert, and active than full-term infants.

5. Parents of preterm children take a more active role than parents of full term children.

6. Parents of very low birth weight or preterm infants who have a lasting illness are more likely to establish secure relationships than parents of full term infants.

7. Parents of preterm infants tend to provide more stimulation to their infants than parents of full-term infants.

66 Study Guide for Exploring Child Development

Use these words to complete the following paragraphs:

| Asian-American | low | African-American | prenatal | mortality |
| higher | family support | Caucasian-American | twenty | |

In the United States, the infant mortality rate is relatively _____(137). However, _____(138) other developed countries have lower rates than the U.S. Within the US, some groups have higher rates of infant _____(139). For example, infant mortality is much _____(140) for _____ (141) infants than for Caucasian American infants. _____(142) infants have a lower mortality rate than _____(143) infants. It is unknown why these groups differ in infant mortality, although _____(144) and postnatal care, as well as cultural values and _____(145), may account for some differences.

---

1 Minute Quiz

1. "Premature" and "low birth weight" mean essentially the same thing. True/False.

2. The percentage of low birth weight children living in poverty who were adaptive and resilient is <u>low/ high</u> *(circle one)*.

3. Most infants who are born too early or weight too little at birth:
   a. develop normally.
   b. have moderate learning disabilities.
   c. have severe intellectual, emotional, and social problems.

4. Except for the first few weeks, parenting a high-risk infant is not much different from parenting a normal infant. True/False.

5. The United States has the lowest infant mortality rate in the modern world. True/False.

☐ Complete the crossword puzzle in Appendix 1 – Crossword Puzzles.

☐ Go to the beginning of this chapter, and on a separate sheet of paper, write out the answers to the lesson objectives.

sAGE Advice

"Write down examples and sayings in the text margin to help you remember."

STUDY QUESTIONS

Multiple Choice (The following questions are identified as being "F," *factual questions* that rely on the recall of facts or "A", *applied questions* that rely on the ability to apply a concept to a real-life situation).

1. The baby is born in the _____ stage of labor. (p. 100; F)
   a. first   b. second   c. third   d. fourth

2. Jonathon and Liza are attending birthing classes that teach relaxation techniques. Most likely, they are attending: (pp. 102 - 104; A)
   a. Lamaze classes.
   b. Leboyer classes.
   c. neonatal classes.
   d. Montessori classes.

3. During labor, Jonathon and Liza hear the midwife say, "Yikes, the baby is coming out with its arm and shoulder first!" This type of birth is referred to as a _____ and usually _____. (p. 106; A)
   a. normal presentation; involves a normal vaginal delivery.
   b. breech presentation; leads to longer periods of labor but normal delivery.
   c. transverse presentation; involves longer periods of labor but normal delivery.
   d. transverse presentation; results in a Cesarean delivery.

4. Which of the following factors has NOT been identified as contributing to the "baby blues?" (p. 107; F)
   a. hormones
   b. fatigue
   c. loss of attention
   d. All of the above contribute to baby blues.

5. Newborns face four challenges after birth: Breathing on their own, controlling their body temperature, ingesting food, and: (p. 110; F)
   a. integrating their reflexes.
   b. bonding with a caregiver.
   c. changing their blood circulation.
   d. looking pretty ugly.

6. Santini is very proud of his newborn son. His son, he explains, got a "9" on his first test 1 minute following delivery and a "Perfect 10" on the same test 5 minutes later. The test Santini is referring to is probably the: (p. 111; A)
    a. Apgar scale.
    b. Brazelton Neonatal Assessment Scale.
    c. Test of Neonatal Reflexes.
    d. Newborn Effective Response Diagnostic Inventory (NERDI).

7. Grandma claps her hands with delight, and Baby Robert reacts to her clap by arching his back, flinging out his arms, and pulling his arms back to his chest. This is an example of: (pp. 112-113; A)
    a. Babinski Reflex.   c. Moro Reflex.
    b. Tonic Neck Reflex.   d. Rooting Reflex.

8. On average, newborns sleep about _____ hours a day. (pp. 114-116; F)
    a. 8   b. 12   c. 16   d. 20

9. It is important to understand arousal states of infants because: (p. 114; F)
    a. states of arousal influence infants' interactions with others and with their environment.
    b. infant states provide information about individual differences.
    c. the regularity of states provides a window on the maturity of the nervous system.
    d. All of the above.

10. Myelination occurs first in the parts of the brain that control: (p. 120; F)
    a. reflexes.   b. motor skills.   c. voluntary movements.   d. the senses.

11. Research has linked myelination to: (p. 120; F)
    a. behavioral development.   c. both behavioral and cognitive development.
    b. cognitive development.   d. neither behavioral nor cognitive development.

12. Sandi is concerned because her baby sustained a mild head injury in a car accident, even though the doctor told her not to worry. You tell Sandi, (p. 120; A)
    a. "While there is reason to be concerned because there probably will be some minor impairment, there are many things you can do to minimize the effects of the damage."
    b. "I'd be concerned, too, because damage to a baby's head results in more problems later on. Adults with brain injuries have fewer problems because they have already learned the important stuff."
    c. "Infant brains are very plastic and more flexible than adult brains. Your doctor is right and your baby will show no ill-effects."
    d. "Increase the amount of folic acid in your baby's diet. Proper nutrition can counteract the effects of brain damage."

13. Which of the following environmental factors probably has little impact on brain development? (pp. 120-121; F)
    a. nutrition
    b. exposure to diseases
    c. little to no social interaction
    d. All of the above can cause disruption in brain development.

14. Maybelle heard the doctor say that her newborn baby has visual acuity of 20:300. Based on what you read in your textbook, you know that: (pp. 121-122; A)
    a. the baby's vision is normal for its age and will continue to improve over the next 6 months.
    b. the baby's vision is normal for its age and will continue to improve over the next 12 months.
    c. the baby's vision is abnormal for its age, but can be corrected with glasses.
    d. the baby's vision is genetically related to the parents' nearsightedness, but can be corrected with glasses.

15. Regarding hearing in infancy, newborns: (pp. 122-123; F)
    a. can hear softer sounds that adults.
    b. prefer low-pitched sounds of short duration.
    c. are unable to localize sounds, such as a rattle coming from the left or right.
    d. seem particularly attuned to human voices.

16. Babies born prior to 38 weeks of pregnancy are referred to as: (p. 125; F)
    a. at-risk.   c. premature.
    b. low birth weigh. d. All of the above.

17. Bradley, et al (1994) found that the percentage of low birth weight children living in poverty who were adaptive and resilient was: (p. 125; F)
    a. very low compared to such children in more affluent, nonpoverty households.
    b. about the same as such children in more affluent, nonpoverty households.
    c. very high compared to such children in more affluent, nonpoverty households.

18. Most children who are born too early or weigh too little at birth: (pp. 126-127; F):
    a. are more likely to show a variety of physical problems, such as subnormal growth.
    b. display more difficulties in school.
    c. have more behavior problems, such as hyperactivity or poor social skills.
    d. will develop normally.

19. You get a job at a modern neonatal intensive care unit. Compared with such units of the past, you are likely to find that: (pp. 128-129; A):
    a. these units are much more sterile and there is an increased concern about germs.
    b. the unit mimics the conditions of the prenatal environment, with low lighting and infants swaddled in hammocks.
    c. there is increased reliance on well-developed formulas, rather than breastfeeding.
    d. parent interaction with infant is discouraged until the infant has gained the appropriate weight.

20. Sam's wife just had a premature and low birth weight baby that is going to require some long-term care. It is likely that Sam and his wife will: (pp. 130-131; A):
    a. find that this experience will initially bring them closer together as a couple.
    b. experience financial problems and stress.
    c. take on a more active role than parents of full term infants.
    d. B and C only.

True/False Questions (If a statement is FALSE, correct it).

1. The first stage of labor is marked by Braxton-Hicks contractions. (p. 100) True/False.

2. Adolescent girls and older women are at risk for complications during delivery. (p. 103) True/False.

3. High levels of stress hormones during the birthing process help the newborn to be alert and attentive following birth. (p. 108) True/False.

4. Scientific evidence supports the idea for a critical period for parent-infant bonding. (pp. 108-109) True/False.

5. Sleep and wake cycles of the infant may indicate brain development. (p. 116) True/False.

6. Newborns react to, but cannot imitate, facial expressions. (pp. 116-117) True/False.

7. Infant brains are less plastic than adult brains. (p. 120) True/False.

8. The pruning of neurons and connections between neurons are influenced only by environmental factors. (p. 120) True/False.

9. Infants who have depressed mothers and who receive less social interaction have brains that are less active. (p. 121) True/False.

10. Infants are born with the same ability as adults to perceive sight, sound, textures, smells, and tastes. (pp. 121-124) True/False.

11. The least-developed sense at birth is hearing. (pp. 122-123) True/False.

12. Newborns feel pain and show signs of distress when they are in pain. (p. 124) True/False.

13. Low birth weight usually is a more significant risk factor than prematurity. (p. 125) True/False.

14. High risk infants usually develop into healthy children. (p. 126) True/False.

15. Infant mortality in the United States is higher among Native-American Indians, African-Americans, Hispanics, and Asian-Americans than Caucasian-Americans. (p. 132) True/False.

☐ REWARD YOURSELF! Phone home (and be grateful the following true story isn't about you ☺).

In Colorado Springs, a young man walked into a little corner store with a shotgun and demanded all the cash from the cash drawer. After the cashier put the cash into a paper bag, the robber saw a bottle of scotch that he wanted behind the counter on the shelf. He told the cashier to put it in the bag as well, but the cashier refused, saying, "I don't believe you are over 21."

The robber insisted he was, but the clerk still refused to give it to him because he didn't believe him. At this point, the robber took out his driver's license and presented it to the clerk. The clerk looked it over, agreed that the man was indeed over 21, and put the scotch into the bag. The robber then ran from the store with his loot.

The cashier promptly called the police and gave the name and address of the robber that he taken off the license. The robber was arrested two hours later.

ANSWERS - Chapter 4 Birth and Neonatal Development

How is a Baby Born? (pp. 99-106)
(1)280, (2)first, (3)last period; (4)on; (5)one; (6)37 and 41; (7)girls; (8)boys; (9)shorter; (10)hormones; (11)oxytocin; (12)lightening; (13)pelvic cavity; (14)primiparous; (15)longer; (16)multiparous; (17)Braxton-Hicks; (18)false labor; (19)exercise
(20) (1) dilation of the cervix; (2) birth of the baby; (3) expulsion of the placenta
(21) episiotomy - c; (22) crowning - e; (23) epidural block - f; (24) transition - b; (25) bloody show - d; (26) molding - a
(27)Stage 1: dilation of cervix; mother relatively passive; 30-60 second contractions at 5-20 minute intervals; cervix dilates from .3 cm to 10 cm; water breaks; lasts 12 to 24 hours in primiparous woman; 4-6 hours in multiparous woman; mucous plug dislodged; transition; contractions most severe at end
(28)Stage 2: expulsion of fetus; begins with cervix fully dilated; ends with baby's birth; contractions about 60 seconds, 1-3 minutes apart; crowning; episiotomy; 5 minutes or less for multiparous woman, 1-2 hours for primiparous woman; mother begins intense physical effort
(29)Stage 3: expulsion of placenta; occurs 15-30 minutes after delivery; contractions continue to move placenta through canal
(30)methods; (31)placenta; (32)affect; (33)restless; (34)withdrawn; (35)learning disabilities; (36)low; (37)benefits; (38)affects
Lessons in Real Life: (39) Lamaze; (40) LeBoyer; (41) birthing center
(42)adolescents; (43)older; (44)diseases; (45)multiple
(46)Cesarean Section; (47)abdomen; (48)increased; (49)5; (50)21; (51)repeat; (52)malpractice; (53)expensive; (54)longer; (55)infection; (56)pitocin; (57)induce; (58)transverse; (59)breech; (60)longer
1 Minute Quiz: 1. d; 2. F; 3. e; 4. e; 5. a; 6. b

How is Childbirth Experienced? (pp. 106-110)
(61) 1. biological changes; 2. fatigue; 3. loss of attention; 4. increased demands at home; 5. sense of anticlimax; 6. feelings of inadequacy
(62) Baby blues rarely more than a week or two and go away without treatment; postpartum depression is marked by intense feelings of sadness, anxiety, despair and disrupt the new mother's ability to function and interact with her child.
(63)coaches; (64)closer; (65)mother's; (66)anxious; (67)medication; (68)stress; (69)catecholamines; (70)lungs; (71)breathing; (72)metabolism; (73)alertness; (74)bonding; (75)sensitive; (76)bond; (77)more; (78)greater; (79)critical; (80)long
(81)medical personnel, father, close family members or friends
(82)the entire community
(83) Birth obviously is a physical event, as the baby leaves the mother's body. It is also a social event, as it involves mother, father, child, and other relatives/friends and roles begin to change (wife/mother; husband/father; mother/grandmother, etc.). In some cultures, the entire village watches the birth of a baby; in the United States, birthing rooms are allowing any family members/friends in to witness and take part in the entire process. Not only that, typically parents bring in a VIDEO CAMERA, and presumably watch the film after dinner parties. How much more social can you get? ☺
1 Minute Quiz: 1. baby blues; 2. d; 3. T; 4. helpful; 5. critical

What are the Characteristics of a Newborn? (pp. 110-118)
(84) 1. Breathing on their own; 2. Changing blood circulation; 3. Controlling body temperature; 4. Ingesting food
(85) vernix caseosa; (86) enlarged; (87) 19 to 21; (88) 7 to 7½; (89) Apgar; (90) 1. respiration; 2. reflex responsiveness; 3. muscle tone; 4. color; 5. heart rate; (91) 8; (92) 4; (93) 10
(94) a-4, 3; (95) b-1, 4; (96) c-5, 1; (97) d-2, 5; (98) e-3, 2
(99) 1. States of arousal influence infants' interactions with others and with their environment; 2. infant states provide information about individual differences; 3. The regularity of states provides a window on the maturity of the nervous system.
(100) 16; (101) 2 to 3; (102) longer; (103) less; (104) brain development; (105) imitate; (106) one; (107) six; (108) imitate; (109) deferred imitation; (110) Neonatal Behavioral Assessment Scale; (111) reflexes; (112) motor; (113) attention; (114) interaction; (115) intervention
1 Minute Quiz: 1. newborn; 2. Apgar Scale, 10; 3. survival; 4. b; 5. False

How Does Early Brain Development Proceed? (pp. 118-121)
(116) Neurons-b; (117) dendrites-g; (118) axon-e; (119) synapses-f; (120) myelination-d; (121) plasticity-a; (122) pruning-c
(123) Early experiences actually change the structure and function of the brain. Animals that have not been stimulated by the environment have been found to have brains with fewer synaptic connections between neurons. Number of neurons, myelination, and synaptic connections are all affected by the environment, including experience.

Chapter 4 Birth and Neonatal Development 73

(124) 1. Permanent reduction in brain size; 2. A reduction in the number of neurons; 3. Reduced myelination of cells; 4. Decreased numbers of synaptic connections; (125) stimulation

How Do Neonates Perceive Their Worlds? (pp.121-124)
(126) Newborn: Vision - 20:300+, improves to 20:20 in 6 months; track slow moving objects; eye movements jerky
Adult: Vision - 20:20; very small, rapid movements when scanning
(127) Newborn: Sound - Structure for hearing more developed than vision; by one year of age similar to adult; can hear whispered speech; prefer high pitched sounds, can localize; attuned to human speech
Adult: Sound - can hear softer sounds than newborn, can hear sounds of short durations
(128) Newborn/Adult: Taste - can distinguish sweet, salty, bitter, sour; prefer sweet; infants have wider distribution of taste buds than adults
(129) Newborn/Adult: Smell - can distinguish between smells, turn away from unpleasant smells, turn toward more pleasant smells; one of first connections between newborn and caregiver
(130) Newborn/Adult: Touch - prenatal response to touch; parts of the nervous system that processes touch information develop early; feel pain;
(131) infant responds to caregiver and caregiver responds to infant
1 Minute Quiz: 1-c; 2-a; 3-True; 4-a

Why are Some Newborns at Risk? (pp. 125-132)
(132) "preterm" or "premature" infants - born prior to 38 weeks; "low birth weight" infants - born after 38 weeks but weighing less than 5½ pounds
(133) If a newborn is premature and brought into a culture that values children and an environment that is enriched, the child is more likely to overcome difficulties and reach his or her potential; premature babies who are brought into a poverty-stricken environment are not as likely to have the enriched environmental stimuli to encourage growth and development.
(134) 1. Subnormal growth; 2. Mental retardation; 3. Blindness; 4. Deafness; 5. Cerebral palsy; 6. Health problems; 7. Greater risk of having lower intelligence scores; 8. More difficulties in school; 9. More behavior problems
(135) Today, neonatal intensive care units have an abundance of specialized machines and equipment to care for infants; however, a major change is the overall environment. Neonatal intensive care units are more likely to attempt to mimic the conditions of the prenatal environment, with low lighting, hammocks for the infants, and medical personnel who know when to encourage or limit infant interactions. Parents are also encouraged to be part of their infant's early life.
(136) *Cross out 4 and 6.;* (137) Low; (138) twenty; (139) mortality; (140) higher; (141) African-American; (142) Asian-American; (143) Caucasian-American; (144) prenatal; (145) family support
1 Minute Quiz: 1-False; 2-low; 3-a; 4-False; 5-False

STUDY QUESTIONS
Multiple Choice: 1-B; 2-A; 3-D; 4-D; 5-C; 6-A; 7-C; 8-C; 9-D; 10-A; 11-C; 12-C; 13-D; 14-A; 15-D; 16-C; 17-A; 18-D; 19-B; 20-D

True/False Questions:
1. False - True Contractions
2. True
3. True
4. False - does not
5. True
6. False - can imitate
7. False - more plastic
8. False - Environmental and genetic
9. True
10. False - not born
11. False - vision
12. True
13. True
14. True
15. False - not higher among Asian-Americans

Glenn Beck's Toddler Miracle Diet*

Flabby Americans are always on the lookout for a new diet. The trouble with most diets is that you don't get enough to eat (the starvation diet), or you don't get enough variation (the liquid diet), or you go broke (the all-meat diet). Consequently, people tend to cheat on their diets, or quit after 3 days, or go right back to stuffing their faces after it is all over. Is there nothing you can do but give up and tell your friends you have a gland problem? Or is there a slim <groan> hope?

Such is the new Toddler Miracle Diet! Over the years you may have noticed, as I have, that most two-year-olds are trim. It came to me one day over a cup of black coffee and a carrot that perhaps their diet is the reason. After consultation with pediatricians, X-ray technicians, and distraught moms, I was able to formulate this new diet. It is inexpensive, offering great variety and sufficient quantity. Before embarking on this diet, however, be sure to check with your doctor ... otherwise you might have to see him afterward. Good luck!

DAY ONE
- Breakfast - One scrambled egg, one piece of toast with grape jelly. Eat 2 bites of egg, using your fingers; dump the rest on the floor. Take 1 bite of toast, then smear the jelly over your face and clothes.
- Lunch - Four crayons (any color), a handful of potato chips, and a glass of milk (3 sips only, then spill the rest).
- Dinner - A dry stick, two pennies and a nickel, 4 sips of stale beer. Bedtime Snack – Toast piece of bread and toss it on the kitchen floor.

DAY TWO
- Breakfast - Pick up stale toast from kitchen floor and eat it. Drink half bottle of vanilla extract or one vial of vegetable dye.
- Lunch - Half a tube of "Pulsating Pink" lipstick and a cigarette (to be eaten, not smoked). One ice cube, if desired.
- Afternoon Snack - Lick an all-day sucker until sticky, take outside, drop in dirt. Retrieve and continue slurping until it is clean again. Then bring inside and drop on the rug.
- Dinner - A rock or an uncooked bean, which should be thrust up your left nostril. Pour iced tea over mashed potatoes; eat with a spoon.

DAY THREE
- Breakfast - Two pancakes with plenty of syrup, eat with fingers, rub in hair. Glass of milk: drink half, stuff pancakes in glass. After breakfast, pick up yesterday's sucker from rug, lick off fuzz, and put it on the cushion of your best chair.
- Lunch - Three matches, peanut butter and jelly sandwich. Spit several bites onto the floor. Pour glass of milk on table and slurp up.
- Dinner - Eat crumbs off kitchen floor and dining room carpet. Find that sucker and finish eating it.

Good luck!!!

*From Glenn Beck at http://www.glennbeck.com. Reprinted with permission.

Chapter 5
Physical and Cognitive Development in Infancy and Toddlerhood

My mother taught me TO MEET A CHALLENGE...
"What were you thinking?! Answer me when I talk to you...Don't talk back to me!"

Objectives

When you have completed this chapter, you will be able to
- outline the physical development of infants and toddlers;
- describe the major milestones of motor development in infants and toddlers;
- discuss how changes in motor development influence the entire family system;
- describe ways to promote healthy growth and development in infants and toddlers within a safe environment;
- define failure to thrive syndrome and state its causes and impact on development;
- summarize the perceptual abilities of infants;
- describe changes in the cognitive abilities of infants and toddlers, including how they learn and what they remember;
- discuss the six substages of sensorimotor development and identify the substage a child is in given specific examples of behaviors;
- compare and contrast Piaget's theory of cognitive development with Vygotsky's theory of cognitive development;
- describe normal language development in children, including the age children are expected to acquire specific speech and language skills;
- discuss the theories that have been used to explain how children acquire speech and language;
- describe ways caregivers encourage speech and language development; and
- define the key terms and concepts listed on page 178 of your text.

☑ Study Check List

☐ Read Chapter 5 Physical and Cognitive Development In Infancy and Toddlerhood.

☐ Re-read the Chapter 5 Summary to refresh your memory.

☐ Read the Chapter 5 Objectives listed above.

☐ Complete the following items:

How Do Infants and Toddlers Develop Physically? (pp. 141 - 146)

Children's growth during the first two years is dramatic. In fact, aside from prenatal growth, there is no other period of life in which children grow as quickly as they do during the first year. The infant's proportions are very different than older children's and adults'. A newborn's head makes up about _____(1) percent of its body! Imagine if your head were that big!

In the first five months of life, the infant's birth weight _____(2). By the end of the first year, its birth weight has _____(3). And by 30 months, the infant's birth weight has _____(4). At age 2, children have reached about _____(5) of their adult height. Suppose Jane's baby is 7 pounds at birth, and the baby grew according to the average growth rate. *Fill in the following table:*

Jane's Baby

Birth Weight	_____	(6)
5 Months Old	_____	(7)
1 Year Old	_____	(8)
2 ½ Years Old	_____	(9)

If Jane's baby was 36 inches tall at age two and lives in a healthy environment, he could be ____(10) feet tall when he is an adult. Both genetic and environmental factors will influence the growth patterns of the baby.

Put the following motor skills in the correct chronological order and match with the appropriate age:
walking, crawling, lifts head, sits alone, turns head to side, stands with support, sits with support, creeping; first month, sixth month, 12-15 months, ninth month, third month, second month, one week, eight month (11)

Ability	Age
_____	_____
_____	_____
_____	_____
_____	_____
_____	_____
_____	_____
_____	_____
_____	_____

Chapter 5 Physical and Cognitive Development in Infancy and Toddlerhood 77

The normal range for motor development is very large. One infant may progress quickly, while another infant progresses slowly. A wiry, curious infant may be off and running at 11 months; but a roly-poly laid-back infant may wait until he's 15 months to walk. However, *both* infants could be normal. It should be noted that all infants do develop from "head to tail," or rather in a ceph_____(12) direction.

Once an infant begins walking, the world changes for both the infant and the caregivers. *Describe some common changes associated with the child and the parent when the child begins walking:* (13)

_____

_____

_____

_____

During these early years, toilet training is a concern for many parents. The ability to be toilet trained increases at the end of the s_____(14) year or beginning of the th_____(15) year. Usually, toddlers gain control over bo_____(16) movements before they control urination. Only 2 percent of children are not toilet trained by the age of _____(17). B_____(18) usually take longer to be toilet trained than girls.

---

1 Minute Quiz

1. **If Sammy weighs 8 ½ pounds at birth and grows normally, he will probably weigh _____ at 1 year.**
   a. 17 pounds   c. 25 ½ pounds
   b. 20 pounds   d. 36 pounds

2. **Children usually begin walking at around _____ months of age.**

3. **Infants who can walk show (circle one) greater/ lesser levels of distress when separated from their caregivers and (circle one) greater/ lesser affection when in their presence.**

78 Study Guide for Exploring Child Development

What Factors Influence Infant Health and Safety? (pp.146 - 150)

To promote healthy development, children should see a pediatrician for a well-child check _____(19) times during the first year of life, and then _____(20) times over the next four years. The child's check-up should include: (21)

1. _____
2. _____
3. _____
4. _____

LESSONS IN REAL LIFE - LESSONS IN REAL LIFE - LESSONS IN REAL LIFE - LESSONS IN REAL LIFE

Infants are also at risk for many types of accidents. Your textbook gives several examples of common ways infants are hurt and suggests that parents and caregivers "babyproof" their homes. Suppose you are a first time parent. For each of the following hazards, write one way to avoid injury to your infant:

Car Accident: _____(22)

Backyard Pool: _____(23)

Toilet bowl cleaner under sink: _____(24)

Stairs and walkers: _____(25)

Antique crib with widely spaced slats: _____(26)

5 gallon bucket filled with water for cleaning: _____(27)

Crib next to a curtain pull: _____(28)

LESSONS IN REAL LIFE - LESSONS IN REAL LIFE - LESSONS IN REAL LIFE - LESSONS IN REAL LIFE

Adequate nutrition is essential for healthy infant development. Most infants will be adequately nourished from br_____ m_____(29) or f_____(30). However, the best nutrition for an infant is b_____ m_____(31). Even malnourished mothers can produce adequate breast milk.

Write 5 benefits of breast milk to infants: (32)

1. _____
2. _____
3. _____
4. _____
5. _____

Write 5 benefits of breast-feeding to mothers: (33)

1. _____
2. _____
3. _____
4. _____
5. _____

Breastfeeding is more common among c_____(34) educated and h_____(35) income women, and today about _____(36) percent of mothers breastfeed. Some mothers should not breastfeed their infants because they are taking certain m_____(37) or they have certain diseases, such as A_____(38). Formula-fed infants can also be healthy and using a bottle allows other f_____(39) members to participate in caring for the baby. No matter what method a parent chooses, most pediatricians recommend that the baby be fed on d_____(40) and not be placed on the rigid 4-hour feeding schedules of the past.

Infants should not be given solid foods until they are about _____ to _____ (41) pounds or between ____ and ____ (42) months of age. The first foods should be s_____(43) because babies are unable to chew well until their second year. Most parents give their babies c_____(44) to start, followed by f_____(45) and v_____(46). Protein foods, such as cheese, yogurt, egg yolks, and pureed meats can be introduced at _____ to _____(47) months, but whole eggs and milk should be delayed until the baby is _____ (48) year old. With age, the toddler will develop more mature eating habits; however, their diet must include nutrient dense foods. Parents **should/ should not** *(circle one)* (49) restrict fat from a toddler's diet.

Failure-to-thrive syndrome is _____

_____

_____(50)

What are 3 causes of failure-to-thrive (FTT) syndrome? (51)

1. _____

2. _____

3. _____

Failure-to-Thrive is more than a growth problem. Children with FTT are also likely to: (52)

1. _____

2. _____

3. _____

4. _____

5. _____

6. _____

7. _____

What are 3 outcomes of FTT and what can affect these outcomes? (53)

1. _____

2. _____

3. _____

_____

_____

Chapter 5 Physical and Cognitive Development in Infancy and Toddlerhood 81

How Do Infants' Perceptual Abilities Develop? (pp. 151 - 152)

For each of the following pairs, circle what an 8-month-old infant would prefer looking at:

a. a face	a flower	(54)
b. face with distorted features	face with typical features	(55)
c. attractive face	unattractive face	(56)
d. moving object	stationary object	(57)
e. simple patterns of motion made by people	complex patterns of motion made by people	(58)

The visual cliff apparatus has been used to test infants perception of d_____(59). By

_____(60) months, most infants will avoid the cliff area of the apparatus, suggesting that infants respond

to changes in d_____(61). Prior to this age, infants may or may not avoid the cliff. The

ability to detect depth and distance is probably to due to changes in the infant's vi_____(62) system.

How Do Infants and Toddlers Learn and Remember? (pp. 152 - 156)

Apply the correct terms/concepts to the following situations:

habituation, classical conditioning, infantile amnesia, deferred imitation, operant conditioning

1. Justin's parents took Justin to Disneyland when he was 18 months old because they wanted him to "Experience Disneyland and celebrate Donald Duck's 35th Anniversary!" However, Justin is now 12 and wants to go to Disneyland because he says he's never been there. Justin's inability to recall going to Disneyland is referred to as _____(63).

2. Samantha was given her measles vaccination by a nurse wearing a white coat. Now, whenever Samantha sees someone wearing a white coat, she begins to cry and whimpers, "No shot! No shot!" Samantha has come to associate the white coat and the shot through _____(64).

3. Gary is trying to keep his infant daughter quiet in church. He repeatedly waves a colorful doll in front of her. Although the doll appeared interesting at first, his daughter begins fussing and appears bored with the doll. This behavior provides evidence of _____(65).

4. 18-month-old LaShawna saw a young child throw a huge temper tantrum in the grocery store. A week later at the grocery store, LaShawna throws a very similar tantrum. LaShawna is evidencing _____(66).

5. Little Christopher randomly made a "growling" noise that resulted in his older sister paying attention to him and telling him to stop. He continued to make the noise and laugh while his sister, obviously perturbed, continued telling him to stop. Christopher apparently associated his actions with his sister's response, meaning that he was learning through _____(67).

82 Study Guide for Exploring Child Development

Infants' memories appear to be con_____(68) bound. Under what circumstances are young children more likely to remember an event? (69)

_____

_____

_____

_____

---

1 Minute Quiz

1. Unfortunately, most childhood accidents and health problems cannot be prevented. True/False.

2. One of the benefits of bottle-feeding an infant rather than breastfeeding an infant is that bottle-feeding is cleaner and more sanitary. True/False.

3. The most common causes of Failure-To-Thrive are _____ and _____.

4. By 12 weeks of age, infants prefer to look at _____.

5. Long-term memories in toddlers have yet to be documented. True/False.

How Do Cognitive Abilities Develop During the Sensorimotor Period? (pp. 156 - 165)

Use these words to complete the following paragraphs:

reflexes	Piaget	combine	cognitive
intentional	object permanence	primary circular reactions	intelligence
problem-solvers	symbols	tertiary circular reactions	goal
six	sensorimotor	secondary circular reactions	previous

According to _____(70), infants and toddlers undergo rapid changes in _____(71) development. Piaget referred to the first period of cognitive development as the _____(72) period, and divided this period into _____(73) substages. Each stage builds on the skills acquired in the _____ (74) stage. In stage 1 (1 month), infants learn about the world through their use of _____(75). Their behavior is not yet purposeful. During stage 2 (1 to 4 months), infants engage in repetitive actions centered on their bodies. These actions are referred to as _____(76). During stage 3 (4 to 8 months), infants begin to _____(77) their actions and begin to explore the qualities of objects rather than their own body. Infants will repeat actions over and over in an effort to reproduce sounds or sights. Repeating actions with objects is called _____(78).

As infants move into stage 4 (8 to 12 months), they show the first signs of _____(79), marked by truly _____(80) behavior. Infants often start an action with a _____(81) in mind. Infants at this stage also begin to develop _____, (82) understanding that things continue to exist even when they are out of sight.

At stage 5 (12 to 18 months), infants become creative _____(83). They now will develop new strategies to solve a problem. Using _____(84), infants will systematically modify their behaviors in subtle ways to explore the effects of those modifications. Through trial-and-error, the infant learns about the world; leading Piaget to dub the child at this stage the "Little Scientist." At stage 6 (18 to 24 months), the child is able to use _____(85) for the first time, to represent objects in their minds. Now, the child can imagine actions and consequences beforehand.

Place the following behaviors in the correct order, identify the sensorimotor stage, and indicate the average age for each behavior:

pretending to feed a baby
flushing different objects down the toilet
grasping anything placed in its hand
repeatedly "blowing raspberries"
repeatedly tossing their bottle on the floor
spying the dog, then crawling over to it to whack it with the plastic cup

84 Study Guide for Exploring Child Development

Substage	Behavior	Age
I.		(86)
II.		(87)
III.		(88)
IV.		(89)
V.		(90)
VI.		(91)

Memory Jog ⇒ "Sensorimotor Period" - infants learn about the world through their senses (i.e., sensori-) and their actions (i.e., -motor) on the objects around them.

Memory Jog ⇒ "Primary" and "Secondary" Circular Reactions - "circular" refers to repeating over and over; "primary" involves one's own body and "secondary" involves objects outside of one's body.

> **Hint from Mom...**
> Don't play "Peek-a-Boo" by hiding outside the sight of a baby who has not yet obtained object permanence. When you suddenly reappear, shouting "Peek-a-boo!", baby will startle and scream! After all, when you were out of sight, you were also out of mind. ☺

Piaget believed that infants form concepts from their direct experience with objects; Mandler believes that infants may develop basic concepts about the world around them from their p_____ l_____ k_____(92) alone. Mandler posits that infants form primitive notions based on visual appearances of objects. These primitive notions are called i_____ s_____(93). From image schemas, infants may develop perception-based concepts that help them learn about the world without direct interaction with it.

Recall that according to Russian Lev Vygotsky, social interactions are essential for learning and infants' cognitive development is acquired through interactions with their more skilled and experienced caregivers. One informal teaching method used by caregivers is sc_____(94). In scaffolding, a parent initially provides a lot of support and guidance; however, as the infant learns the activity, the

Chapter 5 Physical and Cognitive Development in Infancy and Toddlerhood 85

parent provides less help and/or introduces new skills. Suppose a parent buys a ring-toss game for his toddler. *Describe how, through scaffolding, the parent might teach the toddler to use this toy.* (95)

_____

_____

_____

_____

_____

---

1 Minute Quiz

1. According to Piaget, infants don't show signs of true intelligence until Stage ____, when infants can _____ apply a scheme to reach a goal.

2. Angela dropped her rattle outside her crib. Although she cannot see it, she cries for it. It is evident that Angela shows signs of:
   a. habituation.
   b. object permanence.
   c. secondary circular reactions.
   d. being spoiled.

3. Mandler believes that infants can develop basic concepts about the world through perceptual knowledge alone, and infants don't need to directly act on objects to learn about them. True/False.

4. In general, caregivers who are responsive and sensitive to their children's interactions encourage cognitive development. True/False

---

How Do Infants and Toddlers Develop Language Skills? (pp. 165 - 170)

Match the following:

_____ phoneme   a. sentences omitting the little words, such as "the" or "a"
(96)

_____ semantics   b. motherese
(97)

_____ syntax   c. one's understanding of language
(98)

86 Study Guide for Exploring Child Development

_____ pragmatics (99) d. smallest meaningful unit of language consisting of basic sounds

_____ receptive language (100) e. practical rules guiding communication

_____ expressive language (101) f. single word that stands for a whole sentence

_____ holophrase (102) g. word meaning

_____ Language Acquisition Device (103) h. grammar or rules of the language, word order

_____ Child-Directed Speech (104) i. ability to produce language

_____ telegraphic speech (105) j. in-born guide or blueprint for recognizing language

Place the following language accomplishments in the appropriate row and column: understands "No!", consonant-vowel combinations (babbling), 2-word sentences, says first word, coos, vocabulary explosion begins (106)

Language Development Table

	Receptive Language	Expressive Language
2 months		
6 months		
9 months		
12 months		
18 months		
24 months		

Memory Jog ⇒ 1st Word - Age 1
2-Word Sentences - Age 2

LESSONS IN REAL LIFE - LESSONS IN REAL LIFE - LESSONS IN REAL LIFE - LESSONS IN REAL LIFE

I. Jenn tells you that her son was just seen by a speech-language pathologist, who found that her son's expressive language is delayed. Jenn says that she can't remember exactly what the term was; however, her son appears to have difficulty putting words in the correct order. For example, instead of saying "Is Daddy coming home?" her son says, "Daddy is coming home?" This problem is a disorder of **phonemes/semantics/syntax/pragmatics** *(circle one)*. (107)

II. Three-year-old Sheila has learned that if she wants something from Grandma, she should say, "May I please have it, Gramma?" However, when she wants something from her 5-year-old brother, she says,

Chapter 5 Physical and Cognitive Development in Infancy and Toddlerhood 87

"Gimme!" It appears that Sheila understands the **phonemic/semantic/syntactic/ pragmatic** *(circle one)* aspect of language. (108)

III. Four-year-old Jacob has difficulty following basic commands, such as "Sit on the chair" or "Put the book on the table." Jacob's difficulty is in the area of **expressive/receptive** *(circle one)* language. (109)

How is Children's Language Acquisition Explained? (pp. 170 – 177)

Language acquisition has been explained by theorists in terms of nature (i.e., biology) vs. nurture (i.e., learning). Sk_____(110) believed that language was learned through re_____(111). Other behaviorists suggested that language could also be learned through ob_____(112). Learning-based theories are useful in explaining some aspects of language acquisition, but they do not explain how children learn the rules of gr_____(113). For example, a young child will say "foots" when referring to two feet. The child has never heard a parent use "foots" or been reinforced to produce this word; however, it appears that the child has learned the "plural rule," i.e., adding the "s" sound at the end of a word turns it into a plural. This ability to learn rules appears to be in-born and based in biology.

The leading biological theory of language acquisition was proposed by Ch_____(114). He believes that children are born with a la_____ ac_____(115) device that allows them to understand the properties of all human languages. Chomsky's theory is supported by the fact that children worldwide seem to learn language in the same way and at the same rate. Lenneberg believes that there is a cr_____(116) period for learning language, and that period is from age _____ to _____(117). If language is not learned within this time frame, a person will have difficulty acquiring it.

Social interaction plays an important role in children's acquisition of language. An interesting aspect of how adults interact verbally with children is the adults' use of child-directed speech.

Give 4 characteristics of child-directed speech (see Table 5.5): (118)

1. _____
2. _____
3. _____
4. _____

---

1 Minute Quiz

1. Meanings associated with words are referred to as _____.

2. Children say their first word by age _____.

3. A word that conveys the meaning of a whole sentence is a/n _____.

4. Chomsky believes that children are born with a _____ _____ that gives them the ability to understand the properties of language.

5. _____ is the version of language that caregivers use with their children, consisting of simple, repetitive sentences and higher pitched voice.

☐ Complete the crossword puzzle in Appendix 1 – Crossword Puzzles.

☐ Go to the beginning of this chapter, and on a separate sheet of paper, write out the answers to the lesson objectives.

SAGE Advice

"The night before an exam, just before going to bed, scan the information you have studied. As soon as you wake up, quickly scan it again."

STUDY QUESTIONS

Multiple Choice (The following questions are identified as being "F," *factual questions* that rely on the recall of facts; or "A," *applied questions* that rely on the ability to apply a concept to a real-life situation).

1. By the end of the first year, a child's birth weight usually has: (p. 143; F)
   a. doubled. b. tripled. c. quadrupled. d. stabilized.

2. Jared has just learned to walk. Jared is probably about: (p. 144; A)
   a. 6 months old. c. 18 months old.
   b. 12 months old. d. 24 months old.

3. After their infant learns to walk, parents are likely to: (p. 145; F)
   a. express anger toward their infant and expect the infant to comply with their demands.
   b. hold their infant responsible for his actions.
   c. express more affection toward the infant as a result of his accomplishments.
   d. All of the above.

4. To promote healthy development and growth, children should receive _____ well-child visits to the pediatrician during the first year of life. (p.147; F)
   a. 3 b. 6 c. 9 d. 12

5. Which of the following statements is NOT associated with breastfeeding? (p. 148; F)
   a. Breast-fed infants tend to be more irritable, reactive, physiologically adaptive than bottle-fed babies.
   b. Breast-fed infants have less risk of some diseases later in life, including allergies and diabetes.
   c. Breastfeeding helps mothers recover more quickly from childbirth.
   d. All of the above are associated with breastfeeding.

6. Your friend tells you that her mother says it is okay to start offering cereal to her 6-week-old infant. You tell your friend, (p. 149; A)
   a. "Yes, your mother is correct. Most pediatricians today encourage mothers to offer cereal to infants beginning at 6 weeks."
   b. "Your mother is incorrect. Most pediatricians today recommend delaying solid foods until the child is between 4 to 6 months."
   c. "Your mother is incorrect. Most pediatricians today recommend delaying solid foods until the child is 12 months old."
   d. "Your mother is correct. Begin by offering a variety of foods, however, not just cereal."

7. Which of the following factors is NOT associated with failure-to-thrive syndrome? (p. 150; F)
   a. Undernutrition
   b. Malnutrition
   c. Quality of interactions between the child and the caregiver.
   d. All of the above have been found to be factors in FTT.

8. Your sister just had a baby girl. You decide to give the baby a picture to attach to the side of the crib for the baby to look at. Knowing a little bit about infant visual preferences, you give a picture of: (p. 151; A)
   a. your face.   b. a colorful flower.   c. a red ball.   d. a baby.

9. Using a visual cliff apparatus, it has been found that by _____ months of age, infants show fear of heights and can respond to changes in depth. (p. 152 ; F)
   a. 5   b. 7   c. 10   d. 12

10. Longterm memory in infants: (p. 154; F)
    a. cannot be demonstrated with any reliability.
    b. can be demonstrated under certain conditions, such as testing in the same environment and being given a reminder.
    c. is evident in infants over 6 months of age.

11. Anna's baby sucks anything put in his mouth. This behavior is characteristic of: (p. 157; A)
    a. Stage I - Using Reflexive Schemes
    b. Stage II - Exploring Movements of the Body
    c. Primary circular reactions.
    d. Secondary circular reactions.

12. Lana teases her baby by covering the baby's rubber ducky with a blanket. Lana's baby begins crying and looking around the room for the ducky. It is apparent that: (p. 159; A)
    a. Lana's baby has not yet developed object permanence.
    b. Lana's baby has developed object permanence.
    c. Lana's baby is in Stage IV - Active Problem Solving.
    d. Lana's baby is in Stage VI – Using Symbols to Represent Reality

13. Geoffrey pretends that he is asleep by closing his eyes. This behavior is characteristic of: (p. 160; A)
    a. Stage IV - Active Problem Solving.
    b. Stage V - Creative Problem Solving.
    c. Stage VI - Using Symbols to Represent Reality.

14. When comparing theorists, (p. 164; F)
    a. Piaget believed that infants form concepts from their direct experience with objects, but Mandler believed that infants may develop basic concepts about the world from their perceptual knowledge alone.
    b. Mandler believed that infants form concepts from their direct experience with objects, but Piaget believed that infants may develop basic concepts about the world from their perceptual knowledge alone.
    c. Vygotsky believed infants develop cognitive skills through interactions with others more skilled than themselves.
    d. Piaget, Mandler, and Vygotsky believe that culture has little impact on learning or cognitive growth.

15. Scaffolding: (p. 164; F)
    a. helps children extend their current skills to a higher level of competence.
    b. is used equally effectively by both mothers and fathers.
    c. varies depending on culture.
    d. All of the above.

16. Stephen has just started babbling, combining consonants and vowels. Stephen is probably about _____ months old. (p. 167; A)
    a. 3   b. 6   c. 9   d. 12

17. Woody understands more than he says. Therefore, (p. 169; A)
    a. Woody's expressive language is better than his receptive language.
    b. Woody's receptive language is better than his expressive language.
    c. Woody's receptive and expressive language are probably about the same.
    d. Woody's pragmatic language is poor.

18. Jay-Jay says, "Ball!", meaning "Mommy, throw the ball to me!" This is an example of: (p. 169; A)
    a. semantics.
    b. telegraphic speech.
    c. a holophrase.
    d. receptive language.

19. Learning theories of language acquisition best account for: (p. 173; F)
    a. idioms and dialects.
    b. universal features of language.
    c. creativity in language.
    d. grammar.

20. Your baby is just starting to talk. According to the latest research, if you want to help your baby develop excellent speech and language skills, you should: (p. 174; A)
   a. avoid using simplified sentences with your baby.
   b. avoid speaking in a high pitch with your baby.
   c. slow down the tempo of your speech, use simpler vocabulary, and expand your baby's utterances.
   d. use more words per utterance.

True/False Questions (If a statement is FALSE, correct it).

1. Infants experience a growth spurt in height and weight that is more rapid than any other time in the lifespan except for prenatal development. (p. 143) True/False.

2. Infants gain control over muscles in a cephalocaudal direction. (p. 143) True/False.

3. Walking is one of the first major motor accomplishments that infants master. (p. 144) True/False.

4. Most children have control or awareness of the physical sensations associated with elimination by 12 months. (p. 146) True/False.

5. Compared with the 1970s, fewer mothers are breastfeeding their infants. (p. 149) True/False.

6. With adequate diets, failure-to-thrive infants can grow normally. (p.150) True/False.

7. Infants begin to discriminate colors, recognize patterns, and prefer faces at around 6 months of age. (p. 151) True/False.

8. Habituation involves decreasing responsiveness to repeated and meaningless stimuli. (p. 153) True/False.

9. Long-term memories have not been documented in toddlers. (p. 154) True/False.

10. Primary circular reactions are repetitive actions that focus on the noises or shapes of objects. (p. 157) True/False.

11. According to Piaget, infants do not show the first signs of true intelligence until they can intentionally apply a scheme to reach a goal. (p. 158) True/False.

12. According to Mandler, infants develop concepts from their perceptions of them more than from their direct actions with them. (p. 164) True/False.

13. Semantics refers to the rules of forming sentences. (p. 166) True/False.

14. Infants begin to form two-word sentences when they are around 1 year old. (p.169) True/False.

15. Caregivers support children's language development mainly through the use of simplified and exaggerated speech. (p. 174) True/False.

☐ **REWARD YOURSELF!** Read a book to a child.

94 Study Guide for Exploring Child Development

ANSWERS - Chapter 5 Physical and Cognitive Development in Infancy and Toddlerhood

How Do Infants and Toddlers Develop Physically? (pp. 141-146)
(1) 25; (2) doubles; (3)tripled; (4) quadrupled; (5) ½; (6) 7 lbs, (7) 14 lbs., (8) 21 lbs, (9) 28 lbs. ; (10) 6 feet tall
(11) turns head to side-one week; lifts head-first month; sits with support-third month; crawling/stands with support-sixth month; sits alone-eighth month; creeping-ninth month; walking-12-15 months
(12) cephalocaudal
(13) infants - react with increased frustration/anger; show greater levels of distress when separated from caregivers. Parents - anger expression increases; hold infants more responsible for actions; expect infants to comply; express more affection
(14) second; (15) third; (16) bowel; (17) 4; (18) boys
1 Minute Quiz: 1.C; 2. 12; 3. greater; greater

What Factors Influence Infant Health and Safety? (pp. 146-150)
(19) 6; (20) 6; (21) 1. assessment of growth; 2. review/update medical history; 3. physical exam; 4. general guidance
(22) seat belts; (23) gates; (24) locks; (25) gates; (26) new crib; (27) empty bucket; (28) move crib
(29) breast milk; (30) formula; (31) breast milk; (32) balanced nutritionally, more digestible, more resistant to infections, cleanliness, lower risk of illnesses, higher intelligence; (33) closeness, lose more weight, recover quickly from childbirth, delays ovulation, easy, free
(34) college; (35) higher; (36) 60; (37) medications; (38) AIDS; (39) family; (40) demand; (41) 13-14; (42) 4-6 months; (43) soft; (44) cereals; (45) fruits; (46) vegetables; (47) 6-8; (48) 1; (49) should not
(50) infants who do not appear to be ill or abnormal but who do not grow at the expected rates
(51) undernutrition; malnutrition; quality of interactions
(52) show abnormal behaviors; lack nurturing caregivers; be passive and inactive; be shy and withdrawn; show little expression of emotion; avoid close physical contact; show unusual eating behaviors
(53) lag behind in language development, reading, verbal intelligence, and social maturity; depends on how long child had FTT and ongoing quality of caregiving in home environment

How Do Infants' Perceptual Abilities Develop? (pp. 151-152)
(54) a - face; (55) b - face with typical features; (56) c - attractive face; (57) d - moving object; (58) e - complex patterns of motion
(59) depth; (60) 7; (61) depth; (62) visual

How Do Infants and Toddlers Learn and Remember? (pp. 152-156)
(63) infantile amnesia; (64) classical conditioning; (65) habituation; (66) deferred imitation; (67) operant conditioning
(68) context; (69) events are novel and involve smells, sounds, movements; environment same; reminder
1 Minute Quiz: 1 - False; 2 - False; 3 - undernutrition and malnutrition; 4 - faces; 5 - False

How Do Cognitive Abilities Develop during the Sensorimotor Period? (pp. 156-165)
(70) Piaget; (71) cognitive; (72) sensorimotor; (73) 6; (74) previous; (75) reflexes; (76) primary circular reactions; (77) combine; (78) secondary circular reactions; (79) intelligence; (80) intentional; (81) goal; (82) object permanence; (83) problem-solvers; (84) tertiary circular reactions; (85) symbols
(86) I - grasping anything placed in its hand - birth to one month
(87) II - repeatedly blowing raspberries - 1 to 4 months
(88) III - repeatedly tossing bottle to floor - 4 to 8 months
(89) IV - spy dog, crawl to it to whack it - 8 to12 months
(90) V - flush different objects down toilet - 12 to 18 months
(91) VI - pretend to feed a baby - 18 to 24 months
(92) perceptual knowledge; (93) image schemes; (94) scaffolding
1 Minute Quiz: 1 - 4, intentionally; 2 - b; 3 - True; 4 - True

How Do Infants and Toddlers Develop Language Skills? (pp. 165-170)
(95) Initially, the parent might put the stake of the ring toss toy next to baby, and holding baby's hand, will guide the ring onto the post. The parent will then give the baby the ring and let the baby put the ring on the post by itself. Then, the parent may gradually move the post further and further from the child so that eventually, the child will toss the ring at a distance.
(96) d; (97) g; (98) h; (99) e; (100) c; (101) i; (102) f; (103) j; (104) b; (105) a

(106)	Receptive	Expressive
2 months		coo
6 months		babbling
9 months	understands "No!"	
12 months		Says first word
18 months		Vocabulary Explosion
24 months		2-word sentences

(107) syntax; (108) pragmatics; (109) receptive

How is Children's Language Acquidsition Explained? (pp. 170-177)
(110) Skinner; (111) reinforcement; (112) observation; (113) grammar; (114) Chomsky; (115) language acquisition device; (116) critical; (117) 2 - puberty; (118) high pitch, slow tempo, longer pauses, louder volume, more emphatic stress; simpler vocabulary; idioms; decreased complexity, more repetitions, fewer words per utterance.

1 Minute Quiz: 1 - semantics; 2 - 1 yr; 3 - holophrase; 4 - language acquisition device; 5 - child-directed speech

STUDY QUESTIONS

Multiple Choice: 1 - b; 2 - b; 3 - e; 4 - b; 5 - e; 6 - b; 7 - d; 8 - a; 9 - b; 10 - b; 11 - a; 12 - a; 13 - c; 14 - d; 15 - e; 16 - b; 17 - b; 18 - c; 19 - e; 20 - c

True/False Questions:
1. True
2. True
3. False; is not; babies accomplish many motor skills before walking.
4. False; 18 months
5. False; more
6. True
7. False; 3 months
8. True
9. False; have been
10. False; Secondary circular reactions
11. True
12. True
13. False; Syntax
14. False; 2 years old
15. True

Chapter 6
Social and Emotional Development in Infancy and Toddlerhood

My mother taught me HUMOR...
"When that lawn mower cuts off your toes, don't me running to me."
-Things My Mother Taught Me

Objectives

When you have completed this chapter, you will be able to:
- outline the social and emotional development of infants and toddlers, including the development of smiling and laughter, crying, and anger;
- discuss self-awareness and emotions in toddlers;
- describe how play influences emotional development;
- describe how temperament influences emotional development and state the most widely used components of temperament;
- describe how parent-infant attachments influence development;
- summarize attachment theory;
- describe the attachment process;
- identify four patterns of attachment given a description of a child's behavior in the Strange Situation;
- state caregiver and child factors that affect attachment, including the role of culture;
- summarize the consequences of attachment on later development;
- compare and contrast mother-infant and father-infant interactions and attachment;
- discuss the effects of infant and toddler daycare on the child's development;
- distinguish four categories of child maltreatment;
- describe characteristics of child abuse and neglect victims and child abusers;
- describe the effects of child abuse and neglect on the developing child;
- discuss the various types of child abuse prevention programs and program effectiveness; and
- define the key terms and concepts listed on page 218 of your text.

☑ Study Check List

☐ Read Chapter 6 Social and Emotional Development In Infancy and Toddlerhood.

☐ Re-read the Chapter 6 Summary to refresh your memory.

☐ Read the Chapter 6 Objectives listed above.

☐ Complete the following items:

Chapter 6 Social and Emotional Development in Infancy and Toddlerhood 97

How Do Emotions Develop during Infancy and Toddlerhood? (pp. 181 - 190)

As infants and toddlers adapt to their environment, they develop a wide array of social and emotional skills. Until recently, it was believed that infants were able to express only one emotional state – general excitement. However, research now shows that infants are born with basic emotions.

What three basic emotions are present at birth? (1)

1. _____

2. _____

3. _____

What four emotions develop between birth and eight months? (2)

1. _____

2. _____

3. _____

4. _____

Smiling and Laughter

During the first 6 months of life, sm_____(3) may be one of the most significant aspects of social and emotional development. *Describe the development of smiling from birth to 10 weeks, using the terms* **endogenous, exogenous, social, and instrumental smiles**: (4)

_____

_____

_____

_____

_____

_____

_____

98 Study Guide for Exploring Child Development

At what age do infants first laugh? _____(5)

In one sentence, describe a child's developmental progression in laughter: (6)

_____

_____

Crying

C_____(7) is an infant's most effective way of communicating, from the moment a child is born. The pitch, duration, and pattern of crying may reveal ab_____(8) in a newborn's functioning. For example, newborns with high-pitched, shrill cries may have cr_____ du c_____(9) syndrome, indicating brain damage. Crying begins as a r_____(10) response that has survival value and progressively becomes more controllable.

Mothers can distinguish four types of cries: the _____(11) cry, _____ (12) cry, _____(13) cry, and _____ (14) cry. Crying **increases/decreases** *(circle one)* (15) during the first six weeks of life, then **increases/decreases** *(circle one)* (16). On average, infants cry more in the first _____(17) months of life than at any other time, average about _____(18) hours per day. Some babies cry more than others; however, most babies are fussy **early/mid/late** *(circle one)* (19) in the day. This probably is related to the development of the central nervous system.

Newborns cry primarily in response to physical needs, such as hunger or pain, but at times, some cry for no apparent reason. As infants get older, they are more likely to cry in response to c_____(20) and e_____(21) conditions rather than just p_____(22) ones. Caregivers' perceptions of infant crying also change with age, as they perceive more co_____(23) and in_____(24) needs and motives in their babies' cries. How people respond to an infants' cries vary depending on the person's c_____(25). For example, many Mexican mothers believe crying strengthens the baby's lungs and is good for the baby.

Anger

By the end of the first year, children can and do become a_____(26). This anger typically develops as infants gain a sense of co_____(27). Te_____ t_____(28) are signals of their frustration when things do not go as they like. *What three important changes take place during toddlerhood that contribute to the idea of the "terrible twos"? (29)*

1. _____
2. _____
3. _____

Name and describe two types of temper tantrums: (30)

1. _____
2. _____

Self-Awareness and Emotions

By the time a child is 2 years old, he or she understands that emotions are connected with what one wants or does not want. Toddlers also begin to express s_____(31) emotions, such as pride, shame, embarrassment, and guilt. Self-conscious emotions require important advances in self-awareness and cognitive development, including: (32)

1. _____
2. _____
3. _____
4. _____

Gender differences have been found in emotional expression. **Girls/Boys** *(circle one)* (33) are more likely to show shame when they fail at a task than **boys/girls** *(circle one)* (34), even though the **girls/boys** *(circle one)* (35) performed as well on the task as **girls/boys** *(circle one)* (36). This difference persists throughout life.

100 Study Guide for Exploring Child Development

Play and Emotional Development

Play provides young children with the opportunity to ex_____(37) with emotions in a relatively stress-free environment. Play also helps young children to l_____(38) about their world. Infants' and toddlers' play is often re_____(39) and ri_____(40). Early on, it revolves around the child's b_____(41) and ph_____(42) actions, but by one year of age, children begin to use o_____(43) and involve o_____(44) in their play. Even play that results in neg_____(45) interactions can help children learn about emotional worlds and provides opportunities for learning self-_____(46) and coping with n_____(47) social interactions and feelings.

---

1 Minute Quiz

1. *Circle* the emotions you would <u>NOT</u> expect to see at birth:
   sadness   fear   surprise   interest   anger   disgust

2. Exogenous smiles are triggered by _____.

3. The pitch and duration of crying may reveal an abnormality in a newborn's functioning. True/False.

3. A change that contributes to the defiant reputation of toddlers is:
   a. increased ability to express anger.
   b. limitations in social understanding.
   c. strivings toward autonomy.
   d. All of the above contribute to toddlers' defiance.

4. Boys are more likely to show shame than girls are. True/False.

How Does Temperament Influence Development During Infancy and Toddlerhood? (pp. 190-193)

The predisposition to respond in certain enduring and characteristic ways to one's environment is known as t_____(48).

Identify and describe the nine components of temperament: (49)

1. _____
2. _____
3. _____
4. _____
5. _____
6. _____
7. _____
8. _____
9. _____

Temperament is fairly stable, although it does not always follow a predictable course. The environment may modify the expression of one's temperament.

LESSONS IN REAL LIFE - LESSONS IN REAL LIFE - LESSONS IN REAL LIFE - LESSONS IN REAL LIFE

Thomas and Chess (1985) identified three general patterns of temperamental responding. Given the following information about a child, place each in the appropriate temperamental group:

I. Dustin says that he wasn't quite prepared for the birth of his son. Right from the beginning, Dustin's baby was a handful. He cried louder and longer than the other infants in the infant nursery did. In preschool, his son did not adjust to the new setting as easily as his classmates, and he had temper tantrums when schedules were not kept in order. Dustin and the teacher both describe his son as "a handful," and they are exhausted at the end of the day. _____(50)

II. Janyce describes her daughter as a "watcher" in new situations. Janyce must make sure she prepares her daughter's teachers because some teachers have thought the daughter didn't like them. Janyce tells the teachers that her daughter is quiet initially, but once comfortable in the new situation, her daughter is open, curious, and delightful. Janyce is quick to point out that even as a baby, her daughter did not show extreme positive or negative reactions. _____(51)

102 Study Guide for Exploring Child Development

III.   Clyde believes that his firstborn son was the "perfect" child. Right from birth, his baby seemed able to quickly adapt to the hectic household. His son smiled easily, was easy to comfort, and rarely protested when frustrated. Overall, Clyde's baby was a joy and a pleasure. _____(52)

Not all children can be placed into one of the three temperamental categories; in fact, over 1/3 of infants <u>cannot</u> be classified or placed into one neat category. Culture has also been found to influence perception of infant temperament.

---

1 Minute Quiz

1. The predisposition to respond in certain enduring and characteristic ways to one's environment is referred to as _____.

2. Temperamental traits are thought to be:
   a. stable.
   b. enduring.
   c. somewhat modifiable.
   d. All of the above.

3. According to Thomas and Chess (1985), most infants can be classified as:
   a. easy.   b. difficult.   c. slow-to-warm   d. None of these.

4. Temperament is one characteristic that is rarely influenced by culture. True/False.

How Do Parent-Infant Attachments Influence Development? (pp. 193 - 205)

Use these words to complete the following paragraphs:

| attachment figure | intensity | Attachment | contact | secure base |
| distressed | explore | relationship | safety | seek |

_____(53) is a long-lasting _____(54) that is

distinct from bonding. Evidence of attachment can be seen when children attempt to _____(55)

out and maintain _____(56) with a preferred individual or _____(57).

Young children are more willing to _____(58) their world if an attachment

Chapter 6 Social and Emotional Development in Infancy and Toddlerhood 103

figure is present, and will use the attachment figure as a _____(59). If the child becomes _____(60), he or she will seek out the attachment figure for _____(61) and security. Infants differ in their ability to use attachment figures as a secure base and in the _____(62) and quality of emotions they feel toward the attachment figure.

Complete the table: (63)

	Preattachment	Attachment In Making	Clear-Cut Attachment
AGE			
CHARACTERISTICS			

LESSONS IN REAL LIFE - LESSONS IN REAL LIFE - LESSONS IN REAL LIFE - LESSONS IN REAL LIFE

Suppose you are a researcher studying the effects of daycare on attachment behavior. You observe four children in the Strange Situation and each exhibits a different attachment pattern. Identify the attachment pattern for each child:

I. Eileen went over to a toy, explored it briefly, and then began to take it to her mother. As she approached her mother, she froze and looked apprehensive. When the mother left the room and returned, Eileen started to go toward her, but again, she froze, looked daze, and began to cry. _____(64)

II. George explored the playroom excitedly. He closely examined the toys in the room, frequently running back to his mother to show her the toys. When his mother left the room, George looked very concerned and did not play with the toys. He looked to the stranger in the room and asked, "Where Mommy? Where Mommy?" When his mother returned, he happily ran to her, hugged her, and took her to the toy box to show her a toy. _____(65)

104 Study Guide for Exploring Child Development

III. Suma was reluctant to leave her father's side. When offered a toy, she eyed it suspiciously and explored it in a limited manner. When the father left the room, Suma began screaming and rejected attempts by the stranger to be comforted. When the father returned, Suma ran crying to him, begging to be picked up. However, she kicked and cried when he picked her up, and continued to cry after he put her down. It took several minutes before her father was able to soothe her, after which Suma again began playing with the toys in a limited manner. _____ (66)

IV. Antonio appeared to be quite comfortable in the new situation. He quickly left his mother's side and explored the toys in the playroom. When the stranger entered the room, Antonio simply smiled. He did not appear upset or concerned when his mother left the room and did not appear to notice when she returned. He seemed content playing with the toys and was not bothered by the presence of the stranger. _____ (67)

What are two important factors that influence the quality of attachment? (68)

1. _____

2. _____

What role does culture play in attachment? Give a specific example. (69)

_____

_____

_____

_____

_____

Researchers have found that early attachment is linked with later development. Scholars have found that securely attached children *(check all that apply)*: (70)

a. get along better with their peers. _____

b. tolerate frustrations more successfully. _____

c. express a wider range of emotions. _____

d. follow directions easily. _____

e. seldom cry, fuss, or become angry when frustrated. _____

f. remember positive events better than negative ones. _____

g. are comfortable in seeking help from others. _____

h. approach their environments with interest and pleasure. _____

Fathers/Mothers *(circle one)* (71) spend less time interaction with their infants than **fathers/mothers** *(circle one)* (72). As children grow older, father involvement **increases/stays the same/decreases** *(circle one)* (73). **Fathers/mothers** *(circle one)* (74) typically interact as playmates with their infants, rather than as comforters. Infants treat fathers as at_____ f_____(75), although their reactions generally are **less/more** *(circle one)* (76) intense with their f_____(77). Infants who are securely attached to their mothers tend to be s_____(78) attached to their f_____(79); and infants who are anxiously attached to their mother tend to be a_____(80) attached to their father.

---

1 Minute Quiz

1. **Clear-cut attachment usually occurs when the infant is about:**
   a. 4 months old.   b. 7 months old.   c. 10 months old.   d. 12 months old.

2. **A characteristic of clear-cut attachment is:**
   a. stranger anxiety.
   b. separation anxiety.
   c. Both of the above.

3. **When Tommy is reunited with his mother in the Strange Situation, he runs to her, then pushes her away and ignores her. Tommy's attachment pattern is likely to be characterized as:**
   a. secure.   b. avoidant.   c. ambivalent.   d. disorganized.

4. **Two factors that affect the quality of attachment are:**
   a. _____

   b. _____

5. **What is one outcome of a securely attached child?** _____

106 Study Guide for Exploring Child Development

How Does Day Care Influence Infants' and Toddlers' Development? (pp. 205 - 210)

Draw a line through all statements about day care that are FALSE: (81)

1. Most preschool children of working mothers are cared for in group day care centers.
2. Most preschool children of working mothers are cared for in homes by relatives, such as the father or grandparent.
3. Preschoolers are more likely to be cared for by relatives, especially the father, if the mothers work part time.
4. Mothers who work full time are more likely to rely on organized day care centers than on relatives.
5. The federal government has established regulations for child care and day care centers in the US.
6. Over two-thirds of the childcare centers in the US are "barely adequate" in quality.
7. Infants from low-income families are more likely to receive high quality day care than infants from middle income families.
8. Day care has been found to be detrimental for low-income and middle-class children.
9. The available evidence on day care and its effects on children clearly supports its beneficial effects.
10. The findings on the effects of early childcare are contradictory.
11. Quality of day care may be a better predictor of later functioning than age at which children enter day care.
12. Childcare and its impact on children are influenced by culture, as well as the social, political, and physical environments of the family.

Why Are Children Abused and Neglected? (pp. 210 - 216)

List 4 categories of child maltreatment: (82)

1. _____   3. _____

2. _____   4. _____

Victims of child abuse typically share certain characteristics. *Complete the following statements about child/family characteristics related to child abuse and neglect:*

a. Compared with boys, girls are sexually abused _____ (83).

b. Compared with older children, young children are _____ (84).

c. In terms of child maltreatment, a child's race or ethnicity _____ (85).

d. Children with difficult temperaments may _____ (86).

e. Children from poorer families are _____ (87).

f. Children from larger families are _____ (88).

g. Children with disabilities are _____ (89).

Even though certain characteristics may increase the risk of a child being abused, child abuse crosses all social, racial, religious, and educational boundaries.

Some people are more at risk for committing child abuse than others. *For the following pairs, circle the factor that is associated with increased risk of child abuse:* (90)

    a. biological parents   non-biological caregivers

    b. parents   foster parents

    c. fathers   mothers

    d. single parent   married parent

    e. older caretakers   younger caretakers

    f. isolated adults   adults active in the community

    g. alcoholic parent   drug abusing parent

    h. spouse abuser   non-abuser of spouse

Contrary to popular belief, most children who are abused DO NOT grow up to become abusers themselves; in fact, only about one-third of those who were abused become abusers. However, this proportion is still eight times higher than the general population.

It is important to remember that NO SINGLE PROFILE FITS ALL CHILD ABUSERS. The most consistent conclusion about child abuse is that it results from the tr_____(91) of risk and protective factors that exist at mu_____(92) levels, but the exact conditions that contribute to it v_____(93) from family to family and from situation to situation.

List 5 consequences of child maltreatment: (94)

1. _____
2. _____
3. _____
4. _____
5. _____

What is the difference between primary, secondary, and tertiary prevention programs? How effective are child abuse prevention programs? At what level do you think prevention programs will have the greatest impact? (95)

___

1 Minute Quiz

1. The majority of daycare programs in the US are considered adequate or good in quality. True/False.

2. The word that best describes the research findings on the affects of daycare on young children is:
   a. positive.   b. negative.   c. inconclusive.

3. When a mother works part-time, the person most likely to take care of the baby is:
   a. father.   b. grandparents   c. daycare center

4. The child LEAST at risk of maltreatment is the:
   a. older child.
   b. child from a large family.
   c. child with a disability.
   d. All of the above children are at greater risk of maltreatment.

5. Child abuse results from the t_____ of risk and protective factors that exist at multiple levels.

☐ Complete the crossword puzzle in Appendix 1 – Crossword Puzzles.

☐ Go to the beginning of this chapter, and on a separate sheet of paper, write out the answers to the lesson objectives.

sAge Advice

"Before sitting down to study, gather all the items you will need (pen, pencil, paper, dictionary, drink, snacks). That way, you won't need to interrupt your study time."

STUDY QUESTIONS

Multiple Choice (The following questions are identified as being "F," *factual questions* that rely on the recall of facts; or "A," *applied questions* that rely on the ability to apply a concept to a real-life situation).

1. Emotion/s present at birth is/are: (p. 181; F)
   a. interest   b. sadness.   c. disgust.   d. All of these are present at birth.

2. Your sister calls you and excitedly tells you that her newborn baby already knows how to smile. Being diplomatic (and knowing what a newborn is capable of doing), you reply, (p. 182; A)
   a. "How exciting! Your baby has just produced its first social smile!"
   b. "That's wonderful! Your baby has just produced an exogenous smile!"
   c. "Terrific! Your baby has produced an endogenous smile!"
   d. "Do you realize it's 3 a.m.?

3. An infant's most effective way of communicating is: (p. 184; F)
   a. crying.
   b. through gestures.
   c. smiling.
   d. None of the above.

4. Your neighbor calls you and tells you that her 5-week-old baby seems to cry more now than when he was born. She says she is worried that she is doing something wrong and asks you if crying is "normal" for babies this age. You tell her, (p. 185; A)
   a. "The amount of crying actually decreases over the first six weeks and then increases at about 6 months when the baby starts teething. Perhaps you should call your pediatrician."
   b. "The amount of crying actually increases during the first six weeks, then decreases after that. Hang in there!"
   c. "The amount of crying stays about the same during the first 4 weeks, then gradually decreases. Perhaps you're tired and the baby senses your stress."
   d. "Because your baby is a girl, this is pretty typical. You need not worry."

5. Toddlers often become defiant because: (p. 187; F)
   a. they have increased ability to express their anger.
   b. their social understanding is limited.
   c. They have an increased desire for independence.
   d. All of the above.

6. Temperamental tantrums: (p. 188; F)
   a. are used by children to manipulate others into getting what they want.
   b. occur when some aspect of the child's style of interacting has been violated.
   c. should be handled in the same way as all tantrums.
   d. All of the above.

7. For children to develop self-conscious emotions, children must: (p. 189; F)
   a. have a conscious awareness of themselves as distinct from others.
   b. recognize that there are certain standards, rules, or expectations to be met and evaluate their behavior in relation to these standards.
   c. have a sense of responsibility for meeting or not meeting certain standards.
   d. All of the above.

8. Your friend wants to put her toddler in a preschool. However, she is very concerned because whenever she visits preschools, it appears that all the children are "just playing!" She wants her child to get a head start in academics and asks for your opinion. You tell her, (p. 190; A)
   a. "Children learn about their world through play, and a child's work is their play."
   b. "Play is good for children, as long as it doesn't lead to anger and aggression. Negative social interactions must be avoided."
   c. "Your ideas about toddler play are on target. At this age, children do not need as much play as when they were younger."
   d. "You can supplement the preschool activities with flashcards at home and restrict playtime in the home setting to make up for what your child is not doing at school."

9. Research on temperament reveals that: (p. 190; F)
   a. temperamental differences are present prenatally.
   b. temperament is fairly consistent and stable across time.
   c. temperament does not always follow a predictable course.
   d. All of the above.

10. Which of the following is NOT a component of temperament? (p. 191; F)
    a. persistence.
    b. distractibility.
    c. intensity of reaction
    d. predictability

11. Valorie read a book on baby temperaments and is concerned that her baby does not seem to fall into the three categories provided in the book. Based on what you learned from your text, you tell her, (p. 193; A)
    a. "Your baby does appear to be somewhat shy around new people, but generally she smiles and is easily comforted. She best fits in the 'Easy Child' category."
    b. "Research does not really support classification of temperamental groups."
    c. "Over 1/3 of children cannot be classified in terms of the three temperamental groups. Besides that, most children display a wide range of responses to their environment."
    d. "As your baby gets older, she will fit into one of the three groups."

12. Attachment theory places great emphasis on: (p. 195; F)
    a. the caregiver-child relationship as the foundation for individual differences.
    b. differences in biological dispositions.
    c. the caregiver's ties to the infant.
    d. characteristics of the caregiver.

13. If you did not want to baby-sit an infant who cried when his parents left, you would do best to avoid watching a child who is in what phase of attachment development? (p. 196; A)
    a. preattachment
    b. attachment-in-making
    c. clear-cut attachment
    d. goal-corrected partnership

14. Your mother-in-law moved away from your town when your baby was 1 month old. She used to baby-sit for you. Now, your baby is 8 months old, and your mother-in-law wants to come for a visit. If your baby is typical, how do you think your baby will react to grandma's presence? (p. 197; A)
    a. Baby will be delighted and will laugh and smile when grandma enters the room.
    b. Baby will exhibit stranger anxiety and will be fearful of grandma.
    c. Baby will cry when left alone with grandma.
    d. B and C

15. In the Strange Situation, infants who have been abused or neglected are more likely to be classified as: (p. 201; F)
    a. avoidant.   b. disorganized/disoriented.   c. ambivalent.   d. secure.

16. The quality of attachment is influenced by: (p. 202; F)
    a. caregiver sensitivity.
    b. child characteristics.
    c. culture.
    d. All of the above.

17. Which of the following statements about the effects of attachment on later development is FALSE? (p. 203; F)
    a. Infant attachment relates to later intellectual functioning.
    b. Securely attached children get along better with their peers.
    c. Insecurely attached youngsters express a wider range of emotions than securely attached children.
    d. Insecurely attached children have less tolerance of frustration.

18. In the United States, fathers: (p. 205; F)
    a. spend less time interacting with their infants than mothers.
    b. act as playmates and mothers act as nurturers.
    c. are likely to be attachment figures for their infants.
    d. All of the above.

19. Layton is concerned about putting her toddler in daycare when she returns to work. You tell her that: (p. 206; A)
    a. studies on the effects of daycare on child development have been somewhat inconsistent, with some studies showing an increase in child aggression and decrease in compliance.
    b. daycare may have some beneficial effects on her middle-class child.
    c. when you put a child in daycare is probably not as important as the quality of daycare.
    d. All of the above.

20. Congratulations! You have been appointed to the Governor's Task Force on Child Abuse Prevention. She has given you unlimited access to funds. The approach that will probably have the most impact on child abuse overall is: (p. 216; A)
    a. a primary prevention program.
    b. a secondary prevention program.
    c. a tertiary prevention program.
    d. None of the above. Prevention programs here and abroad have been found to have little impact on child abuse.

True/False Questions (If a statement is FALSE, correct it).

1. At birth, babies are able to express general excitement only. (p. 181) True/False.

2. Infants utilize several different types of cries. (p. 185) True/False.

3. Caregivers who are slower to respond to their infants' crying will have children who do not cry as often or as intensely. (p. 186) True/False.

4. Play provides infants and toddlers with opportunities to explore emotional development. (p. 190) True/False.

5. Temperament is inborn and is not modified by one's social and cultural environments. (p. 191) True/False.

Chapter 6 Social and Emotional Development in Infancy and Toddlerhood 113

6. Attachment refers to the caregiver's emotional tie with the infant. (p. 194) True/False.

7. During the Attachment-In-Making phase, infants show a clear preference of a particular caregiver. (p. 196) True/False.

8. Avoidant attachments are characterized by avoidance, resistance, and bizarre repetitions of behavior. (p. 200) True/False.

9. Infants tend to become securely attached to their mothers but not their fathers. (p. 204) True/False.

10. The majority of children of working mothers are cared for in organized group day care. (p. 205) True/False.

11. The overall effects of daycare on development are not influenced by the quality of the daycare setting. (p. 206) True/False.

12. Reported child maltreatment has decreased in the past decade. (p. 211) True/False.

13. Boys generally are maltreated more than girls, particularly in regard to sexual abuse. (p. 212) True/False.

14. Most child abusers are psychologically disturbed. (p. 212) True/False.

15. Parent training is a relatively effective way to prevent child abuse. (p. 216) True/False.

☐ REWARD YOURSELF!   Go to a climbing gym.

114 Study Guide for Exploring Child Development

ANSWERS – Chapter 6 Social and Emotional Development in Infancy and Toddlerhood

How Do Emotions Develop during Infancy and Toddlerhood? (pp. 181-190)
(1) 1. Sadness; 2. Disgust; 3. Interest
(2) 1. Anger; 2. Surprise; 3. Joy; 4. Fear
(3) Smiling
(4) Infants move from reflexive smiling to social smiling by 6-8 weeks. First smiles are endogenous and triggered by changes in the nervous system (simply reflexive). Exogenous smiles are triggered by external stimuli such as stroking the abdomen, and the social smile appears in response to parent's face or voice. At about 10 weeks, smiling becomes instrumental – smile to achieve a goal and gain control over environment
(5) infants laugh at about 4 months of age
(6) Initially occurring in response to physical stimulation, infants increasingly laugh at visual and social stimuli.
Crying: (7) Crying; (8) abnormalities; (9) crie du chat; (10) reflex; (11) basic, (12) anger, (13) pain, (14) hunger; (15) increases; (16) decreases; (17) 3; (18) 2; (19) late; (20) cognitive; (21) emotional; (22) physical; (23) complex; (24) individualized; (25) culture
Anger: (26) angry; (27) control; (28) Temper tantrums; (29) 1. Increased ability to express anger; 2. Limitations in social understanding; 3. Strivings toward autonomy; (30) 1. Manipulative tantrums; 2. Temperamental tantrums.
Self-Awareness and Emotions: (31) self-conscious; (32) 1. Have a conscious awareness of themselves as distinct form others; 2. Recognize that there are certain standards, rules, or expectations to be met; 3. Evaluate their behavior in relation to these standards; 4. Have a sense of responsibility for meeting or not meeting these standards; (33) Girls; (34) boys; (35) girls; (36) boys.
Play and Emotional Development: (37) experiment; (38) learn; (39) repetitive; (40) ritualistic; (41) body; (42) physical; (43) objects; (44) others; (45) negative; (46) self-control; (47) negative
1 Minute Quiz: 1. Fear, surprise, anger; 2. External stimuli; 3. True; 4. D; 5. False

How Does Temperament Influence Development During Infancy and Toddlerhood? (pp. 190-193)
(48) Temperament;
(49) 1. Rhythmicity; 2. Activity level; 3. Approach-withdrawal; 4. Persistence; 5. Adaptability; 6. Quality of mood; 7. Distractibility; 8. Threshold of responsiveness; 9. Intensity of reaction.
(50) I – Difficult   (51) II – Slow-to-Warm   (52) III - Easy
1 Minute Quiz: 1. Temperament; 2. D; 3. A; 4. False

How Do Parent-Infant Attachments Influence Development? (pp. 193-205)
(53) Attachment; (54) relationship; (55) seek; (56) contact; (57) attachment figure; (58) explore; (59) secure base; (60) distressed; (61) safety; (62) intensity
(63) **Preattachment,** 0 to 2 months, responds the same to everybody; reflex behaviors; responds to social and nonsocial stimuli; **Attachment In Making,** 2 to 6 months, prefers social stimuli, positive response to familiar caregivers but not unfamiliar ones, no single attachment preference observable; **Clear-Cut Attachment,** 7 to 12 months, clear preference for attachment figure; stranger and separation anxiety
(64) I – disorganized/disoriented   (65) II – secure   (65) III- Ambivalent   (67) IV - Avoidant
(68) 1. caregiver sensitivity; 2. Characteristics of the child
(69) Infant care behaviors are slightly different in different cultures. Consequently, infants from different cultural backgrounds display different patterns of attachments. For example, German infants tend to be classified as avoidant; they are raised in an environment that stresses independents. Japanese infants are almost never classified as avoidant; they are raised in an environment that values contact and dependence.
(70) All items should be checked.
(71) Fathers; (72) mothers; (73) increases; (74) Fathers; (75) attachment figures; (76) less; (77) fathers; (78) securely; (79) fathers; (80) anxiously
1 Minute Quiz: 1. B; 2. C; 3. C; 4. Caregiver sensitivity and child characteristics; 5. Get along better with peers

How Does Day Care Influence Infants' and Toddlers' Development? (pp. 205-210)
(81) Draw a line through 1, 5, 8, 9

Why Are Children Abused and Neglected? (pp. 210-216)
(82) 1. Physical abuse; 2. Sexual abuse; 3. Neglect; 4. Psychological maltreatment

(83) a. more often; (84) b. more at risk; (85) c. makes no difference; (86) d. increase risk of abuse; (87) e. more likely to experience maltreatment; (88) f. more likely to be maltreated; (89) g. more likely to be maltreated
(90) a. biological parents; b. parents; c. mothers; d. single parent; e. younger caretakers; f. isolated adults; g. drug abusers; h. spouse abuser
(91) transactions; (92) multiple; (93) vary; (94) 1. Delayed intellectual development; 2. Poor self-esteem; 3. Poor emotional stability; 4. Poor school performance; 5. Depression
(95) Prevention programs are classified as primary, secondary and tertiary depending on how "close" the programs address the actual problem. Primary prevention programs address the population as a whole, such as commercials about hugging children, not hitting, or parenting programs available to everybody. Secondary prevention programs address that part of the population thought to be most at risk for child maltreatment. For example, some programs send social workers/parent counselors to local hospitals to work with poor, single mothers. They guide them to services, rally support for the parent, and answer questions as needed. Tertiary prevention programs are for situations where child maltreatment has already occurred. Child Protective Services are examples of such programs. A child may be placed in foster care while his or her parents take parenting lessons, obtain counseling, and find a safe place to live. Once the family has met certain criteria, the child is returned. Which one is best? All are important pieces to a very complex puzzle. Personally, I would like to see more money put in Secondary Prevention programs.

1 Minute Quiz: 1. False; 2. C; 3. A; 4. A; 5. transaction

STUDY QUESTIONS

<u>Multiple Choice</u> : 1. D; 2. C; 3. A; 4. B; 5. D; 6. B; 7. D; 8. A; 9. D; 10. E; 11. C; 12. A; 13. C; 14. D; 15. B; 16. D; 17. C; 18. D; 19. D; 20. A

<u>True/False Questions:</u>
1. False – interest, sadness, disgust;
2. True
3. False – quicker
4. True
5. False – can be modified
6. False – Bonding
7. False – Clear-Cut Attachment
8. False – disorganized/disoriented
9. False – both;
10. False – relatives
11. False – are
12. False – increased
13. False – girls more than boys
14. False – are not
15. False – ineffective

Chapter 7
Physical, Cognitive, and Language Development in Early Childhood

My mother taught me how to BECOME AN ADULT...
"If you don't eat your vegetables, you'll never grow up."
- Things My Mother Taught Me

Objectives
When you have completed this chapter, you will be able to:
- describe the changes in a young child's body size and appearance;
- describe how the child's brain develops during the early years;
- discuss how gross and fine motor skills develop during early childhood and the influence of culture and race on such development;
- summarize nutritional needs of children, including undernourishment and malnourishment;
- state the leading cause of death in the preschool years and discuss other health hazards to young children;
- summarize cognitive development of preschoolers;
- describe the memory skills of preschoolers;
- describe what is meant by "theory of the mind;"
- discuss children's understanding of pretend and real;
- state how social context and culture influence children's cognitive development;
- describe the educational experiences of young children, including the impact of early intervention programs and educational television;
- summarize language development in preschoolers; and
- define the key terms and concepts listed on page 258 of your text.

☑ Study Check List

☐ Read Chapter 7 Physical, Cognitive, and Language Development in Early Childhood.

☐ Re-read the Chapter 7 Summary to refresh your memory.

☐ Read the Chapter 7 Objectives listed above.

☐ Complete the following items:

Chapter 7 Physical, Cognitive, and Language Development in Early Childhood 117

How Do Children's Bodies and Motor Skills Develop During Early Childhood? (pp. 225 - 229)

During early childhood,

- body fat (1) _____;

- stomachs (2) _____;

- arms and legs (3) _____;

- bodies (4) _____;

- growth is not as (5) _____;

- boys and girls are (6) _____;

- the brain grows to _____(7) of the adult size by age 5;

- myelination (8) _____;

- the left hemisphere (9) _____;

- the right hemisphere (10) _____;

- the connections between the two hemispheres (11) _____;

- eye-hand coordination (12) _____;

- balance (13) _____;

- gross motor skills improve through (14) _____; and

- fine motor skills (15) _____.

  Cu_____(16) and bi_____(17) factors

interact in complex ways to influence children's motor development. *Give one specific example of*

(a) genetic influence on motor development: _____(18)

(b) a cultural influence on motor development: _____(19)

What are the Nutritional and Health Issues for Young Children? (pp. 229 - 233)

How does undernourishment differ from malnourishment? _____

_____(20)

State 5 consequences of undernourishment: (21)

1. _____
2. _____
3. _____
4. _____
5. _____

Undernourishment and malnourishment may have such negative affects on children because of functional isolation. What is meant by "functional isolation? (22)_____

_____

_____

Even children living in well-developed countries can be malnourished due to the availability of junk foods and a reliance on fast-food restaurants.

The leading cause of death in the preschool years is ac_____(23), particularly a_____(24) accidents. When traveling in a car, young children should be restrained in car seats designed for their age, weight, and height. The safest place for a child to ride in a car is in the center b_____(25).

Other accidents that befall young children include dr_____(26), ingesting p_____(27), falling down s_____(28), and being b_____(29) by fire or hot water. Many accidents occur on the pl_____(30), where children are likely to fall off swings or slides. Most accidents can be avoided through childproofing homes and providing safe play spaces.

A common childhood health problem is l_____ p_____(31). Many older homes have lead-based p_____(32), although lead can also be found in g_____(33), f_____(34), w_____(35), dust, and soil. Children who have high levels of lead in their bodies are at risk for many b_____(36) problems, such as h_____(37), im_____(38), and w_____(39). Even l_____(40) levels of lead exposure can increase the risk for social w_____(41) and dis_____(42).

---

1 Minute Quiz

1. **Compared with infants, preschool children are more likely to:**
   a. have large heads relative to body size.   c. be taller and slimmer.
   b. grow at a faster rate.   d. All of the above.

2. **By the age of five, a child's brain has reached _____ of its adult size.**
   a. 25%   b. 50%   c. 90%   d. 100%

3. **An example of an improved <u>fine motor skill</u> in a preschooler is the ability to**
   a. use crayons.   b. kick a can.   c. throw a ball.   d. run.

4. **Motor skill development is influenced by _____ and _____ factors.**

5. **Malnourishment refers to receiving inadequate proteins, vitamins, and minerals. True/False.**

6. **Malnourished children may disengage from their physical and social environments. This disengagement is called _____.**

7. **The leading cause of death in the preschool years is:**
   a. disease.   c. child abuse.
   b. malnourishment.   d. accidents.

120 Study Guide for Exploring Child Development

How Do Young Children Think and Solve Problems? (pp. 235 - 251)

Following the sensorimotor stage, young children enter the pre_____(43) stage of cognitive development, according to Piaget. At this stage, youngsters use sym_____c re_____s (44), which means that they can mentally represent ob_____(45) and pe_____(46) and then manipulate these representations.

In the following examples, identify the appropriate concepts related to preoperational thinking:

- Four-year-old Jonathon finds a dime and a nickel on the ground. Examining the two coins, he chooses to keep the nickel because it's bigger. What concepts related to preoperational thinking is evident in his choice?(47) _____

    Why? _____

    _____

    _____

- Three-year-old Sariah's mother playfully dons a monster mask in front of Sariah and says, "Boo!" Sariah backs up and screams, "I want my mommy!!!!!!!" and starts crying. This is an example of

    _____ (48) because_____

    _____.

- Five-year-old Zahid and his mother are getting ready to go to the store. His mother grabs the umbrella and as they walk outside, it begins to rain. "Mommy," Zahid says. "Next time don't bring the umbrella! I don't like the rain!"

    This is an example of _____(49) because _____

    _____.

- Ted is so happy when his daughter finally calls him "Daddy!" He takes her to the park to show her off, and to his amazement, his daughter starts pointing to various men and saying, "Daddy!" It appears that his daughter believes all men are "Daddy."

    This is an example of having difficulty with _____(50), which

    means that _____.

Chapter 7 Physical, Cognitive, and Language Development in Early Childhood 121

- Catherine has started taking a college class. She tells her 5-year-old son about her "first day at school." Her son asks, "What did you eat for snack time?" referring to his kindergarten class snack time. This is an example of _____ (51) because _____

_____.

- 3-year-old Aisha accidentally pulls off her doll's arm. She cries to her mother that the dolly is hurt and needs help. Her anguished cries indicate that she truly feels her dolly hurts. This is an example of

_____ (52), which is _____

_____

Piaget's research has provided an excellent starting point for understanding thinking in early childhood. However, contemporary researchers have discovered that Piaget **overestimated/underestimated** *(circle one)* (53) children's thinking abilities. When tasks are made simpler, children appear to be <u>more advanced</u> in their problem solving than Piaget believed.

> **DID YOU KNOW...........**
>
> As children grow older, they don't totally leave behind earlier stages of thinking? For example, Piaget, the great researcher and thinker, said that he spent a relatively *small* amount of time using formal operational thought (the highest level of cognitive development). Everyday, YOU show evidence of preoperational thought. Have you ever spoken to your computer or your car? My mom names her cars! These are examples of _____ (54).
>
> Not convinced? Some adults think if a person is handsome, beautiful, or has a great physique, that person must also be smart. This is an example of _____ (55). Other adults think that washing the car will cause it to rain. This is an example of _____ (56).
>
> I'm sure you can think of a dozen more examples (mostly among your friends ☺)!

Why are young children's memory capacities more limited than older children's are? (57)

1. _____

2. _____

3. _____

List three memory strategies that are used to improve memory? (58)

1. _____

2. _____

3. _____

Use these words to complete the following paragraphs:

behavior	older	interactions	experts	pretend	scripts
"theory of mind"	appearance	private speech	identity	consistently	
improves	familiar	six	real	uncommon	
deception	scaffolding	strategies	unfamiliar	guide	

Young children tend to have good memories for things they experience frequently. Concepts that people form about routines involved in everyday interactions and events may be thought of as _____(59). Sometimes, young children will inaccurately recall an _____(60) event because their memory is distorted by a very familiar script. As children grow _____(61), their memory for actual events _____(62). Some children are able to learn a large amount of information about a specific topic; these children become _____(63) in that area. For example, some 5-year-olds can name every "Pokemon" character from the cartoon show and tell you the secrets of the popular Gameboy game. Children are able to remember _____(64) information better than _____(65) information, and when information is familiar, children can use new _____(66) more efficiently.

Preschoolers appear to have ideas about the inner mental events that people experience. They understand that people think, imagine, and pretend; this understanding is referred to as the _____ _____(67). What a great achievement this is! Separating the external world from the inner workings of the mind helps children distinguish between _____(68) and _____(69) events, understand _____(70) and lies, interpret other people's _____(71), and distinguish between beliefs and desires. This ability is still quite limited in early childhood because it lacks sophistication and is not always applied _____ (72).

Chapter 7 Physical, Cognitive, and Language Development in Early Childhood 123

How well can children distinguish between pretend and real situations? It depends. Very young preschoolers might pretend to eat a cookie; however, preschool-aged children have difficulty distinguishing "pretend" and "real" when the outward _____(73) of an object conflicts with its true _____(74). Again, with age, a child's ability to distinguish pretend and real improves, so that by age _____ (75), most children will not scare themselves when they play monster!

Children's cognitive growth relies on their _____(76) with those around them. Parents and caregivers use _____(77) to promote cognitive development. An interesting phenomenon occurs during the preschool years. As children engage in activities, they frequently can be seen "talking to themselves." Vygotsky believed that this _____ (78) is an internalized voice that helps _____(79) a child's thinking. As children get older, their private conversations become quieter.

Children's guided participation within their own culture helps them learn the values and skills important to that specific culture. How do children learn the specific cognitive skills and values associated with their own culture? (80)

1. _____
2. _____
3. _____
4. _____
5. _____

124 Study Guide for Exploring Child Development

LESSONS IN REAL LIFE - LESSONS IN REAL LIFE - LESSONS IN REAL LIFE - LESSONS IN REAL LIFE

Your friend recently had a baby. Knowing that you study child development, he asks you what he can do as a parent to encourage his baby's cognitive development. You tell him that he should: (81)

_____

_____

_____

_____

You emphasize that the MOST IMPORTANT thing he can do to encourage cognitive development in his child is _____(82).

Many children attend preschool. A good preschool _____

_____(83) and does not _____

_____(84). According to research, high quality preschools have: (85)

1. _____

2. _____

3. _____

Often, parents are interested in accelerating their children's cognitive development. However, many developmentalists **support/oppose** *(circle one)* (86) emphasis on early academic training because

(1) _____(87);

and (2) _____(88).

Suppose you were elected to represent your state in the United States Congress, and the Head Start Program is due for renewal. Your colleagues "across the aisle" are against renewing the program because they have learned that the initial boost in intellectual performance fades over time. "We're wasting our money if the program doesn't produce lasting effects!" they tell you. Based on the information in your text, you inform them that: (89)

_____

_____

_____

_____

1½ Minute Quiz

1. Kelly looks at the soda her mother poured into two glasses on the table. One glass is tall and thin and filled almost to the top. A short, fat glass is also filled to the top. Kelly insists on taking the tall thin glass because she says it has more soda. Her mom said that each glass holds 8 ounces and is the same. Kelly apparently has difficulty with:
    a. transductive reasoning.
    b. conservation.
    c. egocentrism.
    d. class inclusion.

2. Later studies on children's cognitive development have determined that:
    a. children are less advanced in their problem solving than Piaget believed.
    b. children are more advanced in their problem solving than Piaget believed.
    c. Piaget was accurate in his estimation of children's problem solving.
    d. using the same tasks, Piaget was wrong in his estimation of children's problem-solving.

3. What are 3 techniques used to improve memory strategies:
   _____, _____, _____.

   Do young children use these strategies effectively? Yes/No

4. Vygotsky believed that the private speech of a young child:
    a. was a sign of egocentrism.
    b. acted as an internalized voice to guide thinking.
    c. indicated poor cognitive growth.

5. The most important way for parents to encourage children's cognitive development is to:
    a. spend time with their children.
    b. put their children in a preschool that focuses on academics.
    c. put their children in a preschool that focuses on play.

126 Study Guide for Exploring Child Development

What Changes Occur in Young Children's Language Development During Early Childhood? (pp. 251 - 257)

Unscramble the following words/concepts, using the definitions provided:

_____ _____ - the way children learn word meaning by associating the sound of the
s f t a   p i m n a g p   word with the concept for which the word stands. (90)

_____ - when children use words to refer to objects outside the bounds
n x s e e e i v r o o t n   of the category named by the word. (91)

_____ - the use of words to refer to a smaller groups than the word
s u o x i n d e n t r e e n   actually names. (92)

_____ - language style where vocabulary develops based mostly on object
l e e e r n t a f i   naming. (93)

_____ - language style where vocabulary develops based on words used in social
v i p e e s s r e x   interactions and few object names. (94)

_____ - application of language rules when they do not
z o o e r e u r a r i g l a t i v n   apply, such as saying "My foots are tired." (95)

The development of speech and language in early childhood is truly amazing. Children learn to associate words with objects and concepts, to pronounce sounds appropriately, and to put words together into sentences, using appropriate grammar. In addition, children also learn conversational rules. What are two examples of "conversational rules?" (96)

1. _____

2. _____

Language learning occurs within a social context. Not only do parents direct their children's language exposure, but also children themselves play an active role.

Hint from Mom...

When a child asks, "Do you know what?", never answer, "Yes, as a matter of fact, I do."

---

1 Minute Quiz

1. Fast mapping helps children understand the more subtle aspects of word meaning. True/False.

2. When a child says, "Look at all the sheeps, Dad!", she is using a/n:
   a. expressive language style.
   b. overextension.
   c. overregularization.
   d. fast mapping.

3. Most young children are surprisingly good at following conversational rules. True/False.

4. Language learning:
   a. occurs within a social context.
   b. is directed by parents.
   c. is directed by children.
   d. All of the above.

☐ Complete the crossword puzzle in Appendix 1 – Crossword Puzzles.

☐ Go to the beginning of this chapter, and on a separate sheet of paper, write out the answers to the lesson objectives.

SAGE Advice

"Take advantage of resources available to students, such as tutors or the writing center."

STUDY QUESTIONS

Multiple Choice (The following questions are identified "F," *factual questions* that rely on the recall of facts; or "A," *applied questions* that rely on the ability to apply a concept to a real-life situation).

1. During the preschool years, growth: (p. 226; F)
    a. is not as rapid as it is during the infant years.
    b. is about the same as it is during the infant years.
    c. is faster than it is during the infant years.
    d. essentially stops for a year, while the child gains weight for future growth.

2. Children do not show true running ability until they are about: (p. 227; F)
    a. 1 to 2 years old.
    b. 2 to 3 years old.
    c. 3 to 4 years old.
    d. 4 to 5 years old.

3. Five-year-old Jennifer can fasten a button, unzip a zipper, and string some beads. These are examples of: (p. 229; A)
    a. fine motor skills.
    b. gross motor skills.
    c. fine and gross motor skills.
    d. Neither fine nor gross motor skills.

4. Caroline is concerned because her 4-year-old seems tired all the time. He has always been a picky eater, preferring "Spaghetti-O's" to meat and vegetables. If he is like many children, he may: (p. 230; A)
    a. only appear fatigued to his mother because at this age children typically slow down.
    b. have marasmus.
    c. have kwashiorkor.
    d. have iron deficiency anemia.

5. The leading cause of death among preschool children in the United states is: (p. 231; F)
    a. influenza and pneumonia.   b. choking.   c. accidents.   child abuse.

6. Young children, unlike older children, adolescents, and adults, are: (pp. 234-235; F)
    a. unable to apply operations.
    b. able to apply operations, but unable to make inferences from them.
    c. less likely to use transductive reasoning.
    d. more likely to solve categorization problems involving class inclusion.

7. Tita took a cookie from the cookie jar without asking permission. As she climbed down from the counter, she fell and hurt herself. Tita believed that taking cookies without permission causes one to get hurt. This is an example of: (pp. 235; A)
    a. animism.   b. transductive reasoning.   c. egocentrism.   d. centration.

8. Which of the following statements is NOT related to young children's memory capacities? (p. 238; F)
    a. Young children are more easily distracted than older children.
    b. Young children use more likely to use memory strategies, including rehearsal.
    c. Young children lack awareness of memory.
    d. Young children are unlikely to use metacognition.

9. A theory of mind helps children: (p. 241; F)
   a. understand that people think.
   b. interpret other people's behavior.
   c. distinguish between pretend and real.
   d. All of the above.

10. You notice that a 3-year-old talks while she is putting a puzzle together. Agreeing with Piaget, you believe that the reason she uses private speech is because she: (p. 243; A)
    a. has not reached the stage of preoperations.
    b. has not reached the stage of concrete operations.
    c. is egocentric.
    d. is using her speech to guide her thinking.

11. Children learn the specific cognitive skills and values associated with their own culture through: (p. 244; F)
    a. exposure to situations associated with cultural scripts.
    b. direct or indirect encouragement by adults of activities valued by the culture.
    c. being given certain responsibilities by their parents or adults.
    d. All of the above.

12. Justo has decided he wants his daughter to be the next Einstein. He asks you what you think is the most important thing he can do. You wisely respond: (p. 246; A)
    a. set limits on television viewing.
    b. sign your child up for the library reading program.
    c. find an excellent preschool that has full-day classes.
    d. spend time with your daughter, listening and answering her questions, reading to her, and visiting museums.

13. Before deciding on a preschool for her son, Lacey visits her local preschools and makes her decision based on research findings for high-quality preschool programs. Which of the following schools probably would **NOT** meet Lacey's standards? (p. 246; A)
    a. Kid's Place, where the teacher-child ratio is 1 teacher per 3 children.
    b. Noah's Arc, where teachers are required to have a college degree in child development and are certified early childhood education specialists.
    c. Jabberwocky, where goals are set for students to master 1st grade reading and math materials.
    d. Mother Goose, where the outdoor play area is well equipped for many activities and is safe.

14. The Head Start program, designed to serve preschool-age children from economically disadvantaged backgrounds, been found to: (p. 250; F)
    a. increase children's intellectual performance throughout elementary and middle school.
    b. increase children's intellectual performance throughout high school.
    c. lead to fewer children being assigned to special education classes.
    d. have little impact on whether or not children were held back a grade in school.

15. When Bambi was learning the word for "flower," he called all bright, colorful things "flower," including a butterfly. This is an example of: (p. 252; A)
    a. fast mapping.   b. overextension   c. underextension.   d. overregularization.

16. Your neighbor's 2-year-old has started naming everything in the environment. "Shoes!" he says. "Car!" he says. "Tree," he says. Commenting on his developing vocabulary, you say, (p. 253; A)
    a. "My, your child has a referential language style!"
    b. "My, your child has an expressive language style!"
    c. "My , your child has a tendency to use overextensions!"
    d. "My, you child is annoying!"

17. Which of the following strategies would probably NOT help a young child learn language? (p. 256; A)
    a. Describing what you are doing as you clean the house.
    b. Repeating back word-for-word any statement the child makes.
    c. Providing the child with several different playmates and interacting with a variety of relatives.
    d. Allowing the child to play the "name game".

18. The language of a child's siblings: (p. 257; F)
    a. includes less reciprocal verbal interchanges.
    b. is not much different from parental verbal interactions.
    c. is more playful.
    d. hinders a child's language development.

True/False Questions (If a statement is FALSE, correct it).

1. Preschool-age children grow slimmer as they develop from toddlerhood. (p. 226) True/False.

2. During the preschool years, the child's brain reaches the 50th percentile of adult size by age 5. (p. 226) True/False.

3. One key factor in the development of motor skills is the development of the child's visual system. (p. 226) True/False.

4. Infants show a hand preference right from birth. (p. 227) True/False.

5. Motor development is not influenced by ethnicity. (p. 229) True/False.

6. Undernourished children are at risk for learning impairments and delayed motor development. (p. 230) True/False.

7. Children today are generally healthier than children of twenty years ago. (p. 231) True/False.

8. Static thinking is the tendency to focus attention on the most obvious and striking characteristics of an object while ignoring others. (p. 234) True/False.

9. Tito wants to give his mother a "Blue's Clues" coloring book for her birthday. This is an example of transductive reasoning. (p. 235) True/False.

10. According to contemporary research, Piaget overestimated children's cognitive abilities. (p. 237) True/False.

11. Children's memory for everyday routines and activities influences how they remember specific information. (p. 239) True/False.

12. Young children have difficulty identifying an object when its appearance conflicts with its true identity. (p. 242) True/False.

13. A good preschool should mimic a good elementary school. (p. 246) True/False.

14. No lasting effects have been found for children who participated in Heat Start programs. (p. 250) True/False.

15. By the age of 5, most children have mastered the basics of phonology, semantics, syntax, and pragmatics. (pp. 251-257) True/False.

☐ REWARD YOURSELF!   Go workout at a health club!

ANSWERS - Chapter 7 Physical, Cognitive, and Language Development in Early Childhood

How Do Children's Bodies and Motor Skills Develop During Early Childhood? (pp. 225 - 229)
(1) decreases to 12%; (2) flatten; (3) grow longer and slimmer; (4) grow in size relative to head; (5) rapid; (6) very similar in their patterns of physical growth and development; (7) 75-90%; (8) increases; (9) develops rapidly around the age of 2; (10) has a growth spurt around age 4 or 5; (11) increase and become more efficient; (12) improves; (13) improves; (14) practice, imitating others, others' expectations and encouragement; (15) develop markedly.
(16) Cultural; (17) biological; (18) length of arms and legs; (19) parenting practices

What are the Nutritional and Health Issues for Young Children? (pp. 229 - 233)
(20) Undernourishment is not having enough food and is closely associated with poverty, poor living conditions, etc.; malnourishment is not eating the appropriate kinds of food; (21) 1. Stunted growth; 2. Delayed motor development; 3. Low levels of attention; 4. Learning impairments; 5. Poor academic and school-related performance.
(22) malnourished children become increasingly disengaged from their social and physical environments
(23) accidents; (24) automobiles; (25) backseat; (26) drowning; (27) poison; (28) stairs; (29) burned; (30) playground; (31) lead poisoning; (32) paint; (33) gasoline; (34) food; (35) water; (36) behavioral; (37) hyperactivity; (38) impulsivity; (39) withdrawal; (40) low; (41) withdrawal; (42) disinterest
1 Minute Quiz: 1. C; 2. C; 3. A; 4. genetic and biological; 5. T; 6. functional isolation; 7. D

How Do Young Children Think and Solve Problems? (pp. 235 - 251)
(43) preoperational; (44) symbolic representations; (45) objects; (46) people
(47) inability to apply conservation, centration; Jonathon is looking at the size and bigger means more
(48) static thinking because Sariah focused on outcome (monster) rather than changes that produced the outcome (putting on the mask); (49) transductive reasoning because children often believe if two events occur together, they are causally related; in other words, the umbrella caused the rain; (50) classification; her classifications are based on partial concepts and young children may categorize on the basis of a single attribute; (51) egocentrism because he assumes that his perspective is shared by his mother and events in his life are the same as in hers; (52) animism, which is attributing lifelike qualities to objects that are not alive. (53) underestimated; (54) animism; (55) centration; (56) transductive reasoning
(57) tendency to be easily distracted; failure to use memory strategies; lack of awareness of memory
(58) rehearsal; organization; elaboration
(59) scripts; (60) uncommon; (61) older; (62) improves; (63) experts; (64) familiar; (65) unfamiliar; (66) strategies; (67) theory of mind; (68) real; (69) pretend; (70) deception; (71) behavior; (72) consistently; (73) appearance; (74) identity; (75) six; (76) interactions; (77) scaffolding; (78) private speech; (79) guide
(80) exposure; practice; regulation; encouragement; assignment of responsibility
(81) Read to your children and let them see you read; visit the library; set limits on television; provide pencils and markers for drawing; listen to your child; take your child to museums and art galleries, encourage them to them critically, play with them. (82) spend time with him.
(83) uses developmentally appropriate practices; (84) mimic older children's elementary education classes
(85) low student-teacher ratio; well-educated staff; developmentally appropriate activities
(86) oppose; (87) children learn best when actively involved in learning and need time to play; (88) children may lose interest in learn, which could have long term consequences.
(89) While intellectual performance effects may not be long lasting, Head Start children benefit in additional ways that are long lasting and important, including less likely to be assigned to special education classes, less likely to be held back a grade, and having fewer school absences. They also have improved physical health, nutrition, family interactions, and social-emotional behaviors.
1½ Minute Quiz: 1. B; 2. B; 3. Rehearsal, organization, elaboration; no 4. B; 5. A

What Changes Occur in Young Children's Language Development During Early Childhood? (pp. 251 - 257)
(90) fast mapping; (91) overextension; (92) underextension; (93) referential; (94) expressive; (95) overregularization; (96) turn-taking; adjusting speech to fit the speaker
1 Minute Quiz: 1. F; 2. C; 3. T; 4. D

STUDY QUESTIONS

Multiple Choice: 1. A; 2. B; 3. A; 4. D; 5. C; 6. C; 7. B; 8. B; 9. D; 10. C; 11. D; 12. D; 13. C; 14. C; 15. B; 16. A; 17. B; 18. C

True/False Questions:
1. True
2. False; 75th to 90th percentile
3. True
4. False; after age 3
5. False; is
6. True
7. True
8. False; Centration
9. False; egocentrism
10. False; underestimated
11. True
12. True
13. False; should not
14. False; omit "No"
15. True – amazing, isn't it?!

Chapter 8
Social and Emotional Development in Early Childhood

My mother taught me ABOUT SEX...
"How do you think you got here?"

- Things My Mother Taught Me

Objectives

When you have completed this chapter, you will be able to:
- distinguish between self-concept and self-esteem;
- outline the development of self-concept and self-esteem in children;
- state specific influences on young children's awareness of self;
- discuss three stages children go through toward understanding gender;
- discuss gender stereotypes and how these stereotypes influence children;
- summarize contemporary theories of gender development;
- outline how emotional development changes during early childhood, including dealing with conflict, anger, and aggression, as well as caring and empathy;
- discuss how certain parental behaviors influence young children's development and what factors influence parental behaviors;
- describe parenting styles posited by Diana Baumrind and the predicted outcomes of these styles;
- discuss the impact of divorce on children, citing factors that affect young children's adjustment to divorce, child custody arrangements, and remarriage;
- state how children's relationships with peers differs from family relationships;
- identify Parten's five forms of play;
- describe young children's relationships with their siblings;
- discuss the influence of television on young children's development, including its influence on aggression and prosocial behavior in children; and
- define the key terms and concepts listed on page 300 of your text.

☑ Study Check List

☐ Read Chapter 8 Social and Emotional Development in Early Childhood.

☐ Re-read the Chapter 8 Summary to refresh your memory.

☐ Read the Chapter 8 Objectives listed above.

☐ Complete the following items:

How Does Self-Awareness Change During Early Childhood (pp. 261 - 266)

Self-_____(1) refers to the mental picture we have of ourselves; self-_____(2) refers to how we feel about that mental picture.

⇒ **MEMORY JOG:** Self-concept is how we THINK of ourselves;
Self-est**ee**m is how we F**EE**L about ourselves.

As children develop, their concept of self becomes more complex. Suppose five children have given a description of themselves. *Based on the information in your text (see page 262), match the age to the description:*

2-year-old; 3-year-old; 4–year-old; 7-year-old; 11-year-old; 14-year-old

- "Sometimes I am good…and then I'm bad. Right now, I'm good." _____(3)

- "I'm fast!" _____(4)

- "I'm pretty intelligent, and generally a caring person." _____(5)

- "I'm good at drawing, but I'm not very good at climbing trees." _____(6)

- "I'm a good helper at home, although sometimes I do forget to take out the trash."

    _____(7)

- "Aaron!" (pointing to a picture of himself) _____(8)

According to research, **self-esteem** is a combination of two qualities. What are these two qualities? (9)

a. _____

b. _____

Mruk (1995) put these two qualities in a matrix of high/low competency and high/low worthiness.

According to Mruk,

- Children, who perceive themselves as being very competent and worthy, have _____(10) self-esteem. These children are better prepared to face challenges.

- Children, who perceive themselves as NOT being very competent and feel unworthy, have _____(11) self-esteem. They often have ineffective interactions with others, as well as feelings of anxiety and unhappiness.

136 Study Guide for Exploring Child Development

- Children who perceive themselves as being very competent but also unworthy have _____ self-esteem _____ (12). They may worry about failing and may not feel satisfied even when they have achieved well. They feel they must constantly prove their worth.

- Children who have little accomplishments or competency but see themselves in terms of high worthiness have _____ self-esteem _____ (13). These children often behave in ways that are labeled as stuck-up or spoiled.

Several factors contribute to children's positive concepts and feeling about themselves, including: (14)

1. _____

2. _____

3. _____

---

1 Minute Quiz

1. The value we attach to the mental pictures of ourselves is referred to as _____.

2. What traits are preschoolers MOST likely to use when describing themselves?
   a. traits that are fairly stable over time
   b. traits that emphasize psychological qualities
   c. traits that can exist simultaneously
   d. traits that are global in nature

3. Self-esteem can be understood as a combination of two qualities: _____ and _____.

4. Which of the following is NOT likely to affect a child's self-concept and self-esteem?
   a. warm, secure relationships with parents
   b. positive peer interactions
   c. physical appearance
   d. All of the above will affect a child's self-concept and self-esteem.

Chapter 8 Social and Emotional Development in Early Childhood 137

How Do Young Children Develop a Concept of Gender? (pp. 266 - 270)

Complete the following table, using the information provided: (15)

gender stability; gender consistency; gender labeling; by 30 months of age; by 3 to 4 years of age; by 4 to 5 years of age; child knows a boy wearing a dress or playing with dolls is still a boy; child knows he will always be a boy; understanding and acceptance that one is a boy or a girl; child calls self a "boy" or a "girl" and uses "he" and "she" to correctly match gender group

Gender Identity: _____

Stage	Age	Description

G_____ s_____(16) are the beliefs people share about the typical characteristics of males and females. As early as age _____(17), children have learned basic stereotypes about the sexes. Gender stereotypes influence children in many ways, including: (18)

1. _____

2. _____

Why do children prefer gender-stereotyped toys? (19)

1. _____
2. _____
3. _____

Observable differences between the behaviors of boys and girls generally have not been found before the age of _____ (20), although parents often say that their sons and daughters are different. Parents may int_____(21) with their sons and daughters differently, setting the stage for sex differences to emerge.

What four **sex differences** were found by Maccoby and Jacklin? (22)

1. _____
2. _____
3. _____
4. _____

What are some other sex differences found by researchers? (23) _____

_____
_____
_____
_____

What are the Contemporary Theories of Gender Development? (pp. 270 – 273)

Indicate to which theory of gender development each of the following statements belongs by writing "biological," "social learning," *or* "cognitive":

- Hormone levels may influence children's abilities, behaviors, and personality. _____(24)

- Children use gender schemas, which are mental representations about the sexes, to guide their behavior. _____(25)

- Children's behavior and thinking tend to match their schemas. _____(26)

- Prenatal androgens may masculinize the brain as it develops, making it more sensitive to certain types of environmental influences. _____(27)

- Children learn gender roles when they are rewarded or punished for engaging in gender related behaviors. _____ (28)

- Gender schemas influence what children pay attention to, what they remember, and how they behave. _____(29)

- Children learn gender roles by observing others. _____(30)

- Children are actively involved in learning gender roles and are motivated to adhere to them. _____(31)

---

1 Minute Quiz

1. Christopher was chosen to play "Mrs. Frog" in the school play. He knows that wearing a dress and being called "Mrs." will not change the fact that he is a boy. It appears that Christopher understands _____; and Christopher is at least _____ years old.

2. Children's gender stereotypes influence what children remember. True/False.

3. With which of the following toys would Freddie, a typical 5-year-old boy, probably choose to play?
   a. a tea set
   b. a deflated kickball
   c. a racecar with "Racing Barbie" driving
   d. a "Rubic's Cube" that is described to Freddy as being liked by girls.

4. _____ theories explain how direct learning and observation mold and shape gender development.

140 Study Guide for Exploring Child Development

How Does Emotional Development Change During Early Childhood (pp. 272 - 276)

Conflict

For young children, conflicts involve struggles over ob_____ and poss_____(32). As children mature, their conflicts tend be related to so_____(33) interactions, such as being ignored or challenged. Children respond to conflict in a variety of ways. Young children may become ph_____(34) aggressive, try to re_____(35) a solution, c_____(36), or go for h_____(37). Physical aggression in response to conflict is **rare/common** *(circle one)* (38) among young children; less than _____ (39) percent of conflicts include acts of aggression such as hitting or kicking. As children learn to talk, they increasingly rely on v_____(40) strategies. They also begin to look for co_____(41) solutions.

Aggression

Maccoby (1980) identified at least five things a child must know before her behavior can be judged as aggressive: (42)

1. _____
2. _____
3. _____
4. _____
5. _____

Match the following: (43)

_____ relational aggression   a. "You're a stupid meanie!!!"

_____ instrumental aggression   b. "Tick tock the game is locked – nobody else can play!"

_____ physical aggression   c. aggression directed against another person, often retaliatory in nature

_____ hostile aggression   d. hitting, kicking, pushing

_____ verbal aggression   e. aggression used for a specific purpose

Chapter 8 Social and Emotional Development in Early Childhood 141

Boys/Girls *(circle one)* (44) have been found to be more physically aggressive than **boys/girls** *(circle one)* (45). **Boys/Girls** *(circle one)* (46) have been found to be more verbally aggressive than **boys/girls** *(circle one)* (47). These gender differences have even been found in other cultures, suggesting a b_____(48) contribution to aggressive behavior.

Prosocial Behavior and Emotions

Pr_____ (49) behavior refers to voluntary actions intended to benefit another person. E_____(50) refers to an emotional state that matches another person's emotional state, and s_____(51) refers to feeling sorry or concerned for other people because of their emotional states or conditions. Empathy and sympathy often mo_____(52) prosocial behaviors and actions.

Very young child will respond to another's need in ways that the child himself finds comforting; for example, a child may offer his baby blanket to his distressed father. As children grow, they develop the capacity to take the per_____(53) of others and respond more appropriately.

Reasons for helping others change during early childhood. Young preschoolers are pra_____(54) motivated. Older preschoolers may be motivated by app_____(55) or even selfishness. As children mature, their reasons for helping become al_____(56), desiring to help others without any apparent personal gain or benefit.

LESSONS IN REAL LIFE - LESSONS IN REAL LIFE - LESSONS IN REAL LIFE - LESSONS IN REAL LIFE

Barbie and Ken are interested in raising children who are empathic, sharing, and caring human beings. They ask their friends, neighbors and relatives for suggestions and then write them down. Barbie and Ken then ask you to read the suggestions and <u>cross out</u> any of the suggestions that would NOT lead to their goal: (57)

a. Develop a warm, secure relationship with your child.
b. Don't be afraid to express anger or physically punish the child.
c. Practice what you preach.
d. Talk to and reason with your child about helping others and show your child how to help.

142 Study Guide for Exploring Child Development

How Do Parenting behaviors Influence Young Children's Development? (pp. 276 – 282)

Children's attachments undergo significant changes, and children enter what Ainsworth termed a g_____ c_____(58) partnership. Now, the child becomes a p_____(59) in planning how the relationship develops. Through parents and other caregivers, children learn the values and behaviors important in their society.

Parents help socialize their children through disciplinary practices. D_____(60) is more than just punishment, however. Discipline refers to *any* attempt by parents to alter children's behaviors or attitudes. The most common methods of discipline fall into three categories - power assertion, love withdrawal, and inductive reasoning. *Place the following behaviors into the appropriate category:* (61)

> Ignoring; spanking; giving a child money for good grades; scolding a child and telling the child how ashamed the parent feels; explaining rules; standing a child in the corner; telling a child, "I don't want to see you – get out of my sight!"; telling the child the potential consequences of a child's behavior; telling a child if he's good, he can have dessert; saying "A helpful child like you picks up his room when asked."

Power Assertion	Love Withdrawal	Inductive Reasoning

Chapter 8 Social and Emotional Development in Early Childhood 143

Frequent use of, or reliance on, power assertion and love withdrawal can have negative consequences on children. Children who are more prosocial and popular and have more internalized values and acceptable behavior tend to have parents who rely more on _____(62).

Hint from Mom...

When bringing up a young child, put away all your china, fine porcelain, and any other object you value. "AN OUNCE OF PREVENTION IS WORTH A POUND OF CURE." (And, if your mother-in-law says, "I didn't put away MY fine things...children must just learn not to touch," remember when *she* was raising children, she didn't *have* any fine things).

What factors determine parents' use of discipline? (63)

1. _____

2. _____

3. _____

Parenting styles are made up of several parenting behaviors. Diana Baumrind is best known for her model of parenting styles based on two important characteristics: _____ and _____(64).

LESSONS IN REAL LIFE - LESSONS IN REAL LIFE - LESSONS IN REAL LIFE - LESSONS IN REAL LIFE

On a trip to the local zoo, you take a break from watching the animals to watch the families visiting the zoo, and you observe the following: (65)

I. Family A. Mom and Dad A watch their children as their children playfully toss rocks at one of the animals. "He's got quite an arm on him, doesn't he!" says Dad proudly. "Hey, Chad...you might try putting a little more arc in your throw." Their youngest child pushes two other children out of the way as she attempts to get a better look. Mom smiles. "Excuse me, Madam," says another mother. "Your child is being very rude and pushy!" "Well," replies Mom A. "I believe children need to learn on their own to stick up for themselves."
This is an example of the _____.

This type of parenting style has been found to lead to children who _____

144 Study Guide for Exploring Child Development

_____

_____

II. Family B. At the food counter, Dad B hands a large drink to his small daughter. "Don't drop it!" he says. He orders his daughter to sit down and finish her drink. After several minutes, he tells the daughter to finish her drink because it is time to go. "I don't want to go!" wails the daughter. "Why do we have to go now?!" "Because I said so!" barks the father, who grabs the near empty drink container and tosses it in the garbage.
This is an example of the _____.

This type of parenting style has been found to lead to children who _____

_____

_____

III. Family C. A young man and woman are seated over a box of French fries and appear engaged in a deep conversation. A little girl, about 3 years old, tugs on the woman's arm and says, "Mama! I go potty!" "Go ahead," replies the woman. "It's over there," waving in the direction of the bathrooms across the courtyard. The 3-year-old looks bewildered and begins wandering about the courtyard, and down a walkway out of sight. The man and woman never break from their conversation. A bystander interrupts them, "Excuse me, but I think your daughter went walking toward the lion exhibit." "Oh," replies the mother. "She'll be all right. She's used to do things on her own."
This is an example of the _____.

This type of parenting style has been found to lead to children who _____

_____

_____

IV. Family D. A young mother of three efficiently herds her children to the drinking fountain. While daughter gets a drink, son pushes her and says, "Hurry up! I'm thirsty." The mother firmly tells her son, "Honey...don't push when someone's getting a drink. You could break their tooth and hurt them." "I'm sorry, Mom," sighs the son. "You're such a polite young man! I know you won't push next time."
This is an example of the _____.

This type of parenting style has been found to lead to children who _____

_____

_____

Chapter 8 Social and Emotional Development in Early Childhood 145

⇒ **MEMORY JOG:** AuthoritaTIVE is how parents should L<u>IVE</u>;
AuthoritariaN is <u>Not</u>

---

1 Minute Quiz

1. Most conflicts among young children include acts of aggression, such as hitting, kicking, or biting. True/False.

2. _____ aggression is aggression used for a specific purpose; _____ aggression is aggression that is design to harm another person.

3. Three-year-old Lindsey tells the child next to her, "Let me help you!" She then reaches over her and helps her cut her clay. Which of the following reasons for Lindsey's helping behavior is probably the LEAST LIKELY?
   a. Lindsey may have helped the child because the child was slow and Lindsey wanted her turn.
   b. Lindsey may have helped the child because she believes if she's helpful, the child will like her.
   c. Lindsey may have helped the child because "She's my friend!"
   d. Lindsey may have helped the child simply because she is altruistic and does not expect any personal gain or benefit.

4. "Discipline with reason" is referred to as _____.

5. Baumrind's model of parenting styles is based on:
   a. demandingness of parents.
   b. responsiveness of parents.
   c. both demandingness and responsiveness of parents.
   d. neither demandingness nor responsiveness of parents.

How Does Divorce Affect Young Children's Development? (pp. 282 – 287)

Use these words to complete the following paragraphs:

| support | age | anxiety | Wallerstein | self-blame | crisis | differently |
| half | | structure | aggression | psychological | year | irritability |

Young children have strong reactions to divorce and have a difficult time understanding the situation.

The changes brought about by a divorce can affect the child in several ways. _____(66)

and Kelly conducted a series of longitudinal studies and found that children respond to divorce

_____(67), according to _____(68).

146 Study Guide for Exploring Child Development

Young preschoolers are likely to show increased _____(69). Middle preschoolers are likely to show increased _____(70), aggression, _____(71), and confusion. Older preschoolers are likely to show increased _____(72) and aggression. Adverse consequences of divorce appear to be greater for **boys/girls** *(circle one)* (73). However, in remarriage, **boys/girls** *(circle one)* (74) are more likely to have difficulty making the transition to the new family than **boys/girls** *(circle one)* (75).

Many of these negative behaviors ended within a _____(76) or two for children in a stable caregiving environment; however, almost _____(77) of the preschoolers continue to show emotional distress and poor _____(78) adjustment a year or two following the divorce. Thus, the first two years following a divorce have been labeled as a _____(79) period for children and adults. Children have special needs during this period, including emotional _____(80) and predictable daily _____(81).

List four factors that affect young children's adjustment to divorce: (82)

1. _____
2. _____
3. _____
4. _____

Draw a line through the statements regarding JOINT CUSTODY that are FALSE: (83)
- In joint custody arrangements, each parent has the child for a portion of the year or in alternating years.
- Joint legal custody has been found to increase the father's decision-making authority or involvement in child rearing.
- Fathers with joint custody are generally more satisfied with their arrangement than noncustodial fathers.
- Joint custody couples have less conflict than sole custody couples.
- Based on the research, joint custody should be encouraged for all divorcing parents.

Chapter 8 Social and Emotional Development in Early Childhood 147

How Do Peer and Sibling Relationships Develop During Early Childhood? (pp. 288 – 295)

Describe how relationships with peers differ in important ways from family relationships. (84)

1. _____
2. _____
3. _____
4. _____

Friendships provide children with opportunities to: (85)

a. _____ ;

b. _____ , and

c. _____ .

As children grow in their use of language and in their cognitive abilities, their friendship patterns change. In early childhood, friendship is based on the exchange of common i_____s and a_____(86). Later on, older children learn that friendship is based on mutual sy_____ and lo_____ (87) and that the relationship can be st_____(88) and enduring.

How children play with each other also changes as they mature. Parten (1932) identified five forms of play based on the child's level of involvement with other children. *Using Parten's categories, identify the type of play in the following situations:* (89)

1. Jenny is sitting in the sandbox, pouring water from a bucket into the sand. Seated next to Jenny is Jared, who is doing the same thing. _____

2. Daniel is creating a "monster" at the clay table, along with several other boys. As Daniel builds his clay monster, he comments on the monster that David is creating. They pass the various colors of clay around when requested and occasionally make "roaring" monster noises at each other. _____

3. Saul watches Bernadette playing in the "kiddie kitchen." Once, he asks her, "What's in the oven?" Most of the time, however, he spends watching her play. _____

4. Valorie is playing by herself with her doll. _____

148 Study Guide for Exploring Child Development

5. Kimball, Taylor, and Heber are building a fort. Taylor and Kimball hold the boards, while Heber carefully guides them in their placement. _____

Most children have brothers or sisters. These relationships vary depending on the spacing of the siblings, as well as their age and developmental level. Three factors have been found to influence the quality of sibling relationships: (1) _____; (2) _____; and (3) _____ (90).

How Does Television Influence Young Children's Emotional and Social Development? (pp. 295 – 298)

You are on the "Jerry Springer Show" as an expert on television and child development! Jerry asks you, "Is it true that families who own television sets spend less time sleeping?" You reply, "Not only do they spend less time sleeping, Jerry, they spend less time _____!" (91)

"Well," says Jerry. "A lot of people talk about violence on television…but is there really scientific evidence that violent television shows can be linked to childhood violence?" You reply, "The link between television violence and children's aggression has been found w_____(92), not just here in America. Jerry, several themes have been found by the research. First, children's aggressive tendencies are likely to be increased when violence on television is portrayed r_____(93). Second, when children have been watching violent television, they tend to behave more im_____. (94) Third, television violence seems to have more of an effect on children who are _____(95).

Finally, TV violence has lon_____(96) consequences!"

Chapter 8 Social and Emotional Development in Early Childhood 149

"But you must admit," intones Jerry. "Some of my shows probably have positive consequences. Not all TV is bad…" "You are right again, Jerry! Programs such as Sesame Street, Barney, and Mr. Rogers' Neighborhood do seem to encourage prosocial behavior in children, but only if there are en_____ c_____ (97) and cle_____ c_____g (98) depictions of prosocial behavior."

"Well, thanks for visiting! Our body guards will show you out!"

☐ Complete the crossword puzzle in Appendix 1 – Crossword Puzzles.

☐ Go to the beginning of this chapter, and on a separate sheet of paper, write out the answers to the lesson objectives.

sAge Advice

"If a teacher provides a study guide, use it; that means you should write out the answers on a separate sheet of paper and study from it."

STUDY QUESTIONS

Multiple Choice (The following questions are identified "F," *factual questions* that rely on the recall of facts; or "A," *applied questions* that rely on the ability to apply a concept to a real-life situation).

1. Self-concept: (p. 261; F)
   a. refers to the value we attach to the mental pictures of ourselves.
   b. refers to an individual's beliefs about the attributes and capacities she or he possesses.
   c. revolves around feelings of good and bad.
   d. has been shown to be a combination of worthiness and competence.

2. According to Mruk (1995), defensive self-esteem II: (p. 263; F)
   a. results in feelings of success and positive worth.
   b. describes children who feel valued despite the fact that they lack the accomplishments to be successful.
   c. is a combination of low worthiness and low competence
   d. is seen in children who have difficulty experiencing satisfaction in their achievements and feel they must constantly prove their worth.

3. Which of the following does NOT influence a child's self-concept and self-esteem: (p. 264; F)
   a. the child's physical appearance
   b. the child's relationships with peers
   c. the culture a child is raised in
   d. All of the above influence a child's self-concept and self-esteem.

4. Martha tells James that when she grows up, she's going to be a daddy. James tells Martha that she can't be a daddy when she grows up because daddies are men and she will be a woman. From this information alone, it appears that James understands: (p. 266; A)
   a. gender identity.   c. gender stability.
   b. gender labeling.   d. gender consistency.

5. Gender stereotypes: (p. 267; F)
   a. influence children's judgments about other people.
   b. have little affect on what children remember
   c. cannot be observed in children until about age 4.
   d. do not develop when parents provide examples of breaking gender stereotypic expectations.

6. You buy your niece an unusual toy that you observed some boys playing with in the park. When you give your niece the toy, you tell her that she'll love it because some boys said it was their favorite plaything. Most likely, your niece will: (p. 268; A)
   a. play with the toy to determine if indeed it is as great as the boys said.
   b. play with the toy for a short time, then put it aside.
   c. avoid the toy and play with her doll.
   d. ask, "What's the catch?!"

7. Maccoby and Jacklin (1974) concluded that there are four sex differences found consistently in children and adolescents. Which of the following is **NOT** one of those sex differences: (p. 269; F)
   a. Males have better math skills.
   b. Females have better visual-spatial skills.
   c. Females have better verbal skills.
   d. Males are more aggressive.

8. You watch your nephew play with his friends. He enjoys wrestling, is very active, tends to stare at others, and seems to smile more than other kids. Based on research findings, your nephew: (p. 269; A)
   a. exhibits typical characteristics seen in boys.
   b. exhibits typical characteristics seen in girls.
   c. exhibits typical characteristics seen in boys, except for smiling more often, which is seen more in girls.
   d. exhibits typical characteristics seen in boys, except for staring more often, which is seen more in girls.

9. In a newspaper article on gender differences, an "expert" is quoted as saying "Children learn gender roles directly when they are rewarded or punished for their gender stereotyped choices and by observing the behavior of others." "Aha!" you say, knowingly. "This expert emphasizes _____ theory in gender development." (p. 271; A)
   a. biological   b. social learning   c. cognitive   d. developmental

10. Gender schemas influence: (p. 272; F)
    a. what children pay attention to.
    b. what children remember.
    c. how children behavior.
    d. All of the above.

11. Your friend just started a job at a local preschool for 4 and 5 year olds. He was very surprised that there was so little physical aggression in response to conflicts on the playground. You inform him, (p. 273; A)
    a. "Physical aggression in response to conflict is rare among young children. Your experience is not unusual at all."
    b. "These children are still too young to show a lot of physical aggression. As they develop their sense of autonomy, you will see an increase in incidents."
    c. "Your presence on the playground probably had a dampening affect on the children's display of aggression. Most children this age resort to physical aggression in response to conflict."
    d. "Most of those kids are boys. If you had a group of girls on the playground, you'd really see a lot of fighting."

12. Caregivers are more likely to have children show prosocial feelings and behaviors if the caregivers: (p. 276; F)
    a. frequently talk to and reason with children about prosocial activities and the importance of thinking about others.
    b. set strict guidelines for behavior and spank children who overstep their bounds or do not show caring behaviors.
    c. allow their children to set their own limits and guide them in appropriate ways.
    d. discuss appropriate behaviors with the children, which is far more important that the caregivers' own behavior.

13. Which of the following behaviors is **NOT** classified as a power assertion technique? (p. 278; F)
    a. spanking
    b. grounding
    c. giving rewards
    d. telling the child to "Get out of my sight."

14. Baumrind identified two important parenting characteristics that became the basis for her model on parental styles. The two characteristics were: (p. 280; F)
    a. competency and worthiness
    b. demandingness and responsiveness
    c. strictness and control
    d. caring and guidance

15. Your neighbor's son is caught shoplifting from a local store. The parents tell their son, "Shoplifting costs everybody money. Is it fair to take money out of the pockets of the storeowner who works so hard or out of our own pockets because we have to pay extra to cover the costs of those who steal? You must go back to the store owner and apologize, work for him for 20 hours to cover the costs of his trouble, and not go out with your friends for 2 weeks." It appears that your neighbors are: (p. 280; A)
    a. authoritative.
    b. authoritarian.
    c. permissive.
    d. uninvolved.

16. Your friends are going through a divorce. They are very concerned about the impact of the divorce on their children. You tell them: (p. 285; A)
    a. "As much as you hate each other, try to treat each other as friends and learn to get along."
    b. "One of the side affects of divorce is that fathers tend to get very authoritative and mothers become more permissive. Both parents should become more authoritarian."
    c. "As much as it hurts, the father should try to stay away from the children. This will avoid conflicts with the mother and allow the mother and children time to adjust to the divorce. Once things have settled down, the father can resume his relationship with the kids."
    d. "Don't worry...most children weather divorce well. It's more important that you work out your own problems first."

17. Which of the following statements about divorce and remarriage is **TRUE**? (p. 287, F)
    a. Adverse consequences of divorce appear to be greater for young girls than for young boys.
    b. Age of children at the time of divorce seems to have little impact on how children respond to it.
    c. Girls have more problems than boys do in making the transition to a remarried household.
    d. Joint physical custody is probably the best custody arrangement for young children.

18. Compared to family relationships, peer relationships are: (p. 288; F)
    a. voluntary relationships chosen by the child.
    b. based on equality and mutual give and take.
    c. better at teaching children about things such as cooperation, reciprocity, competition, and lying.
    d. All of the above.

19. Several children are coloring at the same table. They share the crayons, discuss their pictures, and make comments about the others' pictures. According to Parten (1932), these children are engaging in: (p. 292; A)
    a. parallel play.
    b. associative play.
    c. creative play.
    d. cooperative play.

Chapter 8 Social and Emotional Development in Early Childhood 153

20. Television violence: (p. 297; F)
    a. has been found to have short term consequences on children's behavior; however, long term consequences have not been documented.
    b. is likely to influence all children equally, regardless of whether they are abused, emotionally disturbed, or "normal."
    c. has been found to act "cathartically" for children; that is, it has been found to decrease violent tendencies in aggressive children by providing a safe outlet.
    d. has been linked to children's aggression worldwide.

True/False Questions (If a statement is FALSE, correct it).

1. Although their self-concepts are becoming increasingly complex, young children rarely see themselves in terms of stable traits and qualities. (p. 262) True/False.

2. According to Mruk (1995), self-esteem can be understood as a combination of competence and self-perception. (p. 263) True/False.

3. Children label themselves as boys or girls by 4 years of age. (p. 266) True/False.

4. On average, girls have better fine eye-motor skills and flexibility than boys. (p. 269) True/False.

5. Biological theories view gender development as an outcome of normal cognitive development. (p. 270) True/False.

6. Gender schemas influence what children remember. (p. 272) True/False.

7. As children gain a better understanding of social relationships, they are more likely to realize that "might makes right" and resolve conflicts with physical aggression. (p. 273) True/False.

8. Empathy refers to an emotional state that matches another person's emotional state. (p. 275) True/False.

9. Parents use remarkably similar disciplinary strategies with different children. (p. 279) True/False.

10. Authoritative parents tend to have children who are more socially competent, cooperative, and friendly. (p. 282) True/False.

11. The first two years following divorce have been labeled a "crisis period" for children and adults. (p. 284) True/False.

12. The younger a child is when separated from a parent, the more affected the child is by the loss. (p. 286) True/False.

13. Siblings who are temperamentally different are more likely to have positive relationships with each other. (p. 294) True/False.

14. Except for school, television takes up more of a child's time than any other activity. (p. 295) True/False.

15. Most parents do little to control their children's viewing habits. (p. 296) True/False.

☐ **REWARD YOURSELF!** Sit on the front porch (or an outdoor patio) and watch the world go by!

ANSWERS - Chapter 8 Social and Emotional Development in Early Childhood

How Does Self-Awareness Change During Early Childhood (pp. 261 - 266)
(1) concept; (2) esteem; (3) 7-year-old; (4) 3-year-old; (5) 14-year-old; (6) 4-years-old; (7) 11-years-old; (8) 2-years-old
(9) competency and worthiness; (10) high; (11) low; (12) defensive self-esteem II; (13) defensive self-esteem I
(14) physical appearance, relationships with caregivers and peers, social and cultural conditions
1 Minute Quiz: 1. self-esteem; 2. D; 3. worthiness and competency; 4. D

How Do Young Children Develop a Concept of Gender? (pp. 266 - 270)
(15) Gender Identity: understanding and acceptance that one is a boy or a girl.
Gender labeling, 30 months of age, child calls self a "boy" or a "girl" and uses "he" and "she" to correctly match gender group
Gender stability, 3 to 4 years of age, child knows he will always be a boy;
Gender consistency; by 4 to 5 years of age; child knows a boy wearing a dress or playing with dolls is still a boy;
(16) Gender stereotypes; (17) 2 ½ ; (18) making judgments about other people and what they remember; (19) Because they have a history playing with them; they reinforce their own gender identity; they are discouraged from playing with toys gender-typed for the opposite sex.
(20) 2; (21) interact; (22) males have better visual spatial skills; males have better mathematical reasoning abilities; males are more physically aggressive; females have better verbal skills.
(23) boys more likely to take risks, be more active, engage in rough play, throw a ball better, stare; girls are more likely to have better fine eye-motor skills and flexibility, smile, be more socially oriented and more easily influence, be perceived as more dependent.

What are the Contemporary Theories of Gender Development? (pp. 270 – 273)
(24) biological; (25) cognitive; (26) cognitive; (27) biological; (28) social learning; (29) cognitive; (30) social learning; (31) social learning
1 Minute Quiz: 1. gender consistency, 4-5 years old; 2. True; 3. B; 4. Social learning

How Does Emotional Development Change During Dearly Childhood (pp. 272 - 276)
(32) objects and possessions; (33) social; (34) physically (35) reason; (36) cry; (37) help; (38) rare; (39) 20; (40) verbal; (41) cooperative
(42) that other people experience distress and feel pain, that the child's own actions can cause distress, which actions cause distress in other people, how to carry out distress-producing actions; that distress can cause other people to act the way the child wants them to
(43) relational – b; instrumental – e; physical – d; hostile – c; verbal – a
(44) Boys; (45) girls; (46) Boys; (47) girls; (48) biological; (49) Prosocial; (50) Empathy; (51) sympathy; (52) motivate; (53) perspective; (54) practically or pragmatically; (55) approval; (56) altruistic
(57) Cross out "b"

How Do Parenting behaviors Influence Young Children's Development? (pp. 276 – 282)
(58) goal-corrected; (59) partner; (60) Discipline
(61) power assertion - spanking; giving a child money for good grades; standing a child in the corner; telling a child if he's good, he can have dessert
    love withdrawal - ignoring; scolding a child and telling the child how ashamed the parent feels; telling a child, "I don't want to see you – get out of my sight!"
    inductive reasoning - explaining rules; telling the child the potential consequences of a child's behavior; saying "A helpful child like you picks up his room when asked."
(62) inductive reasoning; (63) nature of the misbehavior; characteristics of the child; cultural, ethnic, and social values
(64) demandingness and responsiveness
(65) Family A – permissive; children tend to be immature, demanding rebellious, impulsive, aggressive, and less socially competent; Family B – authoritarian; children tend to be aggressive, anxious, resistant to correction and have low levels of self-control and independence; Family C – uninvolved; children tend to be noncompliant, aggressive, withdrawn, insecure; Family D – authoritative; children tend to be socially competent, friendly, cooperative and confident.
1 Minute Quiz: 1. False; 2. Instrumental; hostile; 3.D; 4. inductive reasoning; 5. Demandingness/responsiveness

How Does Divorce Affect Young Children's Development? (pp. 282 – 287)
(66) Wallerstein; (67) differently; (68) age; (69) aggression; (70) irritability; (71) self-blame; (72) anxiety; (73) boys; (74) girls; (75) boys; (76) year; (77) half; (78) psychological; (79) crisis; (80) support; (81) structure
(82) amount of conflict between parents; effectiveness of the parents; characteristics of the child; relationship of the child with the noncustodial parent
(83) Draw a line through "In joint custody arrangements, each parent has the child for a portion of the year or in alternating years"; "Joint legal custody has been found to increase the father's decision-making authority or involvement in child rearing"; "Joint custody couples have less conflict than sole custody couples"; and "Based on the research, joint custody should be encouraged for all divorcing parents." All of these statements are false.

How Do Peer and Sibling Relationships Develop During Early Childhood? (pp. 288 – 295)
(84) peer relationships are voluntary relationships chosen by the child; peer relationships are based on equality and mutual give and take; children learn things from peers that they are less likely to learn from adults; families tend to love and care for children no matter what
(85) learn effective interpersonal skills; gain experience in displaying and controlling emotions and in responding to others' emotions; share information and ideas and engage in social problem solving.
(86) interests and activities; (87) sympathy and loyalty; (88) stable
(89) 1. Parallel play; 2. Associative play; 3. Onlooker play; 4. Solitary play; 5. Cooperative play
(90) temperaments of the siblings; parental treatment; family life events

How Does Television Influence Young Children's Emotional and Social Development? (pp. 295 – 298)
(91) visiting others, having conversations, cleaning, participating in community or school activities, and pursuing hobbies or sports
(92) worldwide; (93) realistically; (94) impulsively; (95) abused, emotionally disturbed, or predisposed to act aggressively; (96) long-term; (97) environmental cues; (98) clearly contrasting

STUDY QUESTIONS

Multiple Choice: 1. B; 2. D; 3. D; 4. C; 5. A; 6. C; 7. B; 8. C; 9. B; 10. D; 11. A; 12. A; 13. D; 14. B; 15. A; 16. A; 17. C; 18. D; 19. B; 20. D

True/False:
1. True
2. False; competence and worthiness
3. False; 2 ½
4. True
5. False; Cognitive theories
6. True
7. False; resolve conflicts without damaging ongoing interactions
8. True
9. False; parents use different
10. True
11. True
12. True
13. False; temperamentally similar
14. False; omit "Except for school"
15. True

Chapter 9
Physical, Cognitive, and Language Development in Late Childhood

My mother taught me about GENETICS...
"You are just like your father!"

- Things My Mother Taught Me

Objectives

When you have completed this chapter, you will be able to:
- describe the physical growth of children in late childhood;
- summarize the nutritional needs of school-aged children and discuss childhood obesity;
- describe how older children think and solve problems;
- summarize the development of language in older children, including syntactic, semantic, and pragmatic development;
- state the skills children need to become good readers and discuss the controversies about reading instruction;
- define intelligence and identify its components;
- discuss creativity in older children and identify its components;
- describe social perspective taking in late childhood and children's understanding of race and prejudice;
- summarize teaching methods and programs aimed at school-aged children, including multicultural education, bilingual education, and education for children with special needs;
- state the role of family and culture in children's cognitive growth and development; and
- define the key terms and concepts listed on page 341 of your text.

☑ Study Check List

☐ Read Chapter 9 Physical, Cognitive, and Language Development in Late Childhood.

☐ Re-read the Chapter 9 Summary to refresh your memory.

☐ Read the Chapter 9 Objectives listed above.

☐ Complete the following items:

How Do Children Develop Physically during Late Childhood? (pp. 307 - 310)

By the time a child reaches the age of 8, her brain is approximately _____(1) percent of its adult size.

158 Study Guide for Exploring Child Development

Throughout the school year, brain functioning continues to im_____(2). Physical growth during the school years **slows down/speeds up** *(circle one)* (3) compared with earlier years, and this **slower/faster** *(circle one)* (4) rate continues until the child approaches adolescence. This **slower/faster** *(circle one)* (5) rate of growth allows children time to become accustomed to their bodies, bringing gains in mo_____ control and _____ (6). Older children have more st_____, a_____, and b_____(7) than younger children. Their f_____ motor skills also improve, resulting in neater writing. Boys and girls perform motor tasks similarly, but boys do have more u_____ b_____(8) strength and girls are more fl_____(9).

A healthy d_____ (10) is important for growing children. During the school years, children need approximately d_____(11) the calories and protein (per pound) that adults need. Children also need adequate amounts of vitamins and minerals. Adult standards **may/may not** *(circle one)* (12) be appropriate for children. *What adult nutritional standards should be NOT be applied to children? (13)*

_____

_____

_____

Some children are ob_____ (14), meaning they are more than _____(15) percent over their ideal weight. In fact, more children are overweight today than in the past. Obese children are at risk for serious health problems, such as _____, _____, _____, and _____ (16). *What are some causes of obesity? (17)*

1. _____
2. _____
3. _____

Chapter 9 Physical, Cognitive, and Language Development in Late Childhood 159

1 Minute Quiz

1. During the school years, children:
   a. grow more slowly than they did as younger children.
   b. continue to grow at the same steady rate as when they were younger.
   c. grow more quickly than they did as younger children.

2. In terms of motor development,
   a. school-aged boys out perform school-aged girls.
   b. school-aged girls out perform school-aged boys.
   c. school-aged boys and girls perform similarly in almost all motor activities.

3. Per pound, school-aged children need _____ the calories and proteins of adults.

4. Obesity in childhood is not affected by genetics. True/False.

How Do Older Children Think and Solve Problems? (pp. 310-314)

According to Piaget, between the ages of 5 and 7, children enter the cognitive stage of

co_____ op_____ (18). For the first time, children are able

to think l_____(19). Their thinking is more fl_____,

rev_____, and less e_____(20). They can now

solve problems of conservation. To do this, they must be able to: (21)

   1. _____
   2. _____
   3. _____

Children also have re_____(22) thinking, that is, the understanding that actions

can be undone; and com_____(23), that is the understanding that one change

can offset another. During the concrete operational stage, children's understanding of categories and

concepts, as well as seriation becomes more sophisticated.

Children's thinking is influenced by their (a) f_____; (b) c_____; and (c) ex_____ (24).

How Do Language and Literacy Develop During the School Years? (pp. 314 – 320)

During school years, children are able to communicate more effectively over a broader range of contexts. Children continue to show improvements in their syntactic, semantic, and pragmatic abilities. Identify each of the following as an improvement in **syntax, semantics, or pragmatics**: (25)

a. Children are better able to maintain a conversation. _____

b. Older children understand passive sentences with non-action-oriented verbs, i.e., "was followed by." _____

c. Children understand the meanings of idioms, such as "Go fly a kite!" _____

d. School-aged children improve in their ability to understand subtle aspects of meaning, such as the various meanings of the word "bright." _____

e. Children are now able to clarify their messages in conversation if a listener does not understand something. _____

During the school years, children learn to read and write, skills that require attention, perception, memory, and background knowledge. To become a successful reader, children need to understand that wri_____

_____(26).

English-speaking children need to learn that (27)

1. _____

2. _____

3. _____

Children also need to master pho_____ aw_____(28), recognizing sounds are associated with letters and blend together to form words.

Chapter 9 Physical, Cognitive, and Language Development in Late Childhood

LESSONS IN REAL LIFE - LESSONS IN REAL LIFE - LESSONS IN REAL LIFE - LESSONS IN REAL LIFE

- Your friend's child has taken an interest in books. Your friend is afraid of being "too pushy" because she read that pushing children to read before they are ready may cause them to become discouraged. *Using the readiness standards set by the National Association for the Education of Young Children (1998), what questions would you ask your friend in order to help her determine if her child is ready to read?* (29)

_____

_____

_____

_____

_____

- Your friend is also concerned about reading methods and does not know which method is best. She's not sure what is meant by "whole language" and wonders if phonics is better. You tell her: (30)

_____

_____

_____

---

1 Minute Quiz

1. **Which of the following characteristics is NOT indicative of children's thinking during the school years?**
   a. flexible   b. reversible   c. egocentric   d. logical

2. **Children's cognitive abilities appear to develop independent of culture. True/False.**

3. **The ability to maintain a conversation indicates development in the area of _____.**

4. **The whole language approach has been found to facilitate reading for most children. True/False.**

162 Study Guide for Exploring Child Development

What Characteristics Define Children's Intelligence and Creativity? (pp. 320 - 324)

What is intelligence and how is it measured? Scholars and laymen alike have debated these controversial questions. The most popular test of children's intelligence is the W_____r I_____ S_____ for C_____ (31), which measures v_____ intelligence and p_____(32) intelligence. Such intelligence tests typically yield "IQ" (I_____ q_____(33)) scores that have been used to predict school _____(34). IQ tests can identify children who need special help in school or are especially bright; however, IQ scores do not pr_____(35) life outcomes for many individuals. Success in life is due to many things aside from IQ, such as mo_____ and so_____ l s_____(36).

Figure It Out! A person's IQ is determined by taking the person's mental age (MA), which is determined by a test such as the WISC, divided by the person's chronological age (CA), and multiplied by 100. In short,

$$\frac{MA}{CA} \times 100 = IQ$$

Suppose a person has a mental age of 72 months and a chronological age of 72 months. That person's IQ would be 72/72 x 100 = **100.**

If a person's mental age is 72 months and chronological age is 36 months, that person's IQ is _____.

If a person's mental age is 144 months and chronological age is 72 months, that person's IQ is _____.

Fun Facts

Marilyn Vos Savant has been cited in the Guinness Book of World Records Hall of Fame as having the highest recorded IQ. At ten years of age, she achieved a ceiling score for 23-year-olds, giving her an effective IQ of 228. Reportedly, the chance of scoring this high is 1 in 1,600,000,000.

Want to take an IQ test? Check out www.brain.com. Wonder what the estimated IQs are of the world's greatest geniuses? Check out http://home8.swipnet.se/~w-80790/Index.htm

Chapter 9 Physical, Cognitive, and Language Development in Late Childhood 163

One of the most common reasons IQ tests are questioned is that they are c_____y b_____(37). Even tests that supposedly are "culture-free" are not truly so. Most scholars and educators today recommend that IQ tests not be used as sole indicators of one's abilities.

According to different theorists, intelligence is made up of several components. In his tri_____c t_____ of i_____(38), Sternberg (1985) proposed three components of intelligence: (39)

1. _____:_____

2. _____:_____

3. _____:_____

Gardner (1983) emphasizes m_____ i_____(40), identifying seven "f_____ of m_____" (41) or distinct areas of skill that are relatively independent of each other. Children who show exceptional abilities at a very young age in one domain of intelligence are called pr_____(42); and people who show exceptional abilities in one domain but are incompetent in other domain are known as s_____(43).

Cr_____(44) is novel and appropriate behavior that is different from what the person has done or seen before. It is difficult to measure creativity. It appears that four components are needed for creativity: (45)

1. _____

2. _____

3. _____

164 Study Guide for Exploring Child Development

---

1 Minute Quiz

1. Intelligence is a single, stable construct that can be accurately measured through paper and pencil tests. True/False.

2. One problem with IQ tests is that fact that many are _____.

3. Sternberg identifies three components of intelligence in his _____ _____ of intelligence.

4. An example of a "savant" is:
   a. Einstein.
   b. a person with autism who can play any musical selection on the piano.
   c. a young child who can play a violin better than an experienced performer.
   d. a great chess player.

How Do Older Children Understand the Social World? (pp. 324 – 325)

Concrete operational children are better at social p_____(46) taking, which is the ability to move away from one's own perspective and recognize another's perspective. Concrete operational children are **less/more** *(circle one)* (47) egocentric, can communicate more effectively, and have a more sophisticated understanding of people. Around age _____(48), children are more likely to think about others in _____ and _____(49) terms. School-aged children are aware that others have thoughts, beliefs, knowledge, and intentions of their own. Some children, such as children with autism, do not consider the mental states of others to help them understand others' actions. These children are referred to as m_____(50). Most children, however, have quite sophisticated mentalistic concepts and can easily understand the feelings, emotions, and beliefs of others.

What is the difference between prejudice and discrimination? (51) _____

_____

_____

_____

Complete the following outline where indicated:

Children's Recognition of Ethnicity

I. **Developmental Changes**

   A. **Six months of age**

      1. Infants can _____(52)

      2. Recognizing differences *does not* indicate understanding ethnicity.

   B. **Two years of age**

      1. Same-race peer preferences _____(53)

      2. Same-race peer preferences become more clearly established in early _____(54)

   C. **Four years of Age**

      1. Children have _____(55) about racial stereotypes

      2. Children are able to distinguish between _____(56)

         but have difficulty with _____(57).

   D. **Between 6 and 8 years of age**

      1. Children use ethnicity to _____(58).

      2. Children begin to use ethnicity to understand and make guesses about _____

         _____(59).

   E. **By age 11**

      1. Children are more _____(60) in their beliefs

      2. Children no longer perceive people to be different because they are of _____

         _____(61).

166 Study Guide for Exploring Child Development

Based on scientific research, explain the role of parents in the formation of prejudice in children: (62)

_____

_____

_____

A theory that has been used to account for the development of prejudice in people is the so_____l c_____ (63) theory. This theory states that the child's perception of the social world is influence by his or her level of _____ d_____ (64).

How Does Schooling Influence Children's Cognitive Development? (pp. 327 – 330)

Match the following:

_____ multicultural education (65)   a. students are taught how to use specific methods of problem solving to integrate new information with pre-existing information

_____ discovery learning (66)   b. programs designed to teach English-language skills to children with limited English proficiency

_____ generative learning (67)   c. curriculum that includes non-European perspectives or improves educational outcomes for minority students

_____ cooperative learning (68)   d. students work together in groups to solve problems

_____ bilingual education (69)   e. students encouraged to determine principles for themselves

---
LESSONS IN REAL LIFE - LESSONS IN REAL LIFE - LESSONS IN REAL LIFE - LESSONS IN REAL LIFE

Your friend tells you in confidence that he told his daughter's first grade teacher that his daughter was recently tested by a psychologist specializing in learning and found to have a very high IQ in the gifted range! In fact, the daughter never did see a psychologist, but the father said he lied to the teacher because he read somewhere that kids do better in school if their teachers think they're smart. According to research: (70)
a. your friend is all wet. Teachers' expectations have been found to have very little influence on children's academic performance.
b. Your friend is partially right; teachers' expectations have been found to influence children's academic performance, but only in the negative direction. In other words, if the teachers thought the child was dumb, the child did poorly.
c. Your friend is partially right; teachers' expectations have been found to influence children's academic performance, but only in the positive direction. In other words, if the teachers thought the child was smart, the child did better.

d. Your friend is correct. Many studies have demonstrated that teachers have different expectations for and act differently toward students they believe to be high and low achievers. However, few teachers are even aware of the preferential treatment they give to some children.

LESSONS IN REAL LIFE - LESSONS IN REAL LIFE - LESSONS IN REAL LIFE - LESSONS IN REAL LIFE

How Do Schools Address Students' Special Needs? (pp. 331 – 337)

Use these words to complete the following paragraphs:

one-third	environmental	controversial	five	special	mainstreamed
eight	varied	diet	combination	learn	medications
adolescence	biological	attention	genetic	ten	seven
behavioral	least	impulsivity	attention deficit hyperactivity disorder		

About _____ (71) percent of children in the educational system have _____ (72) needs, due to physical, psychological, or emotional disabilities. Another _____ (73) percent have special needs because they are gifted or talented. Federal law requires that all public schools meet the specialized needs of these children in the _____ (74) restrictive environment and at public expense. If possible, children with special needs are _____ (75) into regular classrooms, as much as possible. Mainstreaming allows children to interact with children of _____ (76) abilities.

The most common mental disorder among children is _____ _____ (ADHD) (77). Children with ADHD have low levels of _____ (78) and high levels of _____ (79) and activity. These characteristics make it very difficult for these children to _____ (80) effectively. Most children outgrow their hyperactivity after _____ (81), but about _____ (82) continue to have the problem into adulthood. Because there is such a wide range of "normal," it is sometimes difficult to diagnose ADHD accurately. Children must evidence at least _____ (83) specific symptoms, and these symptoms must have been present prior to the age of _____ (84).

ADHD may have a _____(85) basis and may be _____(86). _____(87) factors also may play a role in this problem. ADHD is most often treated with _____(88), such as Ritalin, although such treatment is _____(89). Other treatments include _____(90), as well as _____(91) strategies. For most ADHD children, a _____(92) of treatments is most effective.

Define "mental retardation": _____
_____(93)

- What are the four degrees of severity? (1) _____; (2) _____; (3) _____; and (4) _____ (94)
- Are more males or females diagnosed as mentally retarded? _____(95)
- Can children outgrow their mental retardation as adults? _____(96)
- What causes mental retardation? _____
_____(97)
- Is specific step-by-step skill training the most effective educational strategy for people who are mentally retarded? _____(98)

Define "gifted": _____
_____(99)

- Which gifted children may miss being identified as "gifted" by their teachers? _____
_____(100)
- What are two types of programs used for educating gifted children? _____
_____(101)

Chapter 9 Physical, Cognitive, and Language Development in Late Childhood 169

- Which program seems to be the most successful in increasing students' achievement and academic abilities? _____(102)

How Do Family and Culture Influence Children's Intellectual Development? (pp. 337 – 339)

Why does poverty appear to adversely affect children's intellectual development and school achievement?

_____
_____
_____
_____(103)

What common characteristics have been found in families of successful and talented children? (104)

a. _____

b. _____

c. _____

d. _____

e. _____

At a local school board meeting, a parent stands up and complains about recent newspaper articles describing the fact that Asian children outperformed American children on math tests. The parent demands a change in school district's math curriculum and blames poor teachers for the poor performance of American students. Citing research by Stevenson and others, you respond: (105)

_____
_____
_____
_____
_____
_____

1 Minute Quiz

1. School-aged children are more likely to:
   a. think about others by focusing on external characteristics.
   b. refer to others in concrete terms.
   c. have difficulty viewing social events from the perspective of others.
   d. think about others in internal psychological terms.

2. Children only learn about prejudice from their parents. True/False.

3. In discovery learning:
   a. children work together in groups to solve problems.
   b. students are taught how to use specific methods of problem solving to integrate new information with pre-existing information.
   c. students are encouraged to ascertain principles for themselves.
   d. teachers teach children basic principles in the classroom with instructions to discover how those principles operate in real life.

4. Children's classroom performance is influenced by the _____ the teachers hold about their capabilities.

5. Scientists believe that attention deficit hyperactivity disorder is caused by
   a. environmental factors.
   b. genetics.
   c. biological factors.
   d. All of the above.

6. Enrichment programs have been found to be the most successful in increasing gifted students' achievement. True/False.

☐ Complete the crossword puzzle in Appendix 1 – Crossword Puzzles.

☐ Go to the beginning of this chapter, and on a separate sheet of paper, write out the answers to the lesson objectives.

SAGE Advice

"Success in school? Attend class, do your homework, don't postpone your long-term assignments, and keep in touch with your teachers!

STUDY QUESTIONS

Multiple Choice (The following questions are identified "F," *factual questions* that rely on the recall of facts; or "A," *applied questions* that rely on the ability to apply a concept to a real-life situation).

1. Sal's 9-year-old daughter wants to be on the boy's soccer team. The team refuses, saying that girls cannot compete with boys at this level and could get hurt. Knowing something about child development, Sal says, (p. 308; A)
   a. "You're incorrect. At this age, boys and girls are very similar in terms of their physical and motor development. You will also find that my daughter is probably more agile than the boys."
   b. "You're incorrect. Although boys' physical and motor development is better than girls', girls this age are quicker."
   c. "You're correct. Boys are stronger and more agile than girls at this age; however, with practice, my daughter should be just as good."
   d. "You're correct. Girls at this age have skills that make them exceptional softball and volleyball players."

2. During the school years, children need _____ the calories and protein (per pound) that adults need. (p. 309; F)
   a. the same amount of   b. double   c. triple   d. quadruple

3. The number of overweight children has: (p. 310; F)
   a. decreased since the 1980s.
   b. remained about the same over the past decade.
   c. increased markedly since the 1980s.
   d. increased, while the number of overweight adults has decreased.

4. Which of the following statements is **FALSE** regarding a school-aged child's cognitive development? (p. 311; F)
   a. School-aged children use a single dimension when classifying objects.
   b. School-aged children use reversible thinking.
   c. School-aged children use compensation to solve conservation tasks.
   d. School-aged children understand the logic of serial position.

5. Children raised in non-industrialized countries often appear behind children from industrialized countries in concrete operational thinking. This finding may be due to: (p. 313; F)
   a. poor nutrition, resulting in poorer brain development.
   b. children from non-industrialized countries never having experience with any tasks related to concrete operational thought.
   c. communication difficulties and the types of tasked used to assess cognitive development.
   d. lack of or poorer schooling in the non-industrialized countries.

6. Who is more likely to enjoy the joke, "What's black and white and read all over?" (p. 316; A)
   a. 3-year-old Sonja, who attends preschool and whose father tells jokes
   b. 5-year-old Tanner, who knows his colors
   c. 7-year-old Parley, who is in the second grade
   d. your date

7. Your friend wants his child to be a good reader and asks several people for advice. Which of the following pieces of advice is **WRONG**? (p. 319; A)
   a. "Make sure you read to your child all the time! I put my kids to bed with a bedtime story."
   b. "Read the newspaper, subscribe to magazines, and write letters to friends."
   c. "Do not allow children to 'pretend' to read or write, especially if their writing consists of 'hen scratches'. Teach children write and spell correctly."
   d. "Read aloud with your child. If he makes a mistake, repeat the difficult word and encourage him to repeat it as well."

8. You have been put in charge of teaching a 6-year-old child to read. You discover that this child has a very low initial reading score. Based on this information, you decide to: (p. 319; A)
   a. use a whole language approach because this approach has been found to be particularly beneficial for children with low initial reading scores.
   b. use a phonics approach because this approach has been found to be particularly beneficial for children with low initial reading scores.
   c. use simple and basic materials to study individual words.
   d. wait until the child is older and more "ready" to learn to read.

9. IQ scores: (p. 320; F)
   a. fairly accurately predict life outcomes for many individuals.
   b. fail to predict school achievement and success for many children.
   c. accurately identify children who need special help in school and those who are especially bright.
   d. relate well to success in a career.

10. Your friend is especially good at taking information from one context and applying it to another. As a result, he has come up with some highly innovative ways of doing things. Using Sternberg's triarchic theory of intelligence, it is apparent that your friend excels in the area of: (p. 322; A)
    a. performance.
    b. metacomponents.
    c. knowledge-acquisition.
    d. logico-mathematical.

11. Wolfgang Mozart who composed keyboard pieces at age 5, is a good example of: (p. 323; A)
    a. a savant.
    b. a prodigy
    c. both a savant and a prodigy.
    d. parental influence on special abilities.

12. Concrete operational children: (p. 325; F)
    a. tend to think about others by focusing on external characteristics.
    b. tend to refer to other people in very concrete terms.
    c. believe that people change frequently.
    d. can better imagine what others are thinking and seeing.

13. Perceptions of differences among other ethnic groups arise: (p. 326; F)
    a. by 4 years of age.
    b. between 6 and 8 years of age.
    c. around 11 years of age.
    d. after adolescence.

14. Listening to a group of 6-year-old children talk, you and a friend overhear a couple of them make several negative comments about people of different races. Your friend says, "I think it's rotten what parents teach their children these days!" You reply: (p. 326; A)
    a. "Yes...research has shown that children's prejudice can be explained on the basis of learning from their parents and other adults around them."
    b. "Yes...children learn prejudice from their parents by direct instruction and by observation. These children are simply reflecting what their parents are saying.
    c. "Well...it is unlikely that these children's prejudice can be explained solely on the basis of learning from parents, adults, or peers. Their parents may be just as shocked as we are."
    d. "It's just talk. Children this age are not really prejudiced and have little knowledge about racial stereotypes."

15. Based on the cognitive developmental theories of Piaget and Vygotsky, many teachers today have adopted: (p. 328; F)
    a. back-to-basics approach to learning.
    b. constructivist theories of learning.
    c. multicultural and multilingual education.
    d. proximal theories of learning.

16. Which of the following statements about the impact of teacher expectations on children's school performance is **FALSE**? (p. 330; F)
    a. Teachers act differently toward students they believe to be high and low achievers.
    b. If a teacher believes that a child is a high achiever, that child will receive less criticism for giving wrong answers.
    c. Children who are not expected to perform well in class are given less opportunity to participate.
    d. Most teachers are aware of the preferential treatment they give to some children.

17. While waiting for a haircut, a customer reading a magazine leans over and says, "I think my son has ADHD! He is 10 years old, and since he started the 5th grade this year, I have noticed that he has four of the symptoms listed in this article…he fidgets in his seat, doesn't follow through with instructions, talks to the others kids in class, and loses his pencils! What should I do?" (p. 333; A)
    a. "Talk to the teacher about these behaviors, but I doubt it's ADHD. These problems and more need to have existed before your son turned 7."
    b. "Talk to your pediatrician. You may find that Ritalin will effectively control his ADHD."
    c. "Talk to both the teacher and pediatrician. Working together, his ADHD should be brought under control."
    d. "Excuse me, but you've just described my husband!"

18. Research has shown that: (p. 335; F)
    a. children identified as mentally retarded never "grow out" of their mental retardation as adults.
    b. a leading known cause of mental retardation is very early prenatal events, including exposure to alcohol.
    c. most cases of mental retardation are due to genetic factors.
    d. few mentally retarded people learn to live semi-independently, maintain employment, or develop social relationships.

19. At a school board meeting, discussion centers on the best way to address the needs of gifted students so that they can increase gifted student achievement and academic abilities. The board asks for your input. You say, (p. 337; A)
    a. "We can identify gifted children by their grades. If a child's school performance is excellent, he or she should be placed in a gifted program."
    b. "Gifted children should be placed in enrichment programs to encourage problem solving and creative activities."
    c. "I suggest that we consider an acceleration program to encourage gifted children to more rapidly through their usual coursework."
    d. "Perhaps we should put our gifted children in independent study and programs with individualized instruction. Assigning a mentor would also be beneficial."

20. Which of the following statements about influences on children's intellectual development is **FALSE**? (p. 338; F)
    a. Parents of successful and talented children encourage children to do their best and follow active pursuits.
    b. Parents of successful and talented children create a firmly structured family life.
    c. American parents are more likely than Asian parents to attribute good mathematic skills to hard work.
    d. Compared with Caucasian American mothers and teachers, minority mothers and teachers were more positive about the value of homework, competency testing, and lengthening school days to improve educational opportunities for children.

True/False Questions (If a statement is FALSE, correct it).

1. During the school years, children's physical growth begins to speed up. (p. 307) True/False.

2. School-aged girls and boys perform similarly in almost all motor activities, although girls are somewhat more flexible than boys. (p. 308) True/False.

3. Children on reduced fat diets may develop nutritional deficiencies. (p. 310) True/False.

4. During the school years, for the first time, children show the same type of logical problem solving evidenced in adult thinking. (p. 312) True/False.

5. The school-aged child's increased ability to maintain a conversation shows an improvement in syntax. (p. 316) True/False.

6. Today, most educators recommend the phonics approach to teaching reading. (p. 319) True/False.

7. Within normal ranges, IQ does not relate to career success. (p. 321) True/False.

8. Researchers have been able to construct a culture-free IQ test through the use of pictorial forms. (p. 322) True/False.

9. It is difficult to assess creativity. (p. 324) True/False.

10. Older children are more likely than younger children to think of other people as having internal and stable personalities. (p. 325) True/False.

11. Federal law requires that special needs children be educated in the least restrictive environment. (p. 331) True/False.

12. The most common mental disorder among children is mental retardation. (p. 332) True/False.

13. More females than males are labeled "mentally retarded". (p. 335) True/False.

14. Poverty has little impact on children's intellectual development when children are placed in schools with excellent teachers. (p. 337) True/False.

15. Family and cultural values appear to affect children's overall academic achievement. (pp. 339) True/False.

☐ REWARD YOURSELF!   Eat dinner by candlelight!

Chapter 9 Physical, Cognitive, and Language Development in Late Childhood 177

ANSWERS - Chapter 9 Physical, Cognitive, and Language Development in Late Childhood

How Do Children Develop Physically during Late Childhood? (pp. 307 - 310)
(1) 90; (2) improve; (3) slows down; (4) slower; (5) slower; (6) motor control and coordination; (7) strength, agility, and balance; (8) upper body; (9) flexible; (10) diet; (11) double; (12) may not; (13) children should not avoid fats, cholesterol, red meat, or eggs; (14) obese; (15) 20; (16) heart disease, diabetes, cancer, and respiratory disease; (17) genetics, sedentary lifestyle; family distress
1 Minute Quiz: 1. A; 2. C; 3. Double; 4. False

How Do Older Children Think and Solve Problems? (pp. 310-314)
(18) concrete operations; (19) logically; (20) flexible, reversible, and less egocentric; (21) 1. Mentally represent the action; 2. Focus on more than one dimension; 3. Recognize that appearances can be deceiving
(22) reversible; (23) compensation; (24) family, culture, and experience

How Do Language and Literacy Develop During the School Years? (pp. 314 – 320)
(25) a. pragmatics; b. syntax; c. semantics; d. semantics; e. pragmatics
(26) they must understand that written words they see are related to the language they hear
(27) 1. words are read from left to right; 2. words go from the extreme right of one line to the extreme left of the next line down; 3. Spaces between chunks of letters indicate words
(28) phonemic awareness
(29) Does your daughter attempt to tell stories while looking at and turning pages in a book? Does she understand that stories start at the front of the book and move to the back, page by page? Does she recognize signs? Has she ever pointed out individual letters, like "O"? Does she like to see her name in print?
(30) "Whole language looks at reading as a natural process that occurs within the context of a print-rich environment. Children learn to guess the meanings of words based on the context of the word within the passage, as well as their own knowledge. It assumes that children will gradually improve skills related to writing and reading. To date, there is little research evidence that it facilitates children's reading. Different kinds of children benefit from different kinds of approaches. If it was me, I'd combine the two."
1 Minute Quiz: 1. C; 2. False; 3. Pragmatics; 4. False

What Characteristics Define Children's Intelligence and Creativity? (pp. 320 - 324)
(31) Wechsler Intelligence Scale for Children (WISC); (32) verbal and performance; (33) Intelligence quotient; (34) achievement and success; (35) predict; (36) motivation and social skills
Figure It Out! IQ=200; IQ=50
(37) culturally biased; (38) triarchic theory of intelligence; (39) performance: involves encoding/interpreting information and retrieving it from memory; knowledge-acquisition: involves strategies for gaining and acting on information; metacomponents: abilities that allow for monitoring of task performance and constructing strategies to solve problems.
(40) multiple intelligences; (41) frames of mind; (42) prodigies; (43) savants; (44) creativity; (45) domain skills, creative working style, creative thinking style, and intrinsic motivation.
1 Minute Quiz: 1. False; 2. Culturally-biased; 3. Triarchic theory; 4. B

How Do Older Children Understand the Social World? (pp. 324 – 325)
(46) perspective; (47) less; (48) 8; (49) abstract and internal psychological; (50) mindblind
(51) Prejudice refers to having preconceived ideas about a person or group of people; discrimination is acting in an unfavorable manner toward people because of their affiliation with a group.
(52) perceptually categorize people on basis of physical appearance
(53) are observed at this age; (54) grade school
(55) considerable knowledge; (56) Caucasian and African American; (57) Native Americans, Chinese Americans, or Mexican Americans
(58) group people together; (59) what people are like
(60) flexible; (61) different races
(62) Cannot explain children's prejudice solely on basis of learning from parents, adults or peers; some children do not adopt prejudicial attitudes of parents; others have prejudicial attitudes when parents do not.
(63) social cognitive; (64) cognitive development

178 Study Guide for Exploring Child Development

How Does Schooling Influence Children's Cognitive Development? (pp. 327 – 330)
(65) c;   (66) e;   (67) a;   (68) d;   (69) b;   (70) d

How Do Schools Address Students' Special Needs? (pp. 331 – 337)
(71) ten; (72) special; (73) five; (74) least; (75) mainstreamed; (76) varied; (77) attention deficit hyperactivity disorder; (78) attention; (79) impulsivity; (80) learn; (81) adolescence: (82) one-third; (83) eight; (84) seven; (85) biological: (86) genetic; (87) environmental; (88) medications; (89) controversial; (90) diet; (91) behavioral; (92) combination
(93) subaverage general intellectual functioning and impaired adaptive functioning, with onset during childhood
(94) mild, moderate, severe, profound; (95) males; (96) yes; (97) early prenatal events; environmental influences, and other mental disorders, genetics, and health problems, including lead poisoning; (98) No, better to teach cognitive skills
(99) having at least one outstanding ability, including creativity, intellectual ability, motor skill, or artistic ability
(100) children who do not perform well in school or who are gifted in areas other than academics, minority children
(101) acceleration programs and enrichment programs; (102) acceleration programs
(103) Women living in poverty receive less prenatal care and have more difficulties with their pregnancies. They are more likely to give birth to premature or unhealthy babies. The effects of poverty can be cumulative. Poverty is related to mental retardation; in addition, children raised in poverty are more likely to be undernourished, have substandard housing, have more illnesses, receive less health care and come from more disorganized families. All of these are related to academic achievement and intellectual development.
(104) a. Parents value success and encourage children to do their best; b. Parents supervise practice sessions and training; c. Parents encourage active pursuits, not television or passive pursuits; d. Parents devote time and energy to their children by reading to them, playing with them, teaching them, checking homework, and supervising practice sessions; e. Family life is firmly structured and children are required to share in responsibilities at home.
(105) Asian performance on tests reflects more than just different curriculum and teachers; families play an important role. Parental attitudes differ, with Asian parent attributing good mathematical skill to hard work and American parents attributing them to natural ability. Asian parents mobilize resources to help their children as soon as the children enter school; only a few American parents will do things such as purchase math workbooks. Almost all Asian children are given their own desk and workspace at home compared to slightly over a quarter of American students. Asian parents also monitor their children's homework more, and even though their children are doing well, Asian parents are more likely to express concern with the school system.
1 Minute Quiz: 1. D;   2. False;   3. C;   4. Expectations;   5. D;   6. False

STUDY QUESTIONS

Multiple Choice: 1. A;   2. B;   3. C;   4. A;   5. C;   6. C;   7. C;   8. A;   9. C;   10. B;   11. B;   12. D; 13. B;   14. C; 15. B;   16. D;   17. A;   18. B;   19. C;   20. C

True/False Questions
1. False; is slower than it was before.
2. True
3. True
4. True
5. False; pragmatics
6. False; a combination of approaches
7. True
8. False; even pictorial forms have some culture bias
9. True
10. True
11. True
12. False; ADHD
13. False; more males than females
14. False; poverty has a major impact on intellectual development
15. True

Chapter 10
Social and Emotional Development in Late Childhood

My mother taught me about ROOTS...
"Do you think you were born in a barn?!"
- Things My Mother Taught Me

Objectives
When you have completed this chapter, you will be able to:
- discuss stress in childhood, including children's ability to cope with it;
- describe three emotional and psychological disturbances that affect children in late childhood;
- describe how children's family relationships change during late childhood;
- discuss peer relationships, including peer rejection and the development of social competence, in late childhood;
- summarize the influence of school on children's social and emotional development;
- compare and contrast Piaget's and Kohlberg's theories of moral development; and
- define the key terms and concepts listed on pages 379 to 380 of your text.

☑ Study Check List

☐ Read Chapter 10 Social and Emotional Development in Late Childhood.

☐ Re-read the Chapter 10 Summary to refresh your memory.

☐ Read the Chapter 10 Objectives listed above.

☐ Complete the following items:

How Does Emotional Development Change During Late Childhood? (pp. 343 - 350)

How do younger and older children differ in what they find stressful? In what ways are older children better able to cope with stressful events?

_____

_____

_____

180 Study Guide for Exploring Child Development

_____
_____
_____(1)

Match the following:

(a) emotion-focused coping strategy   (b) problem-focused coping strategies

- In situations where children have little control, these strategies seem the most effective. _____(2)

- Older children are more likely to use these strategies than younger children. _____(3)

- Attempting to fix a toy that is not working properly. _____(4)

- In situations that children have some control over, these strategies seem most effective. _____(5)

- Coping with frustration because "Wally World" is closed. _____(6)

Stress-resistant children are said to have r_____(7), which is the capacity to bounce back or recover from stressful situations. What are three common characteristics of resilient children? (8)

1. _____
2. _____
3. _____

You have been asked to summarize three emotional and psychological disturbances that affect children in late childhood for a school's parent newsletter. Your summary is to include the definition of the problem, a description of the problem (including incidence and developmental course), factors affecting the development of the program, and treatment. Write your summaries below:

Antisocial Behavior

Definition: _____(9)

Scope of the problem: _____
_____
_____
_____(10)

Chapter 10 Social and Emotional Development in Late Childhood 181

Factors Affecting Antisocial Behavior: (11)

1. _____
2. _____
3. _____
4. _____

Treatments for Antisocial Behavior:

At present, _____ (12) single treatment has been found to effectively address antisocial behavior problems. It has multiple causes necessitating multiple approaches to treatment. Treatment may include: _____

_____(13)

The best approach to dealing with antisocial behavior is to P __ __ __ __ __ __ (14) it from developing.

Childhood Depression

Definition: _____(15)

Symptoms of Clinical Depression: (16)
1. _____
2. _____
3. _____
4. _____
5. _____
6. _____
7. _____
8. _____

Symptoms vary with _____ (17). Depressed infants and toddlers _____

_____,

182 Study Guide for Exploring Child Development

after age 6 or 7, children _____;

and by 7 or 8 _____(18).

Factors Affecting the Development of Childhood Depression: (19)

1. _____

2. _____

3. _____

Treatments for Childhood Depression: (20)

Most children with depression _____ substantially following

treatment. Treatment includes _____

_____

_____

Childhood Phobias

Definition: _____(21)

Most common type in late childhood: _____(22)

Treatments for childhood phobias: (23)

_____

_____

_____

_____

The Parent Dictionary

Full name – what you call your child when you are mad at him
Hearsay – what toddlers do when anyone mutters a dirty word
Independent – what we want our children to be as long as they do everything we say
Ow – the first word spoken by children with older siblings
Show-off – a child who is more talented than yours

1 Minute Quiz

1. The type of stress associated with making a transition from one culture to another is referred to as _____.

2. To cope effectively in situations involving other people, children need to understand the intentions of those involved. True/False.

3. Over the course of a lifetime, antisocial behavior begins in the form of _____ and _____, progresses to _____, and culminates in _____.

4. Which of the following has NOT been identified as a cause of childhood depression?
   a. genetic and biological factors
   b. temperament
   c. family and social factors
   d. All of these factors have been identified.

How Do Children's Family Relationships Change During Late Childhood? (pp. 357 - 360)

During late childhood, the amounts of time children spend with their parents **increases/decreases/stays the same** *(circle one)* (24). Parents concerns about their school-aged children also change. Parents are more likely to be concerned about: (25)

   a. _____
   b. _____
   c. _____
   d. _____

Parental supervision of children during late childhood **increases/decreases/stays the same** *(circle one)* (26). Children who are left unsupervised during the day or return home to an empty house after school are referred to as l_____ (27) children.

During late childhood, the amounts of time children spend with their siblings **increases/decreases/stays the same** *(circle one)* (28). Sibling relationships provide children with opportunities to learn

184 Study Guide for Exploring Child Development

_____(29). Sibling caretaking **is/ is not** *(circle one)* (30) the same as parental caretaking because it lacks the richness and c_____(31) of the care provided by parents.

The findings of several studies have found that only children differ from children with siblings in only two of sixteen ways. Only children: (32)

1. _____
2. _____

What Factors Influence Older Children's Peer Relationships? (pp. 360 – 364)

Use these words to complete the following paragraphs:

| distressed | more | aggressive | rejected | critical | long | lonely |
| poor | successful | stable | neglected | social | shy | |

Peer relationships play a _____(33) important role today than in earlier times. Late childhood is a _____(34) time for developing peer relationships, with friendships becoming more _____ (35) and significant. Peer relationships play an important role in children's _____(36) adjustment.

Unfortunately, some children have problems in peer relationships. Some children are _____ (37) children and are overtly disliked by their peers. Other children are _____(38) children, being reasonably well liked yet lacking friends. Rejected children are unpopular for _____(39) periods of time; neglected children's popularity may change form situation to situation. Rejected children are more likely to be _____(40) and feel victimized and are more emotionally _____(41) by poor peer relationships. They tend to be aggressive and depressed. Neglected children tend to have _____(42) social skills and be _____(43).

Chapter 10 Social and Emotional Development in Late Childhood 185

To help rejected children, interventions should reduce the _____(44) or disruptive nature of their interactions. Neglected children need help developing _____(45) skills that help them make and keep friends.

S_____ c_____(46) refers to a child's ability to use age-appropriate social behaviors to enhance peer relationships without harming anyone. To become socially competent, children must be skilled in the following four areas: (47)

1. _____
2. _____
3. _____
3. _____

Many factors influence the development of social competence in children, including having an adaptable, positive, well-regulated t_____ (48); secure a_____(49); and parents who are involved and consistent in their d_____(50).

How Does School Affect Older Children's Social and Emotional Development? (pp. 364 – 368)

Use these words to complete the following paragraphs:

pessimistic * social * Teachers * risk * emotional * overestimate

Not only do schools function to teach children reading, writing, and arithmetic, schools further children's _____ (51) and _____(52) development, as children learn to cooperate with teachers and peers. Children respond different to the increased demands of school. Some children may have an excessively _____(53) view of their own competence; as a result, these children may undermine their own achievement in school by avoiding schoolwork and spending time on non-academic activities. Other children _____(54) their own competence. They, too, will not invest the necessary effort into their academic work, lowering future achievement. Children who do not learn to plan, evaluate, monitor and revise their actions as they

186 Study Guide for Exploring Child Development

adapt to the school environment are at _____ (55) for poor school outcomes.

_____ (56) play an important role in a child's social and emotional development and their adaptation to school.

LESSONS IN REAL LIFE - LESSONS IN REAL LIFE - LESSONS IN REAL LIFE - LESSONS IN REAL LIFE

Your roommate is about to graduate with her degree in education. She is excited but nervous about teaching next year. She tells you that she knows she will play an important role in her students' social and emotional development, as well as in their overall adaptation to school. She wants to make sure that she does it right so she can make a positive difference. "How do I do that?" she asks you. "What can I do to help my students reach their potential?" You tell her that teachers can enhance positive outcomes for students if they: (57)

1. _____
2. _____
3. _____
4. _____
5. _____

For each of the following pairs, circle the students to whom teachers are more likely to respond positively: (58)

Jessica, who comes from a poor family.
Jacqueline who is upper middle class.

Peter who is silent and withdrawn.
Abraham who is agreeable, compliant, and desires to achieve.

Alysa, a girl
Allen, a boy

In short, teachers' response to children depends on the children's (a) b_____,

(b) _____,

and (c) g_____ (59).

1 Minute Quiz

1. Draw an arrow indicating increase(↑) or decrease (↓) for each of the following items related to late childhood:
   a. Parental supervision _____
   b. Time spent with parents _____
   c. Time spent with siblings _____

2. A shy child plays alone on the playground, although other children will state that they like the child. This child would be described as a _____ child.

3. Which of the following skills is not important for social competence?
   a. initiating social interactions
   b. managing conflicts
   c. well-developed communication skills
   d. All of the above are important for social competence.

4. Teachers generally give boys/girls *(circle one)* more attention.

What Changes Take Place in Moral Development During Late Childhood? (pp. 368 - 378)

The most influential theorists in the area of moral development have been P_____(60) and K_____(61). Piaget believed that it is through interactions with **peers/parents** *(circle one)* (62) that children make important advances in moral development, because peer relationships foster re_____ and per_____(63).

Memory Jog ⇒ Heteronomous comes from "heteros" meaning *other* and "nomos" meaning *rule*; therefore, under the rule of others.
Autonomous comes from "autos" meaning self; therefore, under the rule of self.

188 Study Guide for Exploring Child Development

Using Table 10.3 on page 370, identify the stage of moral development for each of the following examples:

- Sunny has little concern for rules; when she plays a game with her brothers and sister, she gets angry when told she cannot do something because it's against the rules. Sunny is probably at the _____ (64) stage.

- Gloria's friend got in trouble at school for sharing her homework with another student. Gloria knows that sharing homework is against school rules, but she said that her friend did it because the student's father had a heart attack and the student had spent much of the night in the emergency room and had been unable to get the homework done. Gloria is probably at the _____(65) stage of morality.

- Sanford has been told that he should not touch anything in the store. Sanford watches as another child reaches to examine an item. Sharply, Sanford says, "Put that down! You're not supposed to touch things in the store!" Sanford is probably in the _____(66) stage of morality.

- Thomas smells his mother's fresh made cookies. He knows he's not supposed to have one without asking, but the temptation is great. He climbs on the counter, grabs a cookie, and starts to climb down. In the process, he falls flat on his back. Thomas believes falling on his back was punishment for stealing the cookie. Thomas is probably in the _____(67) stage of morality, believing in the concept of _____ _____(68).

Studies have shown that Piaget **underestimated/overestimated** *(circle one)* (69) children's ability to take the intentions of others into account; however, there is some support for his theory.

A theorist who was greatly influenced by Piaget and contributed many new insights into moral development was K_____(70). Kohlberg identified th_____(71) levels of moral development, with t_____(72) stages in each level.

Fascinating Facts

Lawrence Kohlberg was born in 1927. Although he was born into wealth, he chose to become a sailor. After World War II, he helped smuggle Jews into Palestine, and it was during this time that he began to think about moral reasoning. When he returned to America, he completed his BA degree in psychology in only one year! In 1957, he completed his doctorate studying moral decision making. Kohlberg contracted a rare, untreatable disease in Central American in 1973, leaving him with severe physical difficulties and depression. It is believed that he took his own life in 1987 by drowning.

Chapter 10 Social and Emotional Development in Late Childhood 189

Memory Jog ⇒ The term "conventional" means arising out of custom and formed by agreement. At the conventional stage, concern is about others and laws. *Before* you are concerned about others, you are concerned about self (i.e., *pre*-conventional). *Later*, you are not as concerned with others as you are about the moral principle (i.e., *post*-conventional). When thinking of Kohlberg's stages, picture development starting from the inside and moving out:

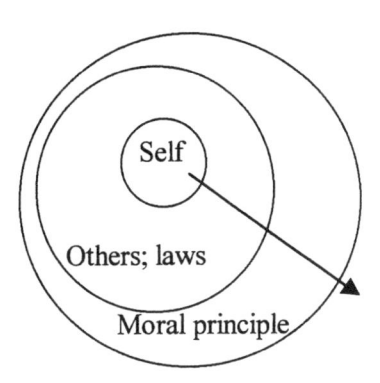

(Concentric circles: Self / Others; laws / Moral principle)

Suppose children were asked if a husband was right in stealing some medicine he could not afford in order to save his wife from dying. Following are their responses. *Place their statements in order: Stage 1 Punishment and Obedience Orientation, Stage 2 Instrumental-Purpose Orientation, Stage 3 Interpersonal Orientation, Stage 4 Social-Order-Maintenance Orientation, Stage 5 Social Contract Orientation, Stage 6 Universal Ethical Principle Orientation.* (73)

_____ "Yes, he was right in stealing it. Our democracy is based on the idea that people have the right to life, liberty, and the pursuit of happiness. Sometimes, the laws don't allow that."

_____ "Yes, he was right in stealing it. If his wife died, who would wash his socks and cook his meals?!"

_____ "Yes, he was right in stealing it. His friends wouldn't think much of him if he let his wife die."

_____ "No, he shouldn't steal it. If he gets caught, he'll go to jail."

_____ "Yes, he should steal it. All humans are have a right to life."

_____ "No, he shouldn't steal it. It's not only against the law, it's against the Ten Commandments."

One's level of moral reasoning **does/does not** *(circle one)* (74) predict moral behavior. Many students may score high in moral reasoning, but may still cheat on an exam. Several factors influence actual behavior. Moral development is also influenced by cu_____(75). Some aspects of moral development are similar across cultures; however, others are not.

1 Minute Quiz

1. The theorist who believed that children go through a premoral stage, followed by a heteronomous, then autonomous stage was _____.

2. According to Kohlberg, if a person is concerned about doing right in order that others will think highly of him or her, that person is in the _____ level of moral development.

3. The level of moral development that one reaches predicts one's moral behavior. True/False.

4. It appears that culture is not related to moral development. True/False.

☐ Complete the crossword puzzle in Appendix 1 – Crossword Puzzles.

☐ Go to the beginning of this chapter, and on a separate sheet of paper, write out the answers to the lesson objectives.

sAGE advice

"Recopy your notes everyday if you can. That way you can organize them, and it'll refresh your memory. Highlight the important points."

… Chapter 10 Social and Emotional Development in Late Childhood …

STUDY QUESTIONS

Multiple Choice (The following questions are identified "F," *factual questions* that rely on the recall of facts; or "A," *applied questions* that rely on the ability to apply a concept to a real-life situation).

1. Which one of the following stressors would probably be the **LEAST** stressful to a school-aged child? (p. 344; A)
   a. flunking a class   b. poor grades   c. scary dream   d. being sent to the principal

2. Which of the following statements is **FALSE**? (p. 345; F)
   a. Emotional-focused coping strategies decrease over the elementary school years.
   b. Problem-focused coping strategies increase over the elementary school years.
   c. In situations where children have little control, emotion-focused coping strategies seem the most effective.
   d. Older children cope better because they are more likely than young children to understand which situations they have control over.

3. A common characteristic of resilient children is: (p. 347; F)
   a. below average intelligence.
   b. positive attractive qualities that elicit positive responses in others.
   c. ability to separate one's self from one's family.
   d. average intelligence.

4. The younger the child, (p. 348; F)
   a. the less likely that child will respond to violence with passivity.
   b. the less likely the child will experience psychological problems in response to traumatic violence.
   c. the more likely it is that safety issues are critical to his or her well being.
   d. the more likely separation from parent during traumatic violence will have little effect.

5. Archie's behavior is aggressive, defiant, uncooperative, and disruptive, not only to himself but to his family and school. It is likely that Archie's behavior would be defined as: (p. 350; A)
   a. depression.   b. attention deficit hyperactivity disorder.   c. phobic.   d. antisocial.

6. Antisocial behavior: (p. 353; F)
   a. does not appear to be related to parents who are stressed or depressed.
   b. may be partially influenced by biological factors.
   c. is more likely to be seen in middle-class neighborhoods than lower-income neighborhoods.
   d. is more prevalent in suburban areas than urban areas.

7. Your friend's dog died, and he is concerned because his son appears to be quite depressed over it. He asks for advice, and you say, (p. 354; A)
   a. "Consider approaching your pediatrician for some antidepressant medication until he is over this hump. At his age, these medications appear to have few side effects."
   b. "Boys are more likely to be depressed than girls."
   c. "Childhood depression is relatively rare – it's nothing to worry about."
   d. "Most children with depression improve substantially with treatment. Consider talking with a counselor who can help your son understand he's not alone in his grief."

8. Six-year-old Ariel has suddenly expressed anxiety about going to school. She gets headaches and stomach aches and tells her Mom she doesn't feel well. Her mother asks you what you would do, and you reply, (p. 357; A)
   a. "Get her to return to school as quickly as possible."
   b. "Have her return to school gradually. Perhaps start her out on half-days, then work up to full days by the end of the month."
   c. "Some cognitive therapy could be particularly useful at her age. Help her see herself as being in control and competent."
   d. "Have you considered homeschooling?"

9. As children enter late childhood, (p. 357; F)
   a. parental concerns center around safety, respect for others, and manners.
   b. there is a decline in the amount of time children spend with their parents.
   c. children spend more time playing.
   d. direct family interaction accounts for about 25 percent of their daily activities.

10. Your co-worker has decided to fire her babysitter and allow her 12-year-old daughter to baby-sit. She asks your opinion, and you say, (p. 359; A)
    a. "I think that's a great idea. Being put in charge of younger siblings has been found to effectively increase responsibility in late childhood."
    b. "I think that idea is sound. Older siblings have been found to take care of, comfort, and support younger siblings as well as adults."
    c. "Perhaps you should re-think this idea. Sibling support and comfort has not been found to be comparable to that provided by parents or other caregivers."
    d. "Why don't you just bring them all down to work?"

11. Only children have been found to be: (p. 360; F)
    a. spoiled and egocentric.
    b. socially awkward and insensitive toward peers.
    c. higher than other children on motivation to achieve and self-esteem.
    d. no different than children with siblings.

12. Which of the following statements is **TRUE**? (p. 362; F)
    a. Neglected and rejected children are disliked by their peers.
    b. Neglected children tend to be unpopular for long periods of time and their status rarely changes.
    c. Rejected children are not likely to feel victimized.
    d. An important aim of intervention for rejected children is to reduce aggressiveness in their peer interactions.

13. Children who are low in social competence: (p. 364; F)
    a. are likely to experience adverse living conditions.
    b. tend to suggest alternative ways of dealing with conflicts.
    c. are more compliant than children high in social competence.
    d. are no more likely to come from a divorced home than a stable two-parent home.

14. Parents and teachers can contribute to children's low perceptions of competence by (p. 367; F)
    a. over-emphasizing grades, achievement, and social comparisons as a basis for self-worth.
    b. providing tutoring to children who need it.
    c. explicitly modeling and explaining criteria that will be used to evaluate children's ability to meet expectations successfully.
    d. letting children participate in goal setting, rather than being given goals by parents and teachers.

15. Which of the following teachers is **LEAST LIKELY** to enhance positive outcomes for students? (p. 368; A)
    a. Ms. Jenkins, who finds ways for students to be successful.
    b. Mr. Farmer, who encourages students to look at their personal progress, not their work in comparison to others.
    c. Mr. Jones, who is strict, aloof, yet holds high expectations.
    d. Ms. Astair, who tells students to focus on their strengths and not their weaknesses.

16. Piaget believed that children make important advances in moral development through their interaction with: (p. 369; F)
    a. parents.   b. siblings.   c. peers.   d. teachers.

17. Cindy decides to surprise Mom by clearing up the dishes. Unfortunately, she breaks a dish. When Mom gets home, Cindy's sister, Marsha, exclaims, "Mom, Cindy broke a plate. She should be punished!" and pouts when Mom refuses to punish Cindy. It appears that Cindy's sister is in the _____ stage of morality. (p. 370; A)
    a. premoral
    b. heteronomous
    c. autonomous
    d. synonymous

18. The concept of immanent justice refers to the idea that: (p. 371; F)
    a. breaking a rule always leads to punishment.
    b. justice must be swift for it to be effective.
    c. justice should be decided by a person of high authority, such as a parent or teacher.
    d. not all justice is fair.

19. Piaget's theory has been criticized because he: (p. 372; F)
    a. did not adequately address gender differences in moral reasoning.
    b. overestimated children's understanding of intentions.
    c. underestimated children's understanding of intentions.
    d. assumed that children needed to be in the stage of preoperations before they could be moral.

20. Reasoning that reflects a belief that goodness or badness is determined by its consequences is considered: (p. 373; F)
    a. preconventional.   b. conventional.   c. postconventional.   d. pseudoconventional.

21. Priscilla is dying from a painful disease and only has days to live. She begs her doctor to give her enough Morphine to allow her to slip away and die. The doctor refuses because the Hippocratic Oath states, "Above all, do no harm." At what level is the doctor's moral reasoning? (p. 374; A)
    a. preconventional   b. conventional   c. postocnventional   d. pseudoconventional

194 Study Guide for Exploring Child Development

True/False Questions (If a statement is FALSE, correct it).

1. Events that cause stress in young children often appear innocuous to older children. (p. 343) True/False.

2. In stressful situations that children have some control over, emotion-focused strategies are more effective. (p. 346) True/False.

3. Resilient children tend to have a positive place in the family. (p. 347) True/False.

4. Children appear to be relatively unaware of community violence. (p. 347) True/False.

5. Children who are antisocial at early ages tend to grow out of it in later years. (p. 350) True/False.

6. Most children with depression improve substantially following treatment. (p. 355) True/False.

7. Girls are more likely to be classified as depressed; boys are more likely to be classified as antisocial. (p. 354) True/False.

8. One of the most common phobias of late childhood is fear of darkness. (p. 356) True/False.

9. Today's parents supervise their children more than in the past. (p. 358) True/False.

10. Only children score higher in the area of self-esteem than children with siblings. (p. 360) True/False.

11. The status and popularity of rejected children changes from situation to situation. (p. 362) True/False.

12. Children with speech and language deficiencies often have low social competence. (p. 363) True/False.

13. Teachers appear to be indifferent to students who are silent or withdrawn. (p. 368) True/False.

14. Higher levels of cognitive development are related to higher levels of moral reasoning. (p. 375) True/False.

15. Culture appears to be unrelated to moral development. (p. 376) True/False.

☐ REWARD YOURSELF! Take a friend to the zoo!

ANSWERS - Chapter 10 Social and Emotional Development in Late Childhood

How Does Emotional Development Change During Late Childhood? (pp. 343 - 350)
(1) "Developmental changes in children's relations to their environments contribute to changes in the contexts that cause stress." Young children may fear being left alone; older children don't. Older children may fear an exam or a bully; young children don't face these situations. Older children are more likely to use emotion-focused and problem-focused coping strategies. They are able to more accurately interpret others' intentions, and so are more likely to respond appropriately.
(2) a; (3) a and b; (4) b; (5) b; (6) a
(7) resilience; (8) above average intelligence; attractive qualities that elicit positive responses in others; positive place in the family

Antisocial Behavior
(9) a pattern of behavior that is aggressive, defiant, uncooperative, irresponsible, and/or dishonest; (10) boys more likely than girls to be referred; nearly half of all children referred to clinics for treatment are referred for this; if children are antisocial at early ages than are more likely to be so in later years; antisocial behaviors progress from noncompliance and temper tantrums in preschool to fighting, stealing, lying in late childhood, to breaking the law in adolescence. (11) biological (temperament, ADHD), family factors (lack of supervision, spousal abuse, mental illness, stress), peer relationships (poor peer relationships; likes attract; peers act as models), and social milieu (urban more than suburban; stressful neighborhood)
(12) no; (13) counseling, behavior modification, family therapy, medication; (14) PREVENT

Childhood Depression
(15) conditions in which children display persistent negative moods and lack pleasure in life.
(16) significant weight loss or gain, insomnia or hypersomnia, motor agitation or retardation, loss of interest or pleasure in usual activities, fatigue or loss of energy, feelings of worthlessness or guilt, impairment in thinking, thoughts of suicide
(17) age; (18) cry or rock, may refuse food, sleep poorly, fail to thrive; by 6-7, begin to describe self as sad or miserable; by 7-8, experience devalued view of themselves.
(19) genetic and biological factors, temperament, family and social factors
(20) improve substantially; counseling, facilitating communication within family, reducing stressors, activities to promote peer acceptance/self-esteem, medications

Childhood Phobias
(21) persistent and irrational fears that significantly affect children's functioning; (22) school phobia; (23) modeling, cognitive techniques

1 Minute Quiz: 1. acculturative stress; 2. True; 3. noncompliance and tantrums, progresses to fighting, stealing, and lying, and culminates in noncompliance with authority and law; 4. D

How Do Children's Family Relationships Change During Late Childhood? (pp. 357 - 360)
(24) decreases; (25) chores, school, friendship choices, values; (26) decreases; (27) latchkey; (28) increases; (29) learn about themselves; (30) is not; (31) complexity; (32) score higher on motivation to achieve and on self-esteem

What Factors Influence Older Children's Peer Relationships? (pp. 360 – 364)
(33) more; (34) critical; (35) stable; (36) successful; (37) rejected; (38) neglected; (39) long; (40) lonely; (41) distressed; (42) poor; (43) shy; (44) aggressive; (45) social
(46) Social competence; (47) initiating social interactions, maintaining social interactions, managing conflicts, communicating for social purposes; (48) temperaments; (49) attachments; (50) discipline

How Does School Affect Older Children's Social and Emotional Development? (pp. 364 – 368)
(51) social; (52) emotional; (53) pessimistic; (54) overestimate; (55) risk; (56) Teachers
(57) Help the students not compare themselves with each other; use cooperative learning in your classroom; help students focus on their strengths rather than their weakness; increase chances for your students to be successful; be warm, encouraging and supportive.
(58) Jacqueline; Abraham; Allen
(59) behaviors; racial, ethnic, and socioeconomic backgrounds; and gender

1 Minute Quiz: 1. Supervision ↓, time with parents ↓, time with siblings ↑; 2. Neglected; 3. D; 4. boys

What Changes Take Place in Moral Development During Late Childhood? (pp. 368 - 378)
(60) Piaget; (61) Kohlberg; (62) peers; (63) reciprocity and perspective taking
(64) premoral; (65) autonomous; (66) heteronomous; (67) heteronomous; (68) immanent justice; (69) underestimated;

(70) Kohlberg; (71) three; (72) two
(73) "Yes, he was right in stealing it. Our democracy is based on the idea that people have the right to life, liberty, and the pursuit of happiness. Sometimes, the laws don't allow that." (Post-conventional; Stage 5)
"Yes, he was right in stealing it. If his wife died, who would wash his socks and cook his meals?!" (Pre-conventional, Stage 2)
"Yes, he was right in stealing it. His friends wouldn't think much of him if he let his wife die." (Conventional; Stage 3)
"No, he shouldn't steal it. If he gets caught, he'll go to jail." (Pre-conventional; Stage 1)
"Yes, he should steal it. All humans are have a right to life." (Post-conventional; Stage 6)
"No, he shouldn't steal it. It's not only against the law, it's against the Ten Commandments." (Conventional; Stage 4)
(74) does not; (75) culture
1 Minute Quiz: 1. Piaget; 2. Conventional; 3. False; 4. False

STUDY QUESTIONS

<u>Multiple Choice</u> : 1. C; 2. A; 3. B; 4. C; 5. D; 6. B; 7. D; 8. A; 9. B; 10. C; 11. C; 12. D; 13. A; 14. A; 15. C; 16. C; 17. B; 18. A; 19. C; 20. A; 21. B

<u>True/False Questions:</u>
1. True
2. False; problem-focused strategies
3. True
4. False; omit "relatively unaware" and replace with "stressed by."
5. False; omit "grow out of it" and replace with "be antisocial"
6. True
7. True
8. False; school phobia
9. False; less
10. True
11. False; neglected
12. True
13. True
14. True
15. False; related

Chapter 11
Physical and Cognitive Development In Early Adolescence

My mother taught me about the WISDOM OF AGE...
"When you get to my age, you'll understand."
  - Things My Mother Taught Me

Objectives
When you have completed this chapter, you will be able to:
- define adolescence and state how the concept of "adolescence" has been recognized historically and culturally;
- outline the physical changes of adolescence for boys and girls;
- discuss the adolescent's response to physical and sexual maturation and how timing of puberty affects later development;
- describe the nutritional needs of adolescence, as well as disturbances in eating;
- describe formal operational thinking in adolescence and the influence of adolescent egocentrism;
- summarize how school influences early adolescent development; and
- define the key terms and concepts listed on page 417 of your text.

☑ Study Check List

☐ Read Chapter 11 Physical and Cognitive Development in Early Adolescence

☐ Re-read the Chapter 11 Summary to refresh your memory.

☐ Read the Chapter 11 Objectives listed above.

☐ Complete the following items:

What is Early Adolescence? (pp. 387 - 390)

Adolescence generally refers to the developmental period between _____ and _____ (1). Adolescence as a stage of development has not always been recognized. Three historical changes have contributed to the acceptance of adolescence as a stage of development: (2)

Chapter 11 Social and Emotional Development in Early Adolescence 199

1. _____
2. _____
3. _____

Match the following:

____ early adolescence (3)   a. 11 to 19 years of age

____ puberty (4)   b. legal term for person not considered an adult under the law

____ youth (5)   c. time during which sexual maturation is taking place

____ late adolescence (6)   d. 11 to 14 years of age

____ juvenile (7)   e. developmental milestone reached when person becomes sexually mature

____ rite of passage (8)   f. younger generation – children through young adulthood

____ adolescence (9)   g. 15 to 19 years of age

____ pubescence (10)   h. initiation into new role

How Do Physical Growth and Sexual Maturation Occur During Early Adolescence? (pp. 390 – 401)

Puberty is brought about by changes in hor_____(11). This biological sequence is:

hy_____ → pi_____ → go_____ (12)
                                                    which release hormones

The balance of hormones changes during adolescence, with girls producing more e_____(13)

and boys producing more a_____(14).

Contrast male vs. female development in each of the following areas:

Beginning growth spurt _____

_____(15)

Body fat and muscle mass _____

_____(16)

200 Study Guide for Exploring Child Development

Primary sex characteristics _____

_____(17)

Secondary sex characteristics _____

_____(18)

Adolescents grow from the outside in, so that their h_____ and f_____(19) and more likely to grow before their tr_____ (20). Pubertal development is not only influenced by biology, but by the en_____ (21) as well. Two powerful influences are h_____(22) and n_____(23), both of which may be responsible for the generational differences observed in the age of pubertal onset. Children today reach puberty about _____(24) years earlier than children did 100 years ago. An interesting environmental factor that may affect when puberty starts is family st_____(25).

*Draw a line through the sentence that is **INCORRECT** in each of the following pairs:* (26)

- Evidence suggests that hormones directly affect behavior in adolescence.
- Evidence suggests that hormones are not direct causes of behavior in adolescence.

- Early maturing boys are more likely than their peers to have problems at school and to use drugs and alcohol.
- Late maturing boys are more likely than their peers to have problems at school and to use drugs and alcohol.

- Early maturing boys are more likely to have higher self-esteem and social status than late maturing boys.
- Late maturing boys are more likely to have higher self-esteem and social status than early maturing boys.

- Early maturing girls are at risk for eating disorders and disturbances.
- Late maturing girls are at risk for eating disorders and disturbances.

- Early maturing girls are more popular and begin dating earlier than later maturing girls.
- Later maturing girls are more popular and begin dating earlier than earlier maturing girls.

- Early maturing girls may have the best situation of all adolescents.
- Late maturing girls may have the best situation of all adolescents.

- Early maturing boys are more likely to have leadership roles later in life.
- Late maturing boys are more likely to have leadership roles later in life.

- Early maturing boys are more likely to report successful marriages than late maturing boys.
- Late maturing boys are more likely to report successful marriages than early maturing boys.

- Girls prepared for menarche report feeling more negative symptoms and have a more negative self-image than girls not prepared for it.
- Girls not prepared for menarche report feeling more negative symptoms and have a more negative self-image than girls prepared for it.

- Boys are fairly well informed about spermarche, or the first ejaculation.
- Boys are not well informed about spermarche, or the first ejaculation.

From Our Family Album...

The onset of puberty does not just affect the child experiencing it, but the whole family. After my daughter and I had gone shopping for her first bra (an experience in itself), we picked up her younger brother from school. As my daughter stepped out of the car, the bra fell out of the bag landing unceremoniously on the driveway. Her brother looked on in surprise, then seizing the opportunity, picked it up, and dangling it, proclaimed, "Our little Bethie is growing up!"

---

1 Minute Quiz

1. **Adolescence/Puberty** *(circle one)* **is a universal phenomenon.**

2. **Which of the following historical changes DID NOT have an affect on the acceptance of adolescence as a stage in development?**
   a. child labor laws   c. public education
   b. criminal laws   d. All contributed to its acceptance.

3. **Who is likely to be taller at age twelve?**   a. Gloria   b. Thomas

4. **Breasts are an example of primary sex characteristics. True/False.**

5. **As adults, boys who matured _____ rate themselves as more rebellious, impulsive, childish, and creative.**

What are the Health Concerns for Young Adolescents? (pp. 401 - 408)

Use these words to complete the following paragraph:

| diets | physical activity | nutrition | boys | protein | anemia |
| calcium | accidents | poor | obesity | cultural | |

The most likely cause of death during adolescence is _____(27), especially for _____(28) and older adolescents. Many of the major health issues for young adolescents relate to _____(29). Because of their rapid growth rate, adolescents need more calories, _____(30), _____(31), and iron. Unfortunately, adolescent eating habits are relatively _____(32), leading to such problems as _____(33). Poor eating habits, combined with lack of _____(34), can lead to _____(35) in adolescence. To lose weight, many adolescents choose to modify their _____(36) rather than their activity, which is a poor strategy for weight control. Many adolescents may skip meals or take appetite suppressants in an effort to achieve the _____(37) ideal.

Place the following information under the correct heading: (38)
binge and purge; eat very little; intense fear of gaining weight; intermittent; negative body image; obese family members; depression; absence of period; perfectionistic; controlled; poor self-esteem; can hide problem for years; parental over-involvement; effective treatment involves reinforcement of weight gain, individual, family, and group therapy; most successfully treated if caught early

Anorexia Nervosa	Bulimia Nervosa

Chapter 11 Social and Emotional Development in Early Adolescence 203

---

1 Minute Quiz

1. Circle all the requirements that adolescents need more of compared to an adult:
   protein   calcium   calories   iron

2. Judy has started severely limiting her food consumption and appears to be obsessed with her weight. She says, "Nobody can be too rich or too thin!" Even though she is extremely thin, she wants to be thinner and worries that her waist is not small enough. She is a highly controlled, perfectionist. From this description, it appears that Judy may have _____ _____.

3. Many people with bulimia maintain a normal body weight and can hide their illness for years. True/False.

4. Relationships with mothers/fathers *(circle one)* are particularly important in conveying messages to daughters about whether their pubertal changes are acceptable.

How Do Young Adolescents Think and Solve Problems? (pp. 360 – 364)

Circle the words that characterize new adolescent thinking abilities: (39)

- thinking only about the here and now
- thinking about possibilities
- reflective abstraction
- thinking about thinking
- hypothetico-deductive reasoning
- logical problem solving with objects
- reversible thinking and compensation
- egocentrism

LESSONS IN REAL LIFE - LESSONS IN REAL LIFE - LESSONS IN REAL LIFE - LESSONS IN REAL LIFE

Sixteen-year-old Cassie just broke up with her boyfriend. As she cries her eyes out, her mother lovingly pats her hand and says, "I know, honey. It's hard to break up with someone you love." "How would you know," wails Cassie. "You've never been in love!" Cassie is showing _____(40).

Fourteen-year-old Arthur is getting ready to go to his first dance. While dressing, a button falls off his pants. His father quickly re-sews the button, using brown thread instead of blue. "I can't wear these pants!" shouts Arthur. "Everybody will laugh at the button! Why didn't you use blue thread?!" Arthur is showing concern for the _____(41).

Fifteen-year-old Morgan saw "Star Wars: Episode 1 Phantom Menace" nine times. He now walks around with a video camera, making his own films. He believes that one day, he will "Out-Spielberg Spielberg" and become the greatest movie director of all time. Morgan is showing _____(42).

204 Study Guide for Exploring Child Development

How Does School Influence Early Adolescent Development? (pp. 411 – 416)

Most adolescents successfully make the transition from elementary to middle or junior high school. However, for some adolescents, this transition begins a downward spiral the may lead to failure in school and dropping out. *What are two reasons for declines in young adolescents' school performance and interest? Explain.* (43)

1. _____
_____

2. _____
_____
_____
_____

During early adolescence, a young person's perception of his or her own academic abilities changes. Instead of being optimistic, early adolescents perceive their abilities more r_____ and sometimes p_____ (44). A drop in grades typically accompanies the transition to middle school, but the drop is grades **does/does not** *(circle one)* (45) match a decline in standardized test scores.

List the three reasons given why Asian children tend to outperform U.S. students: (46)

1. _____
2. _____
3. _____

Academic performance varies in the U.S. among the different racial and ethnic groups. It appears that the poor performance of African American and Hispanic students may be related to the e_____ c_____ and s_____ (47) conditions they grow up in.

1 Minute Quiz

1. When children are able to think in terms of abstract possibilities, they have entered Piaget's stage of _____ _____.

2. "I can't go to school today! Everyone will laugh at the pimple on my nose!" This statement corresponds to the concept of:
   a. personal fable.   b. hypothetico-deductive reasoning.   c. imaginary audience.

3. Typically, the transition to middle or junior high school is accompanied by a drop in both grades and performance on standardized achievement tests. True/False.

4. Compared to Chinese students, American students go to school for _____ hours during the school year.
   a. many more
   b. somewhat more
   c. about the same amount of
   d. fewer

☐ Complete the crossword puzzle in Appendix 1 – Crossword Puzzles.

☐ Go to the beginning of this chapter, and on a separate sheet of paper, write out the answers to the lesson objectives.

sAGE Advice

"If you are unsure about something, make sure you ask your professor!"

STUDY QUESTIONS

Multiple Choice (The following questions are identified "F," *factual questions* that rely on the recall of facts; or "A," *applied questions* that rely on the ability to apply a concept to a real-life situation).

1. Which of the following was **NOT** related to the recognition of the stage of adolescence? (p. 388; F)
   a. changes in child labor laws
   b. passing of laws related to juveniles
   c. mandatory public education
   d. onset of puberty

2. The best example of a rite of passage is: (p. 389; A)
   a. going from the 7th to the 8th grade.
   b. an Autralian aboriginal walkabout
   c. wearing high heeled shoes for the first time.
   d. getting a job.

3. The term "youth" refers to: (p. 390; F)
   a. a broad, nonspecific term for the younger generation.
   b. young people between 13 and 19 years of age.
   c. an individual who is not yet an adult in the eyes of the law.
   d. the period of time during which sexual maturation takes place.

4. James is very concerned because his twin sister, Jamie, is 2 inches taller than he is. You inform James that: (p. 391; A)
   a. because he and his sister are not identical, their different genes affect the onset of puberty.
   b. nutrition and health are important determinants for entering puberty; James should make sure he eats well and starts exercising.
   c. girls enter their growth spurt about 2 years before boys, during which time the girls will be taller. James should sit tight – his turn will come.
   d. both boys and girls enter the growth spurt about the same time, but girls grow faster for the first year, then boys grow faster. James will start growing faster soon.

5. In three months, Bethany went from a size 3 child's shoe to a size 6 woman's shoe. Bethany is probably: (p. 391; A)
   a. at the beginning of her growth spurt.
   b. at the middle of her growth spurt.
   c. at the end of her growth spurt.
   d. not very happy.

6. Which of the following is **NOT** a female primary sex characteristic? (p. 392; A)
   a. uterus
   b. vagina
   c. breasts
   d. ovaries

7. Although the _____ of events associated with puberty is predictable, the _____ of these events varies considerably from one person to another. (p. 393; F)
   a. sequence; timing
   b. timing; sequence
   c. sequence; sequence
   d. timing; timing

8. Regarding nutrition and puberty, (p. 395; F)
    a. nutrition plays a relatively minor role in the onset of puberty because onset is genetically determined.
    b. people who are adequately nourished are likely to enter puberty earlier than those who are not.
    c. people who are inadequately nourished are likely to enter puberty earlier than those who are not.
    d. Nutrition is solely responsible for the onset of puberty.

9. Dolly is 12 ½ years old and recently started her period. Her great-great-great grandmother lived 100 years ago and grew in a manner typical for adolescents of the time. Looking through her great-great-great grandmother's journal, Dolly learned that her great-great-great grandmother: (p. 396; A)
    a. started her period a year earlier than Dolly.
    b. started her period at about the same age as Dolly.
    c. started her period a year later than Dolly.
    d. started her period over two years later than Dolly.

10. Which of the following young people is most likely to use drugs and alcohol, have problems at school, and yet have increased self-esteem? (p. 397; A)
    a. Michael, who is physically less mature than other boys his age.
    b. Junior, who is physically more mature than other boys his age.
    c. Maruka, who is physically less mature than other girls her age.
    d. Julianna, who is physically more mature than other girls her age.

11. A junior high school student asks you for advice about her diet and lifestyle. You tell her, (p. 402; A)
    a. "Compared to adults, you need more calories, calcium, iron, and protein. Don't snack out and get lots of exercise."
    b. "Compared to adults, you need less calories, but more calcium, iron, and protein. Get lots of rest and exercise, too."
    c. Compared to adults, you need about the same number of calories, but more calcium, iron and protein. Exercise and rest are important, too."
    d. Compared to adults, you need about the same number of calories, and more calcium and iron for strong bones. Limit your protein intake, and don't forget to exercise."

12. Which of the following characteristics is probably **NOT** a characteristic of a person with anorexia nervosa? (p. 403; F)
    a. intense fear of gaining weight
    b. absence of menstrual cycle
    c. distorted body image
    d. perfectionistic

13. People with bulimia nervosa: (p. 404; F)
    a. tend to have families with disturbed functioning, especially parents who are intrusive and overly involved in the child's life.
    b. can have the problem intermittently over many years and are often able to hide their problem.
    c. tend to have relatively high levels of self-esteem and a realistic body image.
    d. are more likely to be male; people with anorexia nervosa are more likely to be female.

14. Which concept is **NOT** part of formal operational thinking? (p. 409; F)
    a. abstract problem solving
    b. compensation
    c. reflective abstraction
    d. hypothetico-deductive reasoning

15. Desiree was sitting in her room thinking about school. She then started thinking about the fact that she could think about school. Finally, she laughed as she thought about the fact she was thinking about the fact she was thinking about school. Piaget would refer to Desiree's ability as: (p. 409; A)
    a. compensatory reasoning
    b. heuristic thought
    c. hypothetico-deductive reasoning
    d. reflective abstractoin

16. Gerald is 16 years old and does not use his seatbelt while driving. He has been ticketed for excessive speed and occasionally drag races with his friends. Gerald is evidencing: (p. 411; A)
    a. formal operational thinking.
    b. concern for an imaginary audience.
    C. heuristic thought.
    D. the personal fable.

17. In one study, girls who went to a junior high school rather than staying in a kindergarten through 8th grade school: (p. 412; F)
    a. experienced losses in self-esteem and did poorer academically, even in high school.
    b. experienced gains in self-esteem and did better academically, even in high school.
    c. experienced losses in self-esteem and did poorer academically, but these losses were regained in high school.
    d. experienced gains in self-esteem and did better academically, but these gains were lost in high school.

18. A friend's daughter is about to go to middle school. Your friend asks you what to look for in a "good" middle school. You reply, (p. 413; A)
    a. "Make sure the middle school follows the high school model. If your daughter is put in a small middle school with fewer teachers per year, she will have more difficulty adjusting to high school."
    b. "The structure of the school setting really makes little difference. Girls are likely to do just as well in an elementary, middle, or junior high setting. There is no difference."
    c. "Make sure that the middle school is developmentally appropriate; at this age, children need to have lots of discipline and structure. It is also beneficial to have teachers who teach only one subject, rather than one teacher who teaches many subjects to fewer students."
    d. "The middle school may have guidance and transition programs, team teaching, and cooperative learning and be responsive to the needs of young adolescents; however, girls undergoing physical changes of puberty are still likely to have more problems compared to girls staying in an elementary type setting."

19. Students who transition to middle school show a/n: (p. 414; F)
    a. drop in grades and a decline in performance on standardized achievement tests.
    b. drop in grades but no decline in performance on standardized achievement tests.
    c. improvement in grades, but a decline in performance on standardized achievement tests.
    d. improvement in both grades and performance on standardized achievement tests.

20. Compared with students in China and Japan, students in the United States: (p. 415; F)
    a. spend more time outside of school on academic activities and homework.
    b. have parents who believe more strongly in education as a route to future happiness.
    c. effectively receive up to 6 years less schooling.
    d. believe education is the only avenue to success.

True/False Questions (If a statement is FALSE, correct it).

1. Early adolescence covers the period from 9 to 12 years of age. (p. 388) True/False.

2. Adolescence exists outside the context of culture. (p. 388) True/False.

3. Rites of passage are common in modern U.S. society. (p. 389) True/False.

4. Adolescents grow from the center of their bodies to their extremities. (p. 391) True/False.

5. General health and nutrition influence the onset of puberty. (p. 394) True/False.

6. Hormonal changes that trigger puberty result in adolescents' interest in the other sex, mood swings, and conflict with parents. (p. 396) True/False.

7. As adults, early maturing boys rate themselves as more responsible, warmer, rigid, and conforming than late maturing boys. (p. 399) True/False.

8. Adolescent obesity has decreased since the 1970s. (p. 403) True/False.

9. Research does not clearly support the belief that people with anorexia nervosa have a distorted body image. (p. 403) True/False.

10. Eating disturbances are relatively rare in adolescents. (p. 405) True/False.

11. Formal operational thinking involves the use of hypothetico-deductive reasoning. (p. 409) True/False.

12. Formal operational thinking is used consistently in all problem-solving situations once people reach adolescence. (p. 410) True/False.

13. The personal fable reflects young adolescents' tendency to see themselves as unique and invulnerable. (p. 411) True/False.

14. Most adolescents do not successfully meet the challenges of going from elementary school to middle school to high school. (p. 412) True/False.

15. Cultural values and social conditions have an important influence on school performance. (pp. 416) True/False.

☐   **REWARD YOURSELF!   Play with your pet!**

ANSWERS - Chapter 11 Physical and Cognitive Development in Early Adolescence

What is Early Adolescence? (pp. 387 - 390)
(1) childhood and adulthood; (2) child labor laws; criminal laws; mandatory public education; (3) D; (4) E; (5) F; (6) G; (7) B; (8) H; (9) A; (10) C

How Do Physical Growth and Sexual Maturation Occur During Early Adolescence? (pp. 390 – 401)
(11) hormones; (12) hypothalamus – pituitary - gonads; (13) estrogen; (14) androgens
(15) girls begin growth spurt about 2 years earlier than boys; (16) girls acquire more body fat; boys more muscle mass;
(17) girls' primary sex characteristics include ovaries, uterus, vagina; boys' include penis, testes; (18) girls' secondary sex characteristics include breasts, narrow waist; boys' include facial hair, deep voice, wide shoulders
(19) hands and feet; (20) trunk; (21) environment; (22) health; (23) nutrition; (24) 3; (25) stress
(26) Draw a line through the following sentences; these sentences are false:
   Evidence suggests that hormones directly affect behavior in adolescence.
   Late maturing boys are more likely than their peers to have problems at school and to use drugs and alcohol.
   Late maturing boys are more likely to have higher self-esteem and social status than early maturing boys.
   Late maturing girls are at risk for eating disorders and disturbances.
   Later maturing girls are more popular and begin dating earlier than earlier maturing girls.
   Early maturing girls may have the best situation of all adolescents.
   Late maturing boys are more likely to have leadership roles later in life.
   Early maturing boys are more likely to report successful marriages than late maturing boys.
   Girls not prepared for menarche report feeling more negative symptoms and have a more negative self-image than girls prepared for it.
   Boys are fairly well informed about spermarche, or the first ejaculation.

1 Minute Quiz: 1. Puberty; 2. D; 3. A; 4. False; 5. Later

What are the Health Concerns for Young Adolescents? (pp. 401 - 408)
(27) accidents; (28) boys; (29) nutrition; (30) protein; (31) calcium; (32) poor; (33) anemia; (34) physical activity; (35) obesity; (36) diets; (37) cultural
(38) Anorexia Nervosa: eat very little; intense fear of gaining weight; ; negative body image; perfectionistic; absence of period; controlled; parental over-involvement; effective treatment involves reinforcement of weight gain, individual, family, and group therapy
Bulimia Nervosa: binge and purge; intermittent; obese family members; depression; poor self-esteem; can hide problem for years; most successfully treated if caught early

1 Minute Quiz: 1. Protein, calcium, calories, iron; 2. Anorexia nervosa; 3. True; 4. fathers

How Do Young Adolescents Think and Solve Problems? (pp. 360 – 364)
(39) Only "thinking about the here and now," "logical problem solving with objects," and "reversible thinking and compensation" are not circled. (40) Adolescent egocentrism; (41) imaginary audience; (42) personal fable

How Does School Influence Early Adolescent Development? (pp. 411 – 416)
(43) 1. Adolescents are trying to adjust to both physical changes and school change; 2. Traditional junior high schools are not developmentally appropriate, i.e., larger classes, impersonal classes, teachers don't get to know and trust students, emphasis is on control and discipline, teachers overlook kids who are slipping
(44) realistically and pessimistically; (45) does not; (46) 1. Different cultural values; 2. Different educational policies; 3. Differences in home life; (47) economic and social

1 Minute Quiz: 1. Formal operations; 2. C; 3. False; 4. D

STUDY QUESTIONS

Multiple Choice: 1. D; 2. B; 3. A; 4. C; 5. A; 6. C; 7. A; 8. B; 9. D; 10. B; 11. A; 12. C; 13. B; 14. B; 15. D; 16. D; 17. A; 18. D; 19. B; 20. C

True/False Questions: 1. False, 11-14 years; 2. False, does not; 3. False, are not; 4. False, extremities to center; 5. True; 6. False, only indirectly; 7. True; 8. False, increased; 9. True; 10. False, common; 11. True; 12. False, not; 13. True; 14. False, most do; 15. True

212 Study Guide for Exploring Child Development

Chapter 12
Social and Emotional Development
In Early Adolescence

My mother taught me about the ANTICIPATION...
"Just wait until your father gets home!"
— Things My Mother Taught Me

Objectives
When you have completed this chapter, you will be able to:
- describe changes in self-concept and self-esteem during early adolescence;
- summarize Erikson's and Marcia's theories of identity development;
- discuss gender and ethnic differences in identity formation;
- discuss changes in parent-adolescent relationships during early adolescence;
- describe the characteristics of peer relationships during early adolescents, from friendships to romantic relationships to deviant peer groups;
- summarize findings on the influence of music, computers, and the Internet on early adolescents; and
- define the key terms and concepts listed on page 448 of your text.

☑ Study Check List

☐ Read Chapter 12 Social and Emotional Development in Early Adolescence.

☐ Re-read the Chapter 12 Summary to refresh your memory.

☐ Read the Chapter 12 Objectives listed above.

☐ Complete the following items:

<u>How Do Young Adolescents View Themselves?</u> (pp. 419 - 423)

Use these words to complete the following paragraphs:
possible	self-evaluation	complex	good	self-consciousness	grow
differentiated	fluctuates	eight	discrepancy	teacher	actual

Adolescents have a more _____(1) sense of themselves partly as a result of their new

cognitive abilities. Their circle of significant others continues to _____(2) providing more

opportunities for interactions and self-discovery. One of the most fundamental changes in young adolescents' self-concept is their development of a more _____(3) view of themselves. They are able describe themselves in terms of _____(4) domains – scholastic performance, athletic competence, behavioral conduct, social acceptance, physical appearance, job competence, close friendships, and romantic appeal, reflecting their more diverse social environments. Young adolescents can also distinguish between the _____(5) self (how they see themselves now) and the _____(6) self (how they wish to be in the future). If there is not much _____(7) between these two concepts, then the young person is likely to feel _____(8) about himself or herself and be motivated to improve. Too much discrepancy can result in frustration and sense of hopelessness.

Self-esteem during early adolescence _____(9) as adolescents experience a myriad of physical, social, and cognitive changes. Contrary to what some people believe, self-esteem **does/does not** *(circle one)* (10) provide a protective factor that shelters adolescents from delinquency, academic failure, sexual involvement, or depression. In fact, the reverse may be true. Adolescents who drop out, are delinquent, or become sexually active tend to have **high/low** *(circle one)* (11) self-esteem. Some teens may enhance their self-esteem through high-risk behaviors that win peer approval.

Because of their improved cognitive abilities, young adolescents are able to engage in self-reflection and _____(12), often resulting in increased _____ _____(13). While self-consciousness increases for both boys and girls, it increases more for **boys/girls** *(circle one)* (14). **Boys/Girls** *(circle one)* (15) are especially concerned with their appearance; **boys/girls** *(circle one)* (16) are more concerned with their physical abilities. These concerns reflect our cultural values. School can also undermine girls' self-esteem through _____ (17) interactions. **Boys/girls** *(circle one)* (18) tend to be praised more often, given more feedback, and called on more frequently than girls. Girls are more likely than boys to sit quietly and wait to be called on.

How Do Adolescents Form an Identity? (pp. 424 – 428)

A sense of id_____(19) is developed throughout one's life; however, adolescence is a particularly important time in developing identity as the adolescents' world expands. One of the foremost researchers in identity development was Erik E_____ (20), who believed that adolescents face an identity cr_____ (21). Positive resolution of this crisis leads to identity ac_____(22) and negative resolution results in identity di_____(23).

According to Erikson, adolescence should be a time of psychosocial mo_____(24), during which time young people are relatively free of adult res_____(25) and are able to actively address identity issues. Adolescents who ach_____(26) an identity are able to meaningfully move into adulthood and address new issues there. Students who fail to achieve an identity are like "ships tossed in the wind," lacking direction and meaning in their life. Identity-d_____(27) adolescents are filled with self-doubt and may be vulnerable to problems, such as depression, drug abuse, or delinquency. They may not be prepared for ad_____(28), nor will they be able to engage in healthy, meaningful re_____(29) with others.

Ma_____(30) expanded Erikson's theory and proposed that adolescents' identity status is based on two aspects: _____ and _____(31). Based on the presence or absence of crises (which actually refers to exploration or non-exploration) and the presence or absence of commitment, Marcia was able to identify four identity statuses: (32)

1. _____
2. _____
3. _____
4. _____

Chapter 12 Social and Emotional Development in Early Adolescence 215

LESSONS IN REAL LIFE - LESSONS IN REAL LIFE - LESSONS IN REAL LIFE - LESSONS IN REAL LIFE

Identify the identity status for each of the following individuals*:

Carlos' father graduated from MIT with a degree in engineering. From the time Carlos was born, his parents talked about him going to MIT and becoming an engineer. They even decorated his room in MIT colors, hung a sign over his bed that said "Infinite Corridor" (the heart of MIT campus), and named his dog "Kendall" after Kendall Square. When Carlos graduated from high school, his friends asked him what he was going to do after he graduated. Carlos replied, "Why go to MIT and study engineering, of course." Carlos' identity status would be defined as _____(33).

Meghan has just graduated from high school. She had applied to go to pharmacy school at the University of Arizona, but instead, decides to "Be All That You Can Be!" and join the Army. Meghan tells her parents that she doesn't intend on making this her life's work; it seems interesting, and she will be able to learn many new skills. Additionally, the Army will pay for her schooling when she gets out in four years. She says she may or may not go into pharmacy. She hasn't decided, but she is thinking about it. Meghan's identity status would be defined as _____(34).

From the time he was little, Pete wanted to be teacher. He stayed after school to help his teachers, worked as a teacher's aid in high school and then went to college, majoring in history and hoping to become a history teacher. One summer, Pete worked as a "hot shot" forest fire fighter, and thought seriously about changing his major to forestry. He spent time on the Internet, studying the various programs, and even visited a couple of full time forest rangers to discuss the job. When he returned to school, he decided to finish his degree in history and go on for a master's in education. "I really want to teach," Pete said. Pete's identity status would be defined as _____(35).

Chelsea has graduated from high school, barely having enough credits to graduate. She enjoys spending her time at home watching television, and takes a class or two at her local community college to satisfy her parents. She frequently skips class and spends her time hanging out at the local mall. Occasionally, she will shoplift, not because her parents don't have enough money, but for the "thrill" of it. Although she doesn't seek out drugs, if she is with friends who are using them, she'll go ahead and use them, too. Chelsea's identity status would best be defined as _____(36).

**For each item, ask yourself, "Is this person actively seeking an identity and exploring options or has the person explored options in the past?" If so, then the person has experienced or is experiencing a "crisis." Then ask yourself, "Has this person committed himself or herself to something?" If so, then that person has experienced commitment.*

LESSONS IN REAL LIFE - LESSONS IN REAL LIFE - LESSONS IN REAL LIFE - LESSONS IN REAL LIFE

Males and females have been found to progress through the various identity status categories in a similar manner. One exception to this pattern is in the area of se_____ (37) identity and ca_____ (38) priorities. In these areas, identity formation is more com_____(39) for women due to rapid so_____, unclear ex_____, and con_____ (40).

Minority youth also face special issues with identity. One's sense of belonging to an ethnic group is referred to as e_____(41) identity. Ethnic identity is comprised of five components: (42)

1. _____
2. _____
3. _____
4. _____
5. _____

Members of different ethnic groups may have different identity experiences, but they share a common pathway to identity. Ethnic identity issues may be resolved in four ways: (43)

1. _____
2. _____
3. _____
4. _____

Once a secure ethnic identity is formed, adolescents in each of the four groups have similar levels of self-esteem, mental health, grades, and social competence. The most important influence in formation of ethnic identity is the p_____ (44). Parents should: (45)

1. _____
2. _____
3. _____

1 ½ Minute Quiz

1. *Circle* the word/s that <u>DOES NOT</u> describe changes in adolescents' self-concepts.
      differentiated   complex   all-or-none

2. Helping children gain high self-esteem will "protect" them against gangs and drugs. True/False.

3. Name two theorists associated with adolescent identity:
   a. _____
   b. _____

4. Fill in the blanks with "yes" or "no" to complete the following table:

	Crisis	Commitment
Identity Achieved	Yes	____
Identity foreclosure	____	____
Identity Moratorium	____	____
Identity Confused	____	No

5. Stefan, from Bosnia, has assimilated with the majority culture; Maria, from Mexico, considers herself bicultural.
   a. Stefan is more likely to have good grades, high social competence, and high self-esteem.
   b. Maria is more likely to have good grades, high social competence, and high self-esteem.
   c. Both Stefan and Maria are just as likely to have good grades, high social competence, and high self-esteem.
   d. Neither Stefan nor Maria will have good grades, high social competence, and high self-esteem.

<u>**How Do Family Relationships Change During Early Adolescence?**</u> (pp. 428 – 432)

A majority of adolescents feel **close to/ distant from** *(circle one)* (46) their parents, **value/ devalue** *(circle one)* (47) their parents' opinions, **believe/ don't believe** *(circle one)* (48) their parents love them and care for them, and **respect/ don't respect** *(circle one)* (49) their parents as authority figures.

218 Study Guide for Exploring Child Development

Adolescents also tend to **agree/disagree** *(circle one)* (50) with their parents on attitudes toward work, education, religion, and politics. As adolescents grow and develop, their relationship with their parents must evolve into one that allows greater equality and independence.

- *Cross out the parental behavior that is likely to lead to negative outcomes in adolescents:* (51)

    support ♥ warmth ♥ monitoring ♥ punitiveness ♥ induction ♥ acceptance

- *Draw an arrow that indicates the direction of influence in the parent-adolescent relationship:* (52)

    Parent   Adolescent

- *How much support is there for the existence of a "generation gap"?* (53)

    Little   Moderate   Lots

- Most conflicts that occur between parents and adolescents are related to l_____(54) issues. Most intense conflicts occur during **early/middle/late** *(choose one)* (55) adolescence and may be due in part to changes brought on by p_____(56). Some scholars believe that a certain amount of conflict **fosters/hinders** *(choose one)* (57) adaptive changes in parent-adolescent relationships. Conflict, itself, might not be as much of a problem as how conflict is m_____d and re_____(58).

What are the Characteristics of Early Adolescent Peer Relationships? (pp. 432 - 442)

Peer Culture

Adolescent peer culture emerged during the 20th Century as a result of several social developments, including our age-segregated school systems. What other social developments have supported a peer culture? (59)

a. _____

b. _____

c. _____

Peer cultures vary widely, but all do the following: (60)

1. Provide ways of _____

2. Provide _____

3. Serve as symbols of _____

4. Serve as symbols of _____

5. Allow for the expression of _____

What is the difference between a clique and a crowd? _____
_____
_____(61)

Friendships During Adolescence

Compared to younger children, adolescents are more likely to share se_____,
em_____, and coo_____(62) with friends rather than compete with them. Adolescents demand lo_____(63) in their friendships and express anx_____(64) over the possibility of being rejected.

Gender differences have been observed in adolescent friendship patterns. Girls are more likely to have int_____(65) conversations with friends, prefer more ex_____(66) friendships, and express more em_____(67) than boys. Boys' friendships remain more focused on shared ac_____(68) and expressions of support are often non_____(69).

Peer Popularity and Rejection

What skills do popular adolescents have that are effective in building and maintaining relationships? (70)

1. _____
2. _____
3. _____
4. _____

220 Study Guide for Exploring Child Development

Unpopular and rejected adolescents are at risk for a variety of adverse consequences, including depression, b_____(71), and academic difficulties; and these problems can have long-term consequences.

Dating and Romantic Relationships

Dating relationships are different today than in the past. Today, (72)

1. _____
2. _____
3. _____
4. _____

Dating relationships can help adolescents learn about l_____, l_____, and e_____(73). Boys and girls experience dating differently. Boys emphasize the s_____(74) aspects of dating and the phy_____ _____(75) of the partner; girls focus on the opportunities that dating relationship provides for cl_____, self-_____ , and comm_____(76).

Emerging Sexuality During Early Adolescence

During early adolescence, sexuality tends to revolve around the adolescent's own _____(77). The most common source of orgasm for young teens is m_____(78). Another source of orgasms is no_____ e_____(79). These orgasms are relatively rare.

Sexual interactions between boys and girls also begin during early adolescence, from kissing and hugging to sexual intercourse. Sexual intercourse for young adolescents is sp_____and r_____(80). Fewer than _____ in _____ (81) have sexual intercourse before age 13. Early sexual intercourse is problematic for several reasons: (1) It exposes one to the risk of becoming _____ or acquiring a _____(82); (2) young adolescents often don't understand the _____ (83) of their behavior and are less likely to use _____ (84); and (3) early sexual activity is often part of a larger pattern of high _____ (85) behavior, including use of drugs and alcohol. _____ (86) percent of adolescent girls who had sex before age 14 report that the experience was involuntary.

Deviant Peer Groups: Adolescent Gangs

Gangs are not a recent invention, emerging over 100 years ago and continuing into the 20th century. Gangs are very di_____(87), although most adolescent gangs share the following characteristics: (88)

1. _____
2. _____
3. _____
4. _____

Gang membership often starts off as s_____ (89) involvement. Only a small number of adolescents join gangs and only about _____ (90) percent of juvenile crimes have been described as gang-related. Concern over gang activities has been growing for several reasons. What are two of those reasons? (91)

_____

_____

Many gangs are simply variations of adolescent c_____ and c_____ (92).

How Do Mass Media Influence Young Adolescents' Development? (pp. 443 – 447)

Draw a line through the following statements that are INCORRECT: (93)

- Television viewing drops during adolescence.
- There is little evidence that popular music and its lyrics influence behavior.
- Teenagers understand and agree on the meanings of popular song lyrics.

- A significant relationship exists between adolescents' music and aggressive or sexual behaviors.
- Boys and girls react different to computers.
- Boys view computers as tools and girls view computers as toys.
- Most computer software products for the home are geared toward boys.
- Available research suggests that adolescents who play computer game frequently are no more maladjusted than those who play infrequently.
- Adolescents can be targets of online exploitation.

---

1 Minute Quiz

1. **For most adolescents, family life is marked by struggle and emotional distance. True/False.**

2. **The parenting technique that relies on logical reasoning is:**
   a. support.   b. monitoring.   c. induction.   d. punitiveness.

3. **Alison has 3 friends her age with whom she regularly meets and listens to Ricky Martin. By definition, Alison's peer group is a:**
   a. gang.   b. clique.   c. crowd.

4. **Sexual intercourse during early adolescence is relatively _____.**

5. **A majority/ minority *(circle one)* of inner city youth belong to gangs. True/False.**

6. **There is substantial/ little *(circle one)* evidence that popular music influences adolescents' behavior.**

☐ Complete the crossword puzzle in Appendix 1 – Crossword Puzzles.

☐ Go to the beginning of this chapter, and on a separate sheet of paper, write out the answers to the lesson objectives.

SAGE Advice

"When studying, keep a dictionary by your side. Look up any words you are not familiar with."

STUDY QUESTIONS

Multiple Choice (The following questions are identified "F," *factual questions* that rely on the recall of facts; or "A," *applied questions* that rely on the ability to apply a concept to a real-life situation).

1. A group of concerned citizens want to start a program that will discourage delinquency and dropping out of high school. "We believe the root of the problem is self-esteem," they inform you. "We want to use this program, 'How to Increase Your Child's Self-Esteem.'" You tell them, (p. 420; A)
   a. "Your intentions are good; however, self-esteem among adolescents who drop out, are delinquent, or become sexually active is actually high. We need to consider other alternatives."
   b. "Your intentions are good. Self-esteem has been found to be a protective factor against the types of problems you want to address and more. Let's examine the program."
   c. "Your intentions are good. Self-esteem is low among the groups you mentioned, however, programs such as that are not effective. We need to increase self-esteem in the home."
   d. "Can I get a cut of the royalties?"

2. Adolescent boys: (p. 421; F)
   a. have a greater increase in self-consciousness than adolescent girls during early adolescence.
   b. place more value on what they do than what they look like.
   c. have a high value on their social selves compared to girls.
   d. show a drop in self-esteem due to changes in appearance.

3. During early adolescence, self-esteem: (p. 421; F)
   a. stabilizes.   b. rises.   c. lowers.   d. fluctuates.

4. Your instructor says, "I believe that adolescence is a time of searching for identity. It is a time of crisis, and if the adolescent crisis is not resolved, the adolescent will wander aimlessly in search of self." The theorist most likely to agree with your instructor is: (p. 424; A)
   a. Freud   b. Marcia   c. Erikson   d. Piaget

5. According to Marcia's theory of adolescent identity development, identity status is based on: (p. 425; F)
   a. cognitive growth and experience.
   b. parental guidance and social restraint.
   c. crisis/exploration and commitment.
   d. diffusion and achievement.

6. Clarice is in college. She has changed her major several times. She makes good grades, but has difficulty focusing on what she wants to do. In her words, "I just don't know what I want to be when I grow up!" She has active, healthy relationships with her friends, and is interested in exploring career options. Marcia would probably say that Clarice's identity status is: (p. 425; A)
   a. identity-confused.
   b. moratorium.
   c. foreclosure.
   d. identity-achieved.

7. In terms of progressing through the various identity status categories, adolescent girls differ from adolescent boys in the area/s of: (p. 426; F)
   a. sexual identity and career/family priorities.
   b. moral identity.
   c. religious identity.
   d. political identity

8. Four people from minority ethnic groups have each resolved their ethnic identity in a different way. One person assimilated into the majority culture; another is considered marginalized; the third is separated, identifying only with his culture; and the fourth considers herself bicultural. Each is secure in his or her own ethnic identity. Which of the following statements is **TRUE**? (p. 427; A)
   a. The person that assimilated and the person that considers herself bicultural are more likely to have higher self-esteem, better grades, and be socially competent.
   b. The person who assimilated is more likely than the others to have higher self-esteem, better grades, and be socially competent.
   c. The person who separated is more likely than the others to have higher self-esteem, better grades and be socially competent.
   d. They are all likely to be similar in their self-esteem, grades, and social competence.

9. Raul wants his children to have a secure Hispanic identity. He asks your advice on how to help them. You say, (p. 428; A)
   a. "Avoid discussing ethnic issues with your children because they will be made to feel different from the majority culture. Once they have a strong majority identity, they can then develop their ethnic identity."
   b. "Teach your children to be proud of their heritage and be active in the Hispanic community. Discuss issues of the day, even though some may seem controversial."
   c. "Teach your children to be proud of their heritage and be active in the majority community. They can learn more socially competent skills by watching your participation in that community."
   d. "Make sure your children avoid resolving their identities through being marginalized or separated. They will be happier identifying with both cultures."

10. Your colleague at work tells you that he and his teenage son have an exceptional relationship because they don't fight often and aren't emotionally distant like most families with teenagers. You know that: (p. 428; A)
    a. your colleague's relationship with his son is more typical than atypical.
    b. your colleague's relationship with his son is more atypical than typical.
    c. your colleague has a good relationship because they are the same sex.
    d. your colleague has a good relationship because he rarely sees his son.

11. Your nephew is about to enter adolescence and your sister asks you what kind of parenting behaviors she should or should not use to prevent her son from becoming a delinquent or drug abuser. You say, (p. 430; A)
    a. "Give him some free space to make his own mistakes. You don't need to monitor him as much now that he is older. Telling him where he can and can't go only leads to rebelliousness."
    b. "Hugging and kissing your son should be limited now as he strives to achieve autonomy and develop relationships outside the family realm."
    c. "Avoid the use of induction. Don't worry about appealing to his concern for others. At this point, he has no concern for others and needs strong guidance."
    d. "You should really avoid parental punitiveness. This does not mean avoiding rules, regulations, and limits, but it does mean avoiding slapping, name-calling, and yelling."

12. Parent-adolescent relationships are best described as: (p. 430; F)
    a. unidirectional.
    b. bidirectional.
    c. distant.
    d. stormy and stressful.

13. Occasionally, your young adolescent daughter "talks back" to you and questions your authority. This behavior: (p. 432; A)
    a. is totally unacceptable and is a precursor to worse behavior in the future.
    b. is rare in early adolescence.
    c. may be disturbing and a source of conflict but could actually foster adaptive changes in the parent-adolescent relationship.
    d. discourages revisions in expectations of the parent and adolescent and may foster a lack of family connectedness.

14. Which of the following was **NOT** provided as a reason for the development of the adolescent peer culture? (p. 432; F)
    a. Adolescents need more time to prepare for the adult world and must wait a longer time to participate in it.
    b. Low-wage jobs have been designed specifically for adolescents.
    c. Business has target adolescents for their products.
    d. Adolescents have more in common with their age-mates than with their parents, who come from an entirely different social milieu.

15. For adolescents to be popular, they need all of the following skills, **EXCEPT** the ability to: (p. 436; F)
    a. act appropriately in a variety of social situations.
    b. make their own needs known at the expense of others.
    c. be agreeable, cheerful, and have a sense of humor.
    d. communicate.

16. Dating is different today because: (p. 437; F)
    a. it is less structured, more informal and focused on fun.
    b. parents are more likely to monitor their adolescents' dating.
    c. the purpose of dating today is to find a mate.
    d. dating today rarely involves sex.

17. A 13-year-old student reveals to you that she is concerned because she is "still a virgin." You tell her, (p. 439; A)
    a. "Wow! What a surprise! There are so few of you left!"
    b. "Excuse me, but you are not the only virgin in this classroom. In fact, approximately half of the girls your age still have not had sexual intercourse."
    c. "You may be surprised to learn, but most children your age have not had sexual intercourse. In fact, less than one in ten adolescents have had sex before age 13."
    d. "Yes, most 13-year-olds have had sex, but I don't think it's a good idea."

18. Which of the following statements about gangs is **FALSE**? (p. 441; F)
    a. Gangs have been around since the 19th century.
    b. In high risk areas, approximately 80 percent of adolescents join gangs and gang related activities account for 60 percent of juvenile crime.
    c. Gang membership can be found in low income areas, as well as in suburban middle class neighborhoods.
    d. Gang membership can be a source of status for its members.

19. Music in adolescence: (p. 443; F)
    a. represents a significant topic of discussion among adolescents.
    b. is considered "very important in my life" by only 20 percent of adolescents.
    c. has been found to be a powerful influence over adolescents' behavior and values.
    d. has impact when the lyrics are sexually suggestive or violent.

20. Liam is thinking of buying his children a computer. He wonders what his 13-year-old daughter and 14-year-old son will use it for. You reply, (p. 444; A)
    a. "Adolescents this age use it as a source of entertainment and basic learning only."
    b. "Children who play computer games frequently tend to be maladjusted compared with those who play infrequently; therefore, monitor the amount of time your kids spend on the computer."
    c. "Your daughter is likely to view computers as tools, and your son is likely to view computers as toys and games."
    d. "Your daughter will probably think the computer will enhance her image, but your son may be afraid of being labeled a nerd."

True/False Questoins (If a statement is FALSE, correct it).

1. Adolescents are able to recognize differences between actual and possible selves. (p. 420) True/False.

2. Research suggests that high self-esteem may contribute to risky behaviors and unrealistic perceptions. (p. 421) True/False.

3. Adolescent boys are more at risk for low self-esteem because of physical and social changes than adolescent girls. (p. 421) True/False.

4. Erikson believed that adolescents should be given adult responsibilities early on to help them achieve an identity. (p. 424) True/False.

5. Identity issues are usually resolved completely during adolescence. (p. 425) True/False.

6. Adolescent boys and girls are more alike than different in the ways they form an identity. (p. 426) True/False.

7. An individual who lives within the majority culture but feels alienated or outcast is considered to be separated. (p. 427) True/False.

8. For adolescents, parents have very little influence on the formation of ethnic identity. (p. 428) True/False.

9. Family life during adolescence tends to be marked by constant struggle and emotional distance. (p. 428) True/False.

10. Parents influence adolescents and adolescents influence parents. (p. 430) True/False.

11. Most adolescents are not pressured by peers to use drugs, skip school or engage in delinquent activities. (p. 432) True/False.

12. Some adolescents may be rejected by their peers because they are aggressive, withdrawn, or both. (p. 437) True/False.

13. Dating during early adolescence is usually done in groups. (p. 437) True/False.

14. During early adolescence television viewing decreases. (p. 443) True/False.

15. Girls tend to play with computers and explore them with no particular purpose in mind. (pp. 445) True/False.

☐ REWARD YOURSELF!   Call a friend and just talk!

Chapter 12 Social and Emotional Development in Early Adolescence 229

ANSWERS: Chapter 12 Social and Emotional Development in Early Adolescence

How Do Young Adolescents View Themselves? (pp. 419 - 423)
(1) complex; (2) grow; (3) differentiated; (4) eight; (5) actual; (6) possible; (7) discrepancy; (8) good; (9) fluctuates; (10) does not; (11) high; (12) self-evaluation; (13) self-consciousness; (14) girls; (15) Girls; (16) boys; (17) teacher; (18) Boys

How Do Adolescents Form an Identity? (pp. 424 – 428)
(19) identity; (20) Erikson; (21) crisis; (22) achievement; (23) diffusion; (24) moratorium; (25) responsibilities; (26) achieve; (27) diffused; (28) adulthood; (29) relationships; (30) Marcia; (31) crisis (or exploration) and commitment; (32) achievement, foreclosure, moratorium, confused; (33) foreclosure; (34) moratorium; (35) achievement; (36) confusion (37) sexual; (38) career/family; (39) complicated; (40) social change, unclear expectations, and conflicting priorities about work and family; (41) ethnic; (42) identifying oneself as a member of an ethnic group; developing a sense of belonging to an ethnic group; forming attitudes toward one's ethnic group; having a sense of shared attitudes and values with an ethnic group; following the specific traditions and practices of an ethnic group; (43) assimilation; marginalization, separation, biculturalism; (44) parent; (45) teach adolescents to be proud of their heritage; model participation in the ethnic community; discuss ethnic issues with their adolescents

1 ½ Minute Quiz: 1. All-or-none; 2. False; 3. Erikson and Marcia; 4. Identity Achieved – yes, yes; Identity foreclosure – no, yes; identity moratorium – yes, no; identity diffused – no, no; 5. C

How Do Family Relationships Change During early Adolescence? (pp. 428 – 432)
(46) close to; (47) value; (48) believe; (49) respect; (50) agree; (51) draw a line through "punitiveness"; (52) parent ⟷ adolescent
(53) little; (54) lifestyle; (55) early; (56) puberty; (57) fosters; (58) managed and resolved

What are the Characteristics of Early Adolescent Peer Relationships? (pp. 432 - 442)
(59) increased time necessary for preparing for adulthood; low-wage jobs designed for adolescents; consumer-driven society
(60) provide ways of experimenting with different self-concepts; provide symbols of group membership; serve as symbols of independence from the adult world; serve as symbols of prestige or status within the peer world; allow for the expression of personal beliefs, feelings, and values that are important to adolescents
(61) cliques are small groups of peers, usually of the same sex and age, who interact with one another on a regular basis; crowds are defined by members' activities and social standing
(62) secrets, empathize, and cooperate; (63) loyalty; (64) anxiety; (65) intimate; (66) exclusive; (67) empathy; (68) activities; (69) nonverbal; (70) the ability to act appropriately in a variety of social situations; the ability to perceive and meet the needs of others; being agreeable, cheerful, and having a sense of humor; the ability to communicate effectively; (71) behavior problems
(72) dating is an end in itself, not a practice that leads to marriage; parents are less available to control and monitor adolescents' dating; dating is less structured, more informal, and more focused on leisure-time activities; dating is a means for sexual experimentation, especially when dating relationships last for a while and become exclusive.
(73) love, life, and emotions; (74) sexual; (75) physical attractiveness; (76) closeness, self-disclosure, and communication (77) body; (78) masturbation; (79) nocturnal emissions; (80) sporadic and rare; (81) 1 in 10; (82) pregnant, sexually transmitted disease; (83) consequences; (84) contraceptives; (85) risk; (86) Seventy
(87) diverse; (88) they hang out with one another on a frequent basis; share a common identity, usually expressed through a name; they adopt various status symbols such as styles of dress, colors, hand signals, etc.; are territorial; (89) social; (90) two; (91) higher incidence of gang-related violence; greater access to lethal weapons; greater emphasis on organized criminal activity; trend to stay active in gangs into adulthood; spread of gang culture beyond the inner city; more diverse membership in youth gangs, including females; (92) crowds and cliques

How Do Mass Media Influence Young Adolescents' Development? (pp. 443 – 447)
(93) *Draw a line through:*
- Teenagers understand and agree on the meanings of popular song lyrics.
- A significant relationship exists between adolescents' music and aggressive or sexual behaviors.
- Boys view computers as tools and girls view computers as toys.

1 Minute Quiz: 1. False; 2. C; 3. B; 4. rare; 5. minority; 6. little

STUDY QUESTIONS

Multiple Choice: 1. A; 2. B; 3. D; 4. C; 5. C; 6. B; 7. A; 8. D; 9. B; 10. A; 11. D; 12. B; 13. C; 14. D; 15. B; 16. A; 17. C; 18. B; 19. A; 20. C

True/False Questions:
1. True
2. True
3. False; Adolescent girls
4. False; should not (moratorium)
5. False; are not
6. True
7. False; marginal
8. False; are an important influence
9. False; is not marked
10. True
11. True
12. True
13. True
14. True
15. False; Boys

Chapter 13
Physical and Cognitive Development In Late Adolescence

My mother taught me about RECEIVING...
"You are going to get it when you get home!"
- Things My Mother Taught Me

Objectives
When you have completed this chapter, you will be able to:
- summarize health and safety issues in late adolescence, including automobile crashes, homicides, suicide, sexually transmitted diseases, AIDS, chronic illness, fitness, and exercise;
- describe the changes that occur in older adolescents' thinking and reasoning;
- compare and contrast verbal skills, spatial-visual skills, and math and science skills of boys and girls;
- state the influences on boys' and girls' academic achievement;
- describe the characteristics of high school dropouts;
- design a dropout prevention program using program characteristics that have been found particularly effective; and
- define the key terms and concepts listed on page 481 of your text.

☑ Study Check List

☐ Read Chapter 13 Physical and Cognitive Development in Late Adolescence

☐ Re-read the Chapter 13 Summary to refresh your memory.

☐ Read the Chapter 13 Objectives listed above.

☐ Complete the following items:

What are the Health and Safety Issues in Late Adolescence? (pp. 455 - 466)

Most deaths during late adolescence stem from events that are p_____(1).

In one sentence, summarize the important points in the section on automobile accidents (p. 456): (2)

_____

_____

Did you know...

Automobile safety experts and the U.S. government no longer refer to automobile accidents as "accidents?" Instead, automobile accidents are now called automobile or car "crashes." The term "accident" implies that it was a twist of fate beyond the control of the driver. In fact, most "accidents" can be prevented – even those that aren't your fault! Do you think this change in terminology will help young people become safer drivers?

In two sentences, summarize the important points in the section on homicides (p. 456-457): (3)

_____

_____

The suicide rate among adolescence has almost tr_____ (4) since 1960, especially for Ca_____ (5). Adolescent **boys/girls** *(circle one)* (6) are more likely to commit suicide, but adolescent **boys/girls** *(circle one)* (7) are more likely to attempt it. Fortunately most adolescent suicide attempts are not su_____(8). Risk factors for attempting suicide in adolescence are: (9)

1. _____
2. _____
3. _____
4. _____

Adolescents are also at risk for acquiring s_____(STDs) (10), not only those who are sexually active but also those adolescents who use contaminated n_____ (11) or have bl_____(12). Teens higher risks for these diseases may be due to: (1) _____

_____; (2) _____

_____; and (3) _____(13).

Chapter 13 Physical and Cognitive Development in Late Adolescence 233

Some groups of adolescents are more likely to get AIDS than other groups. At highest risk are

_____

_____ (14).

Additional risk factors for adolescents include having STDs, being s_____,

selling s_____ for survival, not using c_____ , and abusing a_____(15).

About _____(16) percent of adolescents have chronic illness. As a result, these young people

are more likely to miss s_____(17) and other a_____(18).

The number of adolescents with chronic illnesses has **increased/decreased** *(choose one)* (19) as a result of

improved medical treatments that have extended the lives of children. Adolescents with chronic illnesses

may t_____(20) their limits, putting their health at risk; others may make a mistake in their self-

_____ (21). Some adolescents with chronic illness are at **increased/decreased**

(choose one) (22) risk for psychological problems; however, most are mentally h_____ and

w_____(23). When an adolescent has a chronic illness, the whole f_____(24)

is affected. A chronic illness can take a heavy toll on the family's ec_____(25) situation and

cause a lot of family s_____(26). However, f_____(27) play an important

role in helping the adolescent deal with the disease.

During adolescence, young people undergo several physiological changes that affect their fitness level.

These changes include: (a)_____ , (b) _____

_____ , (c) _____ ,

and (d) _____(28).

Place check marks (√) in the appropriate column: (29)

	BOYS	**GIRLS**

Who is most likely to have the
- highest aerobic endurance?
- highest muscle strength?
- greatest flexibility?
- highest percentage of body fat?

234 Study Guide for Exploring Child Development

Exercise is important for adolescents. Adolescents who exercise are more likely to grow up to be h_____(30) adults. Some adolescents participate in sports, but only a few studies have assessed the impact of sports participation on young people. One function of sports is helping the adolescent develop so_____(31) ties with others. Sports also provide positive r_____(32) models and opportunities to engage in eth_____(33) behavior with other people. Young people who participate in sports or regular exercise are less likely to be de_____(34). Perhaps sports and exercise help youth cope with st_____(35). Sports can also help improve adolescents' self-_____ and self-_____(36) and improve their sense of mastery, concentration, and planning.

---

1 Minute Quiz

1. **Boys/Girls (circle one) are more likely to be victims of automobile crashes, homicides, and suicide.**

2. **State one reason why teens are at higher risk for sexually-transmitted diseases.**

   _____

3. **Most chronically ill teens have psychological problems and adjustment difficulties. True/False.**

4. **_____ levels of exercise are best for increasing mental health.**
   a. Low   b. Moderate   c. Strenuous

What Changes Occur in Older Adolescents' Thinking and Reasoning? (pp. 466 – 472)

Due to their cognitive development and increased experience, adolescents are able to think about social relationships. Thinking about people and interpersonal relationships is referred to as s_____ l c_____ (37). One aspect of understanding other people's behavior is forming

Chapter 13 Physical and Cognitive Development in Late Adolescence 235

im_____(38) about them and using impressions to interpret their behavior.

With experience, adolescents show several improvements in how they view other people, including: (39)

1. _____
2. _____
3. _____
4. _____

Adolescents are also much better at viewing a situation from another person's perspective, as skill referred to as s_____ p_____ t_____(40). Between the ages of _____ and _____ (41), adolescents can take a th_____(42) person perspective, viewing a situation from the perspective of a neutral outsider. Later in adolescence, teens are also able to consider cultural and societal perspectives. Although adolescents have these new skills, they do not use them con_____(43). In addition, adolescents vary in their ability to apply their cognitive skills in social situations.

Adolescents' cognitive development affects their moral reasoning skills. To address public perception of a moral crisis among our youth, scholars are attempting to develop a model for educating a complete moral person. Some scholars have tried to identify the char_____(44) of a moral person. Others have studied domains relevant to the development of responsibility and character. Turiel (1983) identified three types of social knowledge: (a) _____, (b)_____ _____, and (c) _____(45).

Match the example to the appropriate domain:

moral domain   social-conventional domain   personal domain

- "I enjoy wearing high heels and having spiked hair." This is part of the _____(46).

- "It is important not to steal from others. Stealing shows a lack of respect and allows one to obtain something that was not earned. It is not right that someone has earned something only to have someone else steal it." This is part of the _____(47).

- "I have noticed that here in America people smile a lot when they meet new people and always say, 'Hello,' 'How are you?', and 'Excuse me.' In Germany, we don't do that." This is part of the _____(48).

Two specific approaches to moral education are (1) Kohlberg's and his colleagues j_____ t c_____ schools; and (2) cha_____ education (49). Briefly describe a "just community school:" (50)

_____

_____

_____

Programs that systematically engage students in moral discussion seem to lead to significant advances in students' moral reasoning abilities; the "jury is still out" as to the effectiveness of character education. It may be that a com_____(51) of the two approaches will have the most impact on students' moral development.

Finally, because of changes in adolescents' thinking abilities, adolescents are able to think about issues they had not thought about before. Two such issues are rel_____ and po_____(52). Adolescents can think in the abstract and think about possibilities. They are much less likely to obey authority figures without question. Their newfound thinking abilities, combined with youthful idealism and lack of experience, can lead to fascinating explorations and discussions.

What Gender Differences are Found in Adolescents' Cognitive Abilities and Achievement? (pp. 472 – 476)

Briefly describe the gender differences in adolescence observed in each of the following areas:

- Verbal skills (53) _____

_____

_____

- Spatial-Visual skills (54) _____

- Math and science skills (55) _____

How are these gender differences explained?

1. _____(56)

2. _____(57)

3. _____(58)

238 Study Guide for Exploring Child Development

---

1 Minute Quiz

1. The ability to think about people and interpersonal relationships is referred to as _____ _____.

2. **Children/ Adolescents** *(circle one)* are more likely to provide justifications for impressions about people.

3. When it comes to social perspective taking:
   a. teens do not use it consistently.
   b. teens vary in their ability to apply cognitive skills in social situations.
   c. teens begin to develop the ability to view a situation from the perspective of a neutral outsider.
   d. All of the above are correct.

4. To advance students' moral reasoning skills, research supports:
   a. teaching character education.
   b. addressing issues in the personal domain.
   c. systematically engaging teens in moral discussions.
   d. ignoring political and religious topics.

What Factors Contribute to Dropping Out of School? (pp. 476 – 480)

Regarding high school dropouts:

- the most common reasons given by boys and girls for dropping out are at_____s _____(59);

- characteristics of students who are likely to drop out are low _____ _____(60);

- girls are more likely to drop out because of _____(61);

- boys are more likely to drop out because of _____(62);

- race, ethnicity, and social class _____(63);

- adolescents living in poverty _____(64);

  and

- cultural factors _____(65).

  Dropping out of high school carries both e_____ and s_____(66) costs to both the individual and society. *Read the characteristics of effective dropout prevention programs on page 479 in your text to answer the following question:*

  Congratulations! You have been elected to head the State Department of Education. One of your campaign promises was to decrease the number of high school dropouts in your state. The governor has given you the "go-ahead" with any program you design and has appropriated unlimited funds for your program. Briefly describe your high school dropout prevention program. (67)

  _____
  _____
  _____
  _____
  _____
  _____
  _____
  _____
  _____
  _____

☐ Complete the crossword puzzle in Appendix 1 – Crossword Puzzles.

☐ Go to the beginning of this chapter, and on a separate sheet of paper, write out the answers to the lesson objectives.

> "Try to tailor information to your own experiences and knowledge. Study your chapter summaries and bold-faced words as often as possible."

STUDY QUESTIONS

Multiple Choice (The following questions are identified "F," *factual questions* that rely on the recall of facts; or "A," *applied questions* that rely on the ability to apply a concept to a real-life situation).

1. The state legislature is proposing a law that would not allow adolescents to drive until they are 18. Based on the research regarding adolescent driving: (p. 456; A)
    a. This idea is sound because adolescents under 18 are more likely than any other age group to die in car accidents.
    b. This idea has some merit because adolescents who are 16 are more likely than any other age group to die in car accidents; perhaps a "graduated" license should be considered to allow students younger than 18 some experience under controlled conditions.
    c. This idea is without merit because adolescents are not more likely to die in car crashes than people of other ages.
    d. This idea should only be considered if people over 60 can't drive either.

2. Which of the following statements regarding homicides is **FALSE**? (p. 456; F)
    a. The most common murder weapon is a gun.
    b. Homicides are twice as likely to occur in rural areas than in urban areas.
    c. Males are much more likely to be murdered than females.
    d. Young African-Americans are more likely to be murdered than any other group and are more likely to be killed by other African-Americans.

3. Which group has the **LOWEST** suicide risk: (p. 457; F)
    a. African Americans   b. Native Americans   c. Hispanics   d. males

4. Sexually transmitted diseases: (p. 458; F)
    a. are transmitted only through sexual contact.
    b. rarely damage the reproductive system.
    c. are an epidemic in the United States and around the world.
    d. are rare in adolescence because most adolescents don't have more than one partner.

5. Brynn is like most adolescents, except for the fact that she has diabetes. If Brynn is like most teens with chronic diseases: (p. 461; A)
   a. Brynn may test limits and eat forbidden foods or take the wrong amount of insulin.
   b. Brynn will accept her chronic illness and follow the guidance provided by her parents and physician.
   c. the disease will affect Brynn's social life, but will have little impact on the family.
   d. the disease will have little affect on Brynn's social life, but major impact on the family.

6. Compared with boys, girls are more likely to: (p. 464; F)
   a. have more aerobic endurance.
   b. have more muscle strength.
   c. have more flexibility.
   d. exercise everyday or almost everyday.

7. _____ exercise is best for increasing mental health. (p. 466; F)
   a. Occasional   b. Moderate   c. Strenuous   d. Mental

8. Lyla wants to ask her parents for her own phone. She thinks about how her parents might react, what they might say, and reasons they might give her for why she shouldn't have one. Lyla did not do this before. Now she is showing evidence of: (p. 467; A)
   a. reversible thinking.   c. compensation.
   b. logical operations.   d. social cognition.

9. When it comes to social perspective taking, teens: (p. 468; F)
   a. are egocentric and unable to take the perspective of another at this age.
   b. are able to use social perspective taking skills fairly consistently.
   c. have difficulty holding both their own and an outside position simultaneously.
   d. may have the ability to understand another person's feelings but not necessarily the ability to solve the problem.

10. Mrs. Anderson wants to talk to her class of high school students about issues related to human welfare, fairness, and justice. Issues such as this are considered to be in the: (p. 469; A)
    a. social-conventional domain.   d. personal domain.
    b. moral domain.   d. spiritual domain.

11. Lief tells you about the new school he is in. He says that the school is small and that he and the other students are the ones who help make decisions about interactions at the school. He said that the students participate in meetings where they discuss what is fair for both students and teachers. You reply: (p. 470; A)
    a. "Oh, it sounds like you are involved in character education, which is designed to help you understand, commit to, and act on shared core moral values.
    b. "I see. It sounds like you are involved in a fad that has not been found to effectively advance students' moral reasoning skills.
    c. "Ah-ha! You are going to a just community school as developed by Kohlberg and his colleagues."
    d. "Hmmm...this school sounds like a social-conventional school designed to enhance moral development."

242 Study Guide for Exploring Child Development

12. When it comes to political and religious thinking: (p. 471; F)
    a. adolescents are more likely to obey authority figures without question because they can take the third party perspective.
    b. adolescent thinking becomes more absolute.
    c. adolescent thinking becomes less tolerant.
    d. adolescents may begin to question ideas taught to them during childhood.

13. You watch a couple of high school students playing a word game that requires participants to think of all the synonyms they can for a word. If research is correct, the most likely person to win this game is: (p. 472; A)
    a. Alicia, a 9th grade girl.
    b. Kim, a 10th grade boy.
    c. Tim, a 9th grade boy and music student.
    d. Gerald, a 9th grade boy and art student.

14. Boys are much better than girls at: (p. 472; F)
    a. finding figures hidden within other figures.
    b. associational fluency.
    c. imagining how object would appear if they were rotated.
    d. locating the horizontal or vertical while ignoring distracting visual information.

15. On math and science skills: (p. 473; F)
    a. the only skill that girls do better on are problem solving skills, probably due to the high verbal content.
    b. girls outperform boys in almost every type of math problem in the third grade.
    c. improved math performance in boys is seen in the United States but not in other countries.
    d. girls increase in confidence but decrease in mathematical performance throughout high school.

16. Which of the following explanations for gender differences in cognitive abilities is **FALSE**? (p. 474; F)
    a. Prenatal sex hormones affect the development and organization of the brain.
    b. Parents' beliefs about children's abilities in math and science have a greater impact on achievement and attitudes than do children's earlier performance in those subjects.
    c. Parental encouragement of hobbies and activities has little to do with academic performance.
    d. Teachers' judgments of what constitutes a "good" student are based more on gender-stereotyped attitudes and expectations than on how well students do in school.

17. Which of the following reasons is **LEAST LIKELY** to be given by a young male high school drop out? (p. 477; A)
    a. "I dropped out of school because I didn't get along with the teachers."
    b. "I dropped out of school because I was expelled."
    c. "I dropped out of school because I was fighting with other students."
    d. "I dropped out of school because I got married and had to support my wife."

18. Low achievement, low ability, and low interest in school appear to have roots in: (p. 477; F)
    a. elementary school.
    b. middle school.
    c. first two years of high school.
    d. transitions between school levels.

19. Which of the following is **NOT** related to dropping out of high school? (p. 478; F)
    a. low self-esteem
    b. culture
    c. ethnicity
    d. poverty

20. The principal at a local high school has decided to decrease the number of school dropouts. He suggests that: (p. 479; A)
    a. teachers and staff increase their expectations and standards for all students.
    b. classrooms become more structured, with an emphasis on basic skills.
    c. teachers be more objective and "professional" in their interactions with students.
    d. occupational training and job training be taken off campus so that students will focus on college preparation.

True/False Questions (If a statement is FALSE, correct it).

1. Accidents are the leading cause of death among adolescents. (p. 456) True/False.

2. Adolescents are more likely than adults to kill or assault strangers. (p. 456) True/False.

3. Adolescent boys attempt suicide more often than adolescent girls. (p. 457) True/False.

4. Sexually transmitted diseases are the most common diseases during adolescence. (p. 460) True/False.

5. The number of adolescents with chronic illnesses has decreased. (p. 461) True/False.

6. Adolescents who exercise are more likely to be healthy adults. (p. 464) True/False.

7. Adolescents are more likely than children to describe people in terms of global evaluations. (p. 467) True/False.

8. Teens are fairly consistent in using social perspective taking skills. (p. 468) True/False.

9. Effective moral education should focus on the moral and personal domains. (p. 469) True/False.

10. Strong evidence supports the use of character education in schools to improve adolescents' moral development. (p. 470) True/False.

11. Girls show higher levels of reading comprehension than boys. (p. 472) True/False.

12. Biology, family interactions, and gender bias in school may contribute to gender differences in academic achievement. (p. 476) True/False.

13. Boys are more likely to drop out of school because of social factors. (p. 478) True/False.

14. Poverty appears to have little impact on dropout rates. (p. 478) True/False.

15. Flexible instruction and skills training for job success may help decrease high school dropout rates. (p. 481) True/False.

☐ REWARD YOURSELF!   Rent your favorite childhood movie!

ANSWERS: Chapter 13 Physical and Cognitive Development in Late Adolescence

What are the Health and Safety Issues in Late Adolescence? (pp. 455 - 466)
(1) preventable;
(2) Driving is one of the riskiest activities for adolescents, with 16-year-olds more likely than any other age group to die in accidents, and the accident rate highest for Caucasian males.
(3) Most adolescent homicide victims and perpetrators are males, with certain groups more likely to be victims (such as African American males). Homicides are more likely to occur in big cities and involve guns.
(4) tripled; (5) Caucasian-American; (6) boys; (7) girls; (8) successful; (9) psychiatric problem, antisocial behavior, and substance abuse, belonging to a family with a history of suicide, experiencing high levels of stress; experiencing family problems or high levels of family conflict.
(10) sexually-transmitted diseases; (11) needles; (12) blood transfusions; (13) multiple sex partners, unprotected intercourse, high-risk partners; (14) homosexuals, drug users, homeless or runaway adolescents, African American and Hispanic adolescents; (15) sexually abused, selling sex for survival, being sexually active without using condoms, and abusing alcohol
(16) 14; (17) school; (18) activities; (19) increased; (20) test; (21) treatment; (22) increased; (23) healthy and well-adjusted; (24) family; (25) economic; (26) stress; (27) families; (28) aerobic endurance, muscle strength and endurance, muscle flexibility, body fat; (29) aerobic endurance – boys, muscle strength – boys, flexibility – girls, body fat – girls; (30) healthy; (31) social; (32) role; (33) ethical; (34) depressed; (35) stress; (36) self-esteem and self-concept
1 Minute Quiz: 1. Boys; 2. Multiple partners, high risk partners, unprotected intercourse; 3. False; 4. Moderate

What Changes Occur in Older Adolescents' Thinking and Reasoning? (pp. 466 – 472)
(37) social cognition; (38) impressions; (39) becoming more differentiated in their impressions; become more abstract in their impressions, basing impression more on indirect evidence and information supplied by others, and providing justifications for impressions
(40) social perspective taking; (41) 10 and 15; (42) third; (43) consistently; (44) character; (45) the moral domain, the social-conventional domain, and the personal domain; (46) personal domain; (47) moral domain; (48) social-conventional domain; (49) just community schools and character education; (50) A just community school provides students with opportunities to interact in a democratic community with decisions made through consensus rather than majority rule. The schools are small in size, providing a sense of belonging, and teachers take leadership roles in discussions to establish norms of fairness for all community members.
(51) combination; (52) religion and politics

What Gender Differences are Found in Adolescents' Cognitive Abilities and Achievement? (pp. 472 – 476)
(53) Gender differences in verbal skills are relatively small; however, females are much better than males in certain verbal skills. Females are much better than males at associational fluency (synonyms).
(54) Boys and girls differ least in spatial visualization but differ most in mental rotation skills.
(55) Boys begin to outperform girls on mathematical problem solving skills early in adolescence, and are much better than girls in high math ability. Girls lack confidence in math and science skills, contributing to their lower performance. Female participation in math and science careers is low.
(56) Biology – hormones may affect brain development and organization; untangling the effects of hormone and environment is difficult but some causal links between hormones and cognitive abilities have been suggested.
(57) Family – Parents' expectations can influence adolescent expectations which can affect academic performance. Parents can also influence adolescent academic performance through activities they provide and encourage.
(58) School gender bias – Teachers hold different expectations for boys and girls and this influences academic performance; teachers also treat boys and girls differently. Guidance students receive at school may also be affected by gender stereotypes.
1 Minute Quiz: 1. Social cognition; 2. Adolescents; 3. D; 4. C

What Factors Contribute to Dropping Out of School? (pp. 476 – 480)
(59) attitudes about school and academic performance; (60) low achievement, low ability, and low interest in school; (61) social factors that limit their choices; (62) behavior problems or being expelled; (63) relate to dropout rates, with minorities more likely to drop out; (64) are eight times more likely to drop out and the poorest families represent over 40 percent of all dropouts; (65) are significantly related to dropping out; for example, Hispanic immigrants are much more likely to drop out than Hispanic youths born in the U.S. (66) economic and social
(67) I would utilize a systems approach to this problem and involve families, peers and the community. Local business could be enlisted to sponsor schools and classrooms and provide mentoring and tutoring. Parents

would be encouraged to become actively involved in the schools beginning in Kindergarten and going all the way through high school. Students not doing well in school would be identified and provided extra help and enrichment activities after school, on weekends, and throughout the summer if needed. High standards would be set and students would be made aware of the standards and given the support necessary to reach those standards. Teachers would be rewarded for innovative programs, and classrooms would be flexible to meet the needs of individual students. Teachers would be encouraged to develop warm and caring relationships with their students and this would be helped through small classrooms and small schools. A variety of education possibilities would be available to students, including vocational training so that those students who do not want to go to college would leave high school prepared to get a job in a field of interest.

STUDY QUESTIONS

Multiple Choice: 1. B; 2. B; 3. A; 4. C; 5. A; 6. C; 7. B; 8. D; 9. D; 10. B; 11. C; 12. D; 13. A; 14. C; 15. B; 16. C; 17. D; 18. A; 19. A; 20. A

True/False Questions:
1. True
2. True
3. False; Adolescent girls
4. True
5. False; increased
6. True
7. False; Children are more likely than adolescents
8. False; inconsistent
9. False; moral and social-conventional domains
10. False; Limited evidence
11. True
12. True
13. False; Girls
14. False; has major impact
15. True

Chapter 14
Social and Emotional Development In Late Adolescence

My mother taught me about JUSTICE...
"One day, you will have kids, and I hope they turn out just like YOU...then you'll see what it's like!"
- Things My Mother Taught Me

Objectives
When you have completed this chapter, you will be able to:
- identify the dimensions of autonomy given real-life examples and state factors that contribute to the development of autonomy;
- summarize how sexuality changes during late adolescence;
- discuss teen pregnancy and its affect on the adolescent, the family, and the community;
- describe types of sex education for adolescents and program effectiveness;
- discuss issues related to gay and lesbian youth;
- describe common behavior problems of late adolescence, including antisocial behavior, depression, substance use and abuse;
- discuss employment in adolescence, citing both positive and negative effects;
- state factors that influence adolescents' vulnerability and resiliency; and
- define the key terms and concepts listed on page 511 of your text.

☑ Study Check List

☐ Read Chapter 14 Social and Emotional Development in Late Adolescence

☐ Re-read the Chapter 14 Summary to refresh your memory.

☐ Read the Chapter 14 Objectives listed above.

☐ Complete the following items:

How Do Older Adolescents Develop Autonomy? (pp. 483 - 485)

As adolescents become more independent and self-governing, they are said to be developing

a_____(1). Adolescents become independent in three major areas:

248 Study Guide for Exploring Child Development

(a)_____, (b)_____,

and (c) _____(2).

LESSONS IN REAL LIFE - LESSONS IN REAL LIFE - LESSONS IN REAL LIFE - LESSONS IN REAL LIFE

Identify the type of autonomy displayed in each of the following examples:

Cody is 15 years old and has started keeping his own checkbook on an account into which his parents provide a monthly deposit. He is responsible for purchasing his own clothes, school supplies, and entertainment expenses. Occasionally, his parents disagree with his managing of the account and his financial priorities. Cody is demonstrating _____(3).

Eighteen-year-old Sharon is pleased that she has the opportunity to vote in the next election. She has studied the issues and weighed the various political parties. Sharon's mother is a Democrat, and Sharon's father is a Republican. Sharon has decided that she agrees most strongly with the Libertarian perspective. Sharon is demonstrating _____(4).

Patty is 17 years old. One day, her mother mentioned that she did not like a particular singer that Patty adores. Patty thought about what her mother had said and was a bit surprised that her mother's disapproval didn't bother Patty. In the past, such disapproval would have caused Patty to break down into tears and brood for hours. In fact, Patty thought that it had been a long time since she cried over something like that. It is apparent that Patty is developing _____(5).

LESSONS IN REAL LIFE - LESSONS IN REAL LIFE - LESSONS IN REAL LIFE - LESSONS IN REAL LIFE

Scan the section "Factors that Contribute to Adolescent Autonomy" on pages 484 to 485, and identify four factors that contribute to adolescent autonomy: (6)

1. _____
2. _____
3. _____
4. _____

How Does Sexuality Change During Late Adolescent? (pp. 485 – 496)

Most adolescents begin having sex during their l_____(7) teens, and the likelihood of being sexually active **increases/decreases** *(circle one)* (8) with age. The majority of adolescents, however, have **few/many** *(circle one)* (9) sex partners during adolescence. Several factors associated with adolescent

Chapter 14 Social and Emotional Development in Late Adolescence 249

sexual activity have been identified. Early and frequent sex if more likely if teens have l_____(10) occupational and education aspirations, perform p_____(11) in school, and live in d_____(12) communities.

What roles do:

- *family relationships play in adolescent sexual attitudes and behaviors?* (13)

  _____
  _____
  _____

- *peers play in adolescent sexual attitudes and behaviors?* (14)

  _____
  _____
  _____

- *partners play in adolescent sexual attitudes and behaviors?* (15)

  _____
  _____
  _____

- *social-psychological context play in adolescent sexual attitudes and behaviors?* (16)

  _____
  _____
  _____

Compared with their peers in other countries, American teenagers are **more/less** *(circle one)* (17) likely to use contraceptives. The use of contraceptives and the type of contraceptives chosen vary with a_____(18).

250 Study Guide for Exploring Child Development

The most common reason adolescents give for not using condoms is *(circle)*: (19)

"I forgot them."
"I got carried away in the heat of the moment.'"
"They take away from the pleasure of sex."
"I didn't think I would get pregnant."
"If you're meant to get pregnant, you're going to get pregnant anyway."

What five steps must adolescents go through to use contraception successfully? (20)

1. _____
2. _____
3. _____
4. _____
5. _____

Who is more likely to be sexually abstinent? (21) (a) Boys/girls *(circle)* (b) younger/older teens *(circle)*

The United States has the **highest/lowest** *(circle one)* (22) teen pregnancy rate among developed nations. Racial and ethnic differences are quite apparent with A_____ and H_____ (23) teens more likely to get pregnant than Caucasian Americans. This difference may be because of differences in cultural mo_____ , at_____, and ex_____ (24) about pregnancy and parenthood.

About _____ (25) of all teen pregnancies end in the actual birth of a child. The remaining are lost through abortion, miscarriage, or stillbirth. Teens are **likely/not likely** *(circle one)* (26) to place their child from adoption. Repeat pregnancies are **common/uncommon** *(circle one)* (27) in adolescence.

What are the negative consequences of teen pregnancy on:

- *the mother?* (28)_____

_____

_____

- *the baby?* (29)_____

- *the community?* (30)_____

Compared to adults, teen parents are more likely to: (31)

1. _____
2. _____
3. _____
4. _____
5. _____

Sex education is the subject of stormy debate, with some advocates supporting programs that encourage ab_____(32) and other advocates supporting programs that include pro_____(33) against pregnancy and disease. Abstinence based programs **have/have not** *(circle one)* (34) been found to reduce adolescent sexual behavior or prevent nonmarital pregnancy.

Effective comprehensive sex education programs include the following: (35)

1. _____
2. _____
3. _____
4. _____
5. _____
6. _____

252 Study Guide for Exploring Child Development

These programs are most effective if presented **before/after** *(circle one)* (36) teens become sexually active. Such programs **have/have not** *(circle one)* (37) been found to increase sexual activity, and **have/have not** *(circle one)* (38) been successful in helping young people postpone intercourse or use contraception.

During adolescence, sexual orientation may be quite ind_____(39) of sexual behavior. Many gay and lesbian youths are os_____(40) by their peers, and some young people endure great st_____(41) because of this. Supportive f_____(42) can help buffer gay and lesbian youths from the stress they face. Although gay and lesbian youths have difficulties, most appear to a_____(43) well and emerge from adolescence with p_____(44) views of themselves, their lives, and their futures.

---

1 Minute Quiz

1. The ability to understand oneself as a person, emotionally distinct from one's parents, is referred to as _____ autonomy.

2. Greater autonomy results when parents are:
   a. distant but supportive.   c. authoritarian.
   b. warm and nurturing.   d. well-educated.

3. Today, boys and girls are about equally as likely to experience sexual intercourse during adolescence. True/False.

4. The most common reason given by adolescents for not using a contraceptive is _____.

5. Sex education programs have been found to increase sexual activity among adolescents. True/False.

Chapter 14 Social and Emotional Development in Late Adolescence 253

What Types of Behavior Problems Occur During Late Adolescence? (pp. 496 – 505)

Match the following:

____ Psychological difficulties in which people act
(45) out against society

a. antisocial behavior

____ Psychological difficulties in which people focus
(46) on or within themselves

b. alcohol

____ Experimenting with drugs, having sex early in
(47) adolescence, delinquent acts, reckless driving

c. externalizing problems

____ Behavior that conflicts with the norms of society
(48)

d. risk-taking behaviors

____ Acts that are illegal for juveniles but not adults
(49)

e. marijuana

____ Symptoms include fatigue, social withdrawal,
(50) apathy, poor school performance

f. status offenses

____ The most commonly used and abused substance
(51)

g. internalizing problems

h. depression

What conclusions about juvenile crime and delinquency have been reached based on available research? (52)

1. _____

2. _____

3. _____

4. _____

5. _____

Most parents **do/do not** *(circle one)* (53) give their teenagers a clear message about not using alcohol.

At this point in time, there is no known "s_____ d_____" (54) of alcohol for adolescents.

Alcohol use may have serious and unpredictable consequences for adolescents because of their low i_____(55) control, em_____(56) volatility, lack of a sense of li_____(57), and feelings of in_____(58).

Your textbook lists several factors associated with tobacco use during adolescence. *What are three of those factors?* (59)

1. _____
2. _____
3. _____

Regular use of illegal drugs other than marijuana is **rare/common** *(circle one)* (60) among adolescents. However, marijuana use among adolescents has **increased/decreased** *(circle one)* (61) since 1990. Many teens believe that marijuana **is/is not** *(circle one)* (62) harmful to their health. The percentage of parents who talk to their children about drugs has **decreased/increased** *(circle one)* (63). The adolescent's relationship with his or her **parents/peers** *(circle one)* (64) plays an important role in adolescents not using drugs, as does the degree to which parents mon_____(65) their children and provide in_____(66) about the physical and moral consequences of using drugs.

---

1 Minute Quiz

1. **Substance abuse is an example of an <u>internalizing/externalizing</u> *(circle one)* problem.**

2. **Which of the following offenses is a status offense?**
   a. shoplifting   c. assault
   b. running away   d. threatening and intimidating

3. **The most commonly used and abused substance is _____.**

4. **Most drug use by adolescents leads to long term problems. True/False.**

Chapter 14 Social and Emotional Development in Late Adolescence 255

How Does Employment Affect Older Adolescents? (pp. 476 – 480)

LESSONS IN REAL LIFE - LESSONS IN REAL LIFE - LESSONS IN REAL LIFE - LESSONS IN REAL LIFE

Your best friend is concerned about his 16-year-old son. He makes mostly Bs and Cs in school and, as he puts it, "just seems a bit lost." Your friend tells you that he thinks a good remedy for this is a job. "When I was young," he says. "I managed to work my father's dairy and go to school at the same time. It taught me responsibility, the value of a dollar, and kept me out of trouble. I think this is just the thing for my son. What do you think?" Based on the information in your text, you reply: (67)

_____

_____

_____

_____

_____

_____

_____

_____

_____

What Factors Influence Adolescents' Vulnerability and Resiliency? (pp. 506 – 510)

Use these words to complete the following paragraphs:

protect	early	relationships	behavior	most	relationships
earlier	adolescence	growth	childhood	severe	personal
middle	beneficial	peers	parents	school	

Relatively few adolescents have _____ (68) and adjustment problems, and many problems they do have during adolescence have roots in _____ (69) development.

Behavior problems that persist from _____ (70) tend to be more _____ (71) and have different causes than problems that arise during adolescence.

A classic study on coping found that _____ (72) qualities (such as temperament) strongly influence outcomes _____(73) in development; and _____(74) and cognitive factors are keys to adjustment during _____(75) childhood; and the ability to develop interpersonal _____(76) is important to adjustment during _____(77).

For _____(78) teens, the demands of adolescence bring opportunities for _____(79). Making friends, learning in school, and accepting new responsibilities can be _____(80) to most adolescents. To face the stress of these new challenges, adolescents can draw on the warm supportive _____(81) with _____(82) and _____(83) which can _____(84) adolescents and turn challenge into opportunity for growth toward adulthood.

---

1 Minute Quiz

1. The "magic number" of hours per week that students should not work over is _____.

2. Many problems that arise during adolescence have their roots in _____ development.

3. Most teens meet the challenges of adolescence and grow up to become healthy adults. True/False.

☐ Complete the crossword puzzle in Appendix 1 – Crossword Puzzles.

☐ Go to the beginning of this chapter, and on a separate sheet of paper, write out the answers to the lesson objectives.

SAGE Advice

"Form a study group. It's amazing how many people can find things you may have missed but need to know."

STUDY QUESTIONS

Multiple Choice (The following questions are identified "F," *factual questions* that rely on the recall of facts; or "A," *applied questions* that rely on the ability to apply a concept to a real-life situation).

1. Stella picks her own clothes to wear and goes to the school activities she chooses. Stella is showing: (p. 484; A)
   a. value autonomy.   b. emotional autonomy.   c. behavioral autonomy.   d. individual autonomy.

2. Reuben's family is Roman Catholic. For part of his adolescence, he began questioning his Roman Catholic beliefs and even questioned the existence of God. However, after some personal soul searching, he has embraced the Catholic religion and is considering entering the priesthood. Reuben is showing: (p. 485; A)
   a. value autonomy.   b. emotional autonomy.   c. behavioral autonomy.   d. individual autonomy.

3. Which of the following factors does **NOT** contribute to adolescent autonomy? (p. 485; F)
   a. acquiring the physical characteristics of adulthood
   b. cognitive development
   c. participation in diverse activities
   d. parents who are not nurturing

4. Which of the following statements is **TRUE**? (p. 486; F)
   a. Adolescents today are generally less accepting of sexual involvement before marriage.
   b. Most adolescents begin having sex in their early teens.
   c. The percentages of girls and boys who are sexually active are about the same.
   d. Adolescents tend to be promiscuous.

5. Which teen is **MOST LIKELY** to become sexually active at an earlier age? (p. 487; A)
   a. Charles, whose parents are controlling and authoritarian.
   b. Winifred, whose parents use moderate levels of control.
   c. Kari, who is the same age as her 14-year-old boyfriend and whose parents monitor their whereabouts.
   d. Landis, whose parents talk to him about sex often and convey conservative values about sexuality.

6. Male sexual behavior tends to be: (p. 488; F)
   a. more dependent on intimate relationships.
   b. initially focused on conquest, peer status, and recreation.
   c. cautious.
   d. subject to guilt and anxiety, as well as pleasure.

7. The most common reasons adolescents give for not using condoms is: (p. 490; F)
   a. lack of availability of contraceptives
   b. fear that parents will find out.
   c. believing that pregnancy will not happen to them.
   d. embarrassment associated with buying contraceptives.

8. Alexis is 15 years old and pregnant. What will be the most likely outcome? (p. 493; A)
   a. Alexis will have a miscarriage or stillbirth.
   b. Alexis will have an abortion.
   c. Alexis will have a baby and put it up for adoption.
   d. Alexis will have a baby and keep it.

9. Teen mothers are at greater risk of: (p. 493; F)
   a. dropping out of school.
   b. having health problems during pregnancy.
   c. having a baby with birth defects or impaired development.
   d. All of the above.

10. You observe two groups of parents. One group consists of parents in their mid-20s; the other group consists of teen parents. Which of the following are you **MORE LIKELY** to see in the teen parent group? (p. 494; A)
    a. knowledge about child development.
    b. calmness and anticipation about parenting
    c. less interaction with the infants
    d. positive exchanges with the infants

11. Which of the following is NOT part of an effective comprehensive sex education program for adolescents? (p. 495; A)
    a. practice in communication, negotiation and refusal skills
    b. activities that address social and media pressures related to sex
    c. general discussion based on teen pregnancy research findings
    d. basic information about methods of avoiding unprotected intercourse

12. Homosexual youth tend to: (p. 496; F)
    a. adapt well and emerge from adolescence with positive views of themselves.
    b. be more promiscuous than heterosexual youths.
    c. not be ostracized or rejected by peers.
    d. have mental problems.

13. An example of an externalizing problem is: (p. 497; A)
    a. depression.   b. truancy.   c. anorexia.   d. anxiety.

14. Which of the following boys committed a status offense? (p. 498; A)
    a. Dustin, who was arrested for assault in a gang fight.
    b. Graham, who was arrested for underage drinking.
    c. Clint, who was arrested for sexual abuse against a minor.
    d. Reed, who was arrested for stealing an expensive car.

15. Which of the following statements is **TRUE**? (p. 498; F)
    a. Younger adolescents are not becoming more violent as popular culture believes.
    b. Few delinquency cases are settled informally or dismissed; most cases result in formal probation or placement in a residential facility.
    c. Significant decreases have occurred in the tendency for adolescents to commit serious crimes, such as aggravated assault, homicide, and manslaughter.
    d. Ethnic differences in delinquency rates disappear or are greatly diminished once social class differences are taken into account.

16. Most teenagers: (p. 501; F)
    a. will engage in binge drinking during their high school years.
    b. will have some experience with alcohol and other drugs.
    c. have parents who actively attempt to dissuade them from drinking.
    d. can handle "safe doses" of alcohol.

17. A factor **NOT** associated with tobacco use during adolescence is: (p. 502; F)
    a. parental indifference.
    b. low academic achievement.
    c. easy access to tobacco.
    d. peers who don't smoke.

18. Daily use of stimulants, hallucinogens, inhalants, cocaine, or steroids among teenagers: (p. 503; F)
    a. is relatively high.
    b. is relatively low
    c. has decreased since the late 1980s.
    d. is greatest among Caucasian youth.

19. Your cousin's daughter just started a job at a local theater, working 30 hours per week during the school year. She asks your opinion, and you say, (p. 506; A)
    a. "As a result of this job, you daughter is less likely to learn about responsibility but more likely to use drugs and alcohol, do worse in school, and have less feelings of self-reliance."
    b. "This job will help your daughter learn about responsibility and self-reliance."
    c. "This job could be beneficial if you make sure that your daughter has control of her own money and can spend it the way she sees fit."
    d. "Can she get me into a movie for free?"

20. Watching a newscast on television, you hear the commentator lamenting about the increasing risks teenagers face today with drugs, sex, violence, and crime and fearing for the future of our country. You send him an e-mail titled: (p. 507; A)
    a. Teen Risks: Most Teens Won't Make It!
    b. Cheer Up! Most Teens Weather the Challenge and Become Healthy Adults!
    c. I Agree – Most Teens have Problems But Interventions are Available to Help Now!
    d. Teens are Better Off With *NO* Stress!

True/False Questions (If a statement is FALSE, correct it).

1. Constructive autonomy means being independent but still close to important others. (p. 483) True/False.

2. Greater autonomy results when parents are warm and nurturing. (p. 485) True/False.

3. Most adolescents are not promiscuous. (p. 486) True/False.

4. Parents who are too strict or too loose are more likely to have teens who engage in earlier and higher rates of sexual activity. (p. 488) True/False.

5. Today, girls are no more likely to feel guilty or anxious about sex than boys. (p. 489) True/False.

6. American adolescents are more likely to use contraception than their peers from other countries. (p. 489) True/False.

7. Most teen pregnancies end in abortion. (p. 493) True/False.

8. Teen mothers are more likely to interact with their babies than older mothers. (p. 494) True/False.

9. Sex education programs do not encourage sexual experimentation or increase sexual activity. (p. 495) True/False.

10. Sexual orientation and sexual behavior can be quite independent of each other. (p. 496) True/False.

11. Adolescents and young adults violate the law less often than older age groups. (p. 498) True/False.

12. Some depression may be related to hormonal activity in the brain and nervous system. (p. 500) True/False.

13. The proportion of teens who see smoking as dangerous has increased since 1993. (p. 502) True/False.

14. Adolescents who work are more likely to have behavior problems and use alcohol or drugs. (p. 506) True/False.

15. Most adolescents grow up to become healthy, well functioning adults. (p. 508) True/False.

☐ **REWARD YOURSELF!** Pat yourself on the back for a job well-done!

262 Study Guide for Exploring Child Development

ANSWERS: Chapter 14 Social and Emotional Development in Late Adolescence

How Do Older Adolescents Develop Autonomy? (pp. 483 - 485)
(1) autonomy; (2) value autonomy, emotional autonomy, and behavioral autonomy; (3) behavioral autonomy; (4) value autonomy; (5) emotional autonomy
(6) 1. Adolescent's changing bodies results in people treating them more as adults and leads adolescents to believe they are mature enough for greater autonomy. 2. Changes in adolescent thinking contribute to development of autonomy. 3. Nurturing and supportive parents contribute to developing autonomy. 4. Widening social circle and exposure to different values, viewpoints, etc., contribute to greater autonomy.

How Does Sexuality Change During Late Adolescent? (pp. 485 – 496)
(7) late; (8) increases; (9) few; (10) low; (11) poorly; (12) disadvantaged
(13) Parents talk (or don't talk) about sexual behavior and values and monitor and supervise young people. Parents who have close relationships with their kids and moderate levels of control have children who are more likely to postpone becoming sexually active. High and low levels of parental control lead to earlier and higher rates of teen sexual activity.
(14) Peers may have more influence than family on initial sexual experience and rate of sexual activity; peer norms legitimize sex and make it more acceptable; some teens feel pressured by peers to have sex.
(15) Some teens feel pressured by partners to have sex; adolescent females tend to have sex with older males
(16) Sex is more than just hormones; social meaning is important. Sexual activity is socially scripted and is scripted differently for males than females. Boys initially experience sex in terms of sexual conquest, peer status, and recreation; girls experience sex in terms of intimacy and relationship issues. Girls more likely to feel guilty and anxious.
(17) less; (18) age; (19) circle "I didn't think I would get pregnant."
(20) acquire, process, and retain contraceptive information; acknowledge the likelihood of sexual intercourse; obtain contraception; communicate contraceptive issues with one's partner; use contraception correctly.
(21) Circle "boys" and "younger teens"
(22) highest; (23) African American and Hispanic; (24) mores, attitudes, and expectations; (25) half; (26) not likely;
(27) common; (28) mothers likely to remain in poverty longer, have fewer educational and job opportunities; dropout, have health problems with the pregnancy; (29) more likely to be premature, have low birth weight, birth defects, cognitive deficiencies and impaired social-emotional development; lower educational levels and less financial independence; more likely to become teen parents; (30) increased tax burden, crime, school and medical support to meet the demands listed.
(31) 1. lack knowledge about child development, 2. be anxious and frustrated about parenting, 3. have little interaction with their infants, 4. have negative exchanges with their children, 5. hold negative attitudes toward parenting.
(32) abstinence; (33) protection; (34) have not; (35) 1. Practice in communication, refusal skills, 2. Focus on reducing sexual behaviors that lead to unintended pregnancies or STDs, 3. Provide basic, accurate info about methods of avoiding unprotected intercourse, 4. Use a variety of teaching methods to personalize information, 5. Taught by trained teachers, 6. Include activities that address social and media pressures related to sex; (36) before; (37) have not; (38) have; (39) independent; (40) ostracized; (41) stress; (42) families; (43) adapt; (44) positive
1 Minute Quiz: 1. emotional; 2. D; 3. True; 4. not thinking they would get pregnant; 5. False

What Types of Behavior Problems Occur During Late Adolescence? (pp. 496 – 505)
(45) c; (46) g; (47) d; (48) a; (49) f; (50) h; (51) b
(52) 1. Relatively small percentage of offenders are responsible for disproportionately large percentage of offenses. 2. Significant increases have occurred in the tendency for adolescents to commit serious crimes. 3. Younger adolescents are becoming more violent. 4. Ethnic difference exist in rates of delinquency but differences disappear when class is taken into account. 5. Most delinquency cases are settled informally or dismissed.
(53) do not; (54) "safe dose"; (55) impulse; (56) emotional; (57) limits; (58) invulnerability
(59) low socioeconomic status; easy access to tobacco; peers/siblings use tobacco; parental indifference; low academic achievement; low self-esteem; lack of knowledge of the health consequences of tobacco use
(60) rare; (61) increased; (62) is not; (63) decreased; (64) parents; (65) monitor; (66) information
1 Minute Quiz: 1. externalizing; 2. B; 3. alcohol; 4. False

How Does Employment Affect Older Adolescents? (pp. 476 – 480)
(67) Perhaps the father should rethink his position. Most jobs that teens hold teach very few skills that are able to carry over to adulthood. Young people who work are more likely to have behavior problems and use alcohol or drugs. They are also more likely to get into arguments with their parents, get inadequate sleep and exercise. School achievement also suffers when adolescents work. There appears to be a causal relationship with these problems being caused by working. Teens who work

and keep the money for themselves tend to spend the money on non-essential items, giving a false impression about the value of money because they are not paying for essentials. The critical number of hours is 20; if adolescents work less than 20 hours per week then it is less likely that such negative outcomes will be observed.

What Factors Influence Adolescents' Vulnerability and Resiliency? (pp. 506 – 510)
(68) behavior; (69) earlier; (70) childhood; (71) severe: (72) personal; (73) early; (74) school; (75) middle; (76) relationships; (77) adolescence; (78) most; (79) growth; (80) beneficial; (81) relationships; (82) parents; (83) peers; (84) protect
1 Minute Quiz: 1. 20; 2. early; 3. True

STUDY QUESTIONS

Multiple Choice: 1. C; 2. A; 3. D; 4. C; 5. A; 6. B; 7. C; 8. D; 9. D; 10. C; 11. C; 12. A; 13. B; 14. B; 15. D; 16. B; 17. D; 18. B; 19. A; 20. B

True/False Questions:
1. True
2. True
3. True
4. True
5. False; more likely
6. False; less likely
7. False; live births that the mother keeps
8. False; less likely
9. True
10. True
11. False; more often than any age group
12. True
13. False; has decreased
14. True
15. True

Appendix 1

Crossword Puzzles

Chapter 1 - Introduction

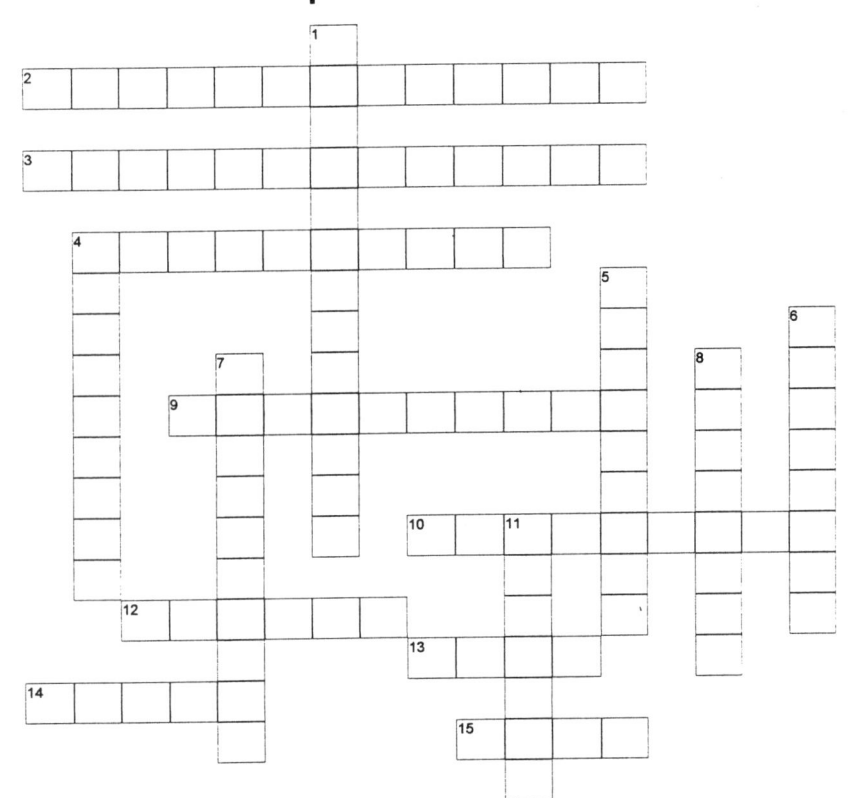

ACROSS

2. Process by which children learn roles and become members of a group
3. Complex interplay between the individual and the environment
4. Development is seen as gradual changes
9. Changes brought about as a result of one's genetic code
10. Periods that are optimal for development of certain functions
12. Changed view of child development with theory of evolution
13. First scientist to use questionnaires with children
14. Multiracial golfer
15. Group whose members share a genetic heritage

DOWN

1. Development is seen as occuring in steps or stages
4. Development that involves mental processes to process information
5. Group whose members share a common cultural heritage
6. Believed children are innately good
7. Locke's idea of a child's mind, blank slate
8. Periods during which events must occur if development is to proceed normally
11. Mom, Dad, and Kids

Chapter 1 - Introduction

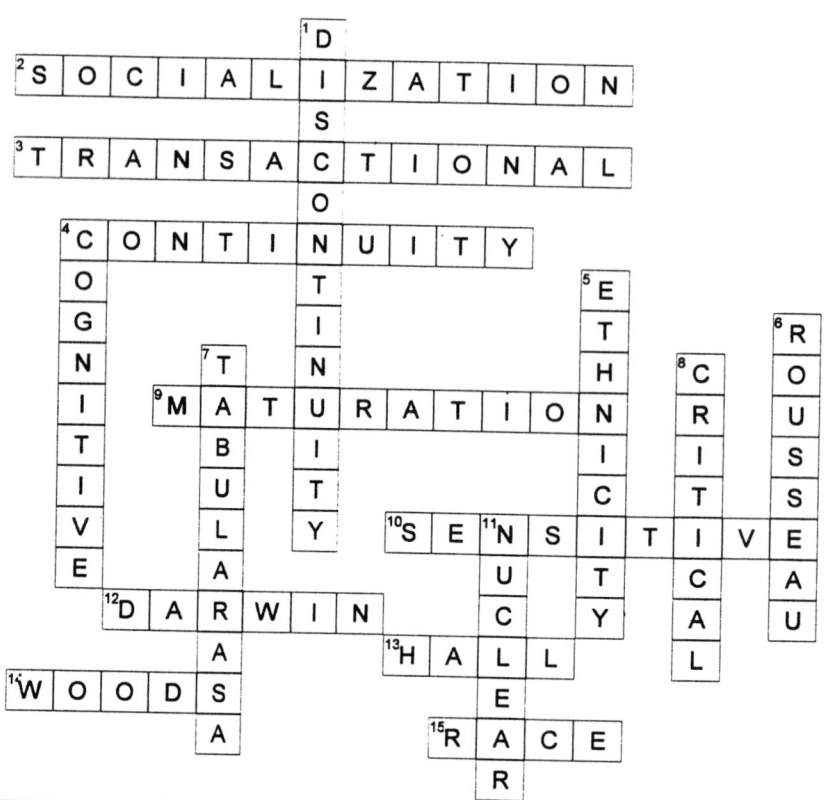

268 Study Guide for Exploring Child Development

ACROSS

2. Process by which children learn roles and become members of a group
3. Complex interplay between the individual and the environment
4. Development is seen as gradual changes
9. Changes brought about as a result of one's genetic code
10. Periods that are optimal for development of certain functions
12. Changed view of child development with theory of evolution
13. First scientist to use questionnaires with children
14. Multiracial golfer
15. Group whose members share a genetic heritage

DOWN

1. Development is seen as occuring in steps or stages
4. Development that involves mental processes to process information
5. Group whose members share a common cultural heritage
6. Believed children are innately good
7. Locke's idea of a child's mind, blank slate
8. Periods during which events must occur if development is to proceed normally
11. Mom, Dad, and Kids

Solved Puzzle

Across:
2. SOCIALIZATION
3. TRANSACTIONAL
4. CONTINUITY
9. MATURATION
10. SENSITIVE
12. DARWIN
13. HALL
14. WOODS
15. RACE

Down:
1. DISCONTINUITY
4. COGNITIVE
5. ETHNICITY
6. ROUSSEAU
7. TABULA
8. CRITICAL
11. NUCLEAR

Chapter 2 - Development

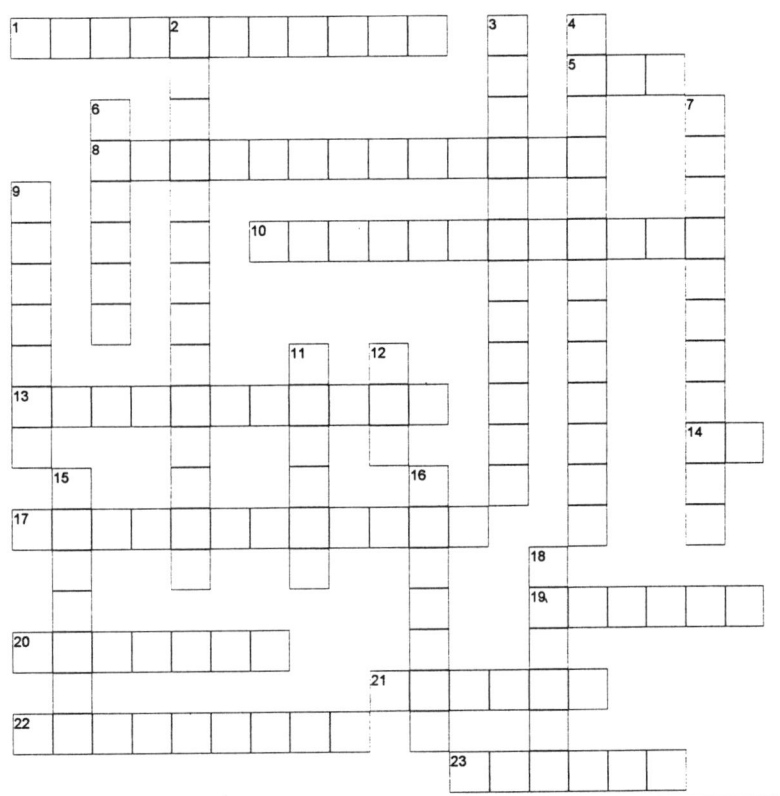

ACROSS

1. Variable that is manipulated by the scientist
5. Source of reason, uses reality principle
8. Changing a scheme to fit new information
10. Piaget's first stage of cognitive development
13. Theories that focus on how behaviors promote survival of the species
14. Primitive instinct
17. Assessing the same group of people over time
19. Group of individuals who are the same age or experience the same events at the same time
20. Expanded Freud's ideas
21. Critical periods in personality development
22. Conditioning that pairs conditioned stimulus with unconditioned stimulus
23. Structured set of ieas that attempts to organize and explain facts

DOWN

2. Theories that emphasize unconscious internal drives
3. Directly processing information that fits a scheme
4. Increases a behavior
6. Studied salivating dogs
7. Comparing participants on two variables to see how they relate
9. Research designed to solve practical problems
11. Source of action and sexual desire
12. Poor Albert's afraid of this!
15. This group wasn't manipulated
16. Social learning theory
18. A cognitive guide or blueprint for processing information about the world

Chapter 2 - Development

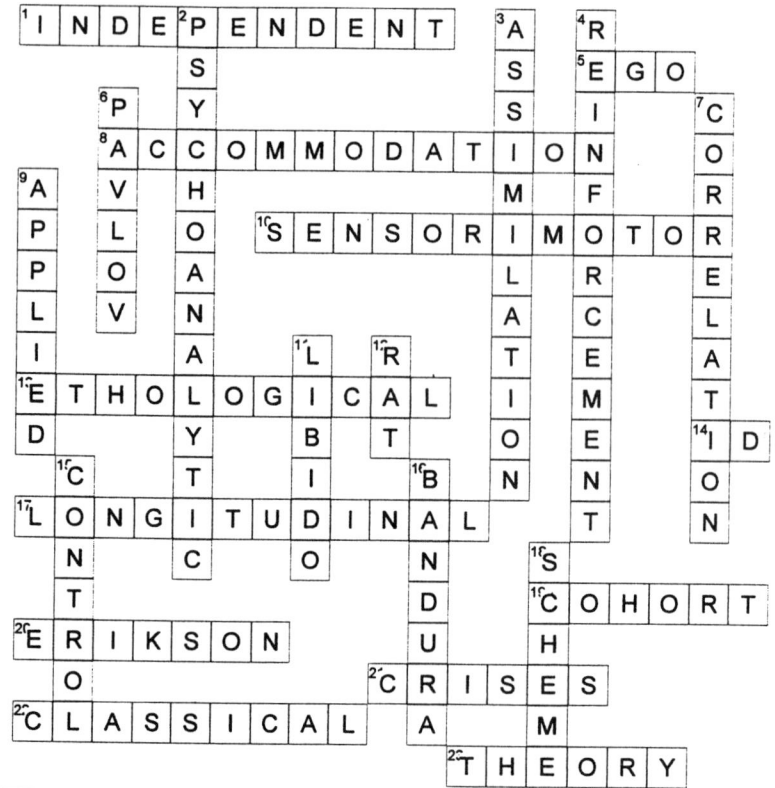

270 Study Guide for Exploring Child Development

Crossword Solution Grid

Across:
1. INDEPENDENT
5. EGO
8. ACCOMMODATION
10. SENSORIMOTOR
13. ETHOLOGICAL
14. ID
17. LONGITUDINAL
19. COHORT
20. ERIKSON
21. CRISES
22. CLASSICAL
23. THEORY

Down:
2. PSYCHOANALYTIC
3. ASSIMILATION
4. REINFORCEMENT
6. PAVLOV
7. CORRELATE
9. APPLIED
11. LIBIDO
12. RAT
15. CONTROL
16. BANDURA
18. SCHEMA

ACROSS

1. Variable that is manipulated by the scientist
5. Source of reason, uses reality principle
8. Changing a scheme to fit new information
10. Piaget's first stage of cognitive development
13. Theories that focus on how behaviors promote survival of the species
14. Primitive instinct
17. Assessing the same group of people over time
19. Group of individuals who are the same age or experience the same events at the same time
20. Expanded Freud's ideas
21. Critical periods in personality development
22. Conditioning that pairs conditioned stimulus with unconditioned stimulus
23. Structured set of ieas that attempts to organize and explain facts

DOWN

2. Theories that emphasize unconscious internal drives
3. Directly processing information that fits a scheme
4. Increases a behavior
6. Studied salivating dogs
7. Comparing participants on two variables to see how they relate
9. Research designed to solve practical problems
11. Source of action and sexual desire
12. Poor Albert's afraid of this!
15. This group wasn't manipulated
16. Social learning theory
18. A cognitive guide or blueprint for processing information about the world

Chapter 3 - Genetics and Prenatal

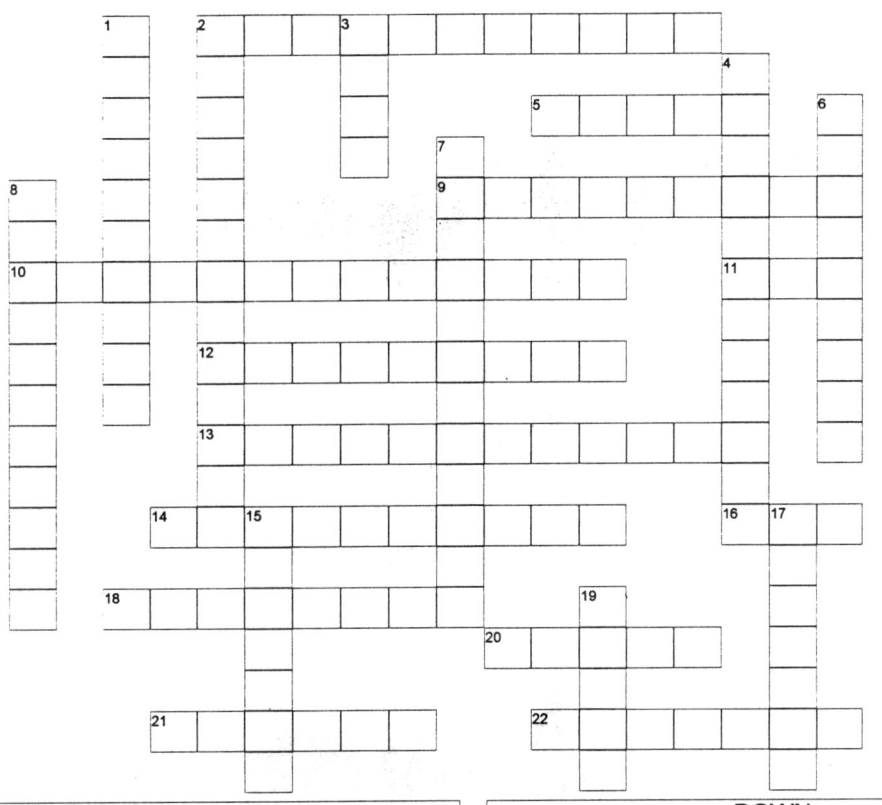

ACROSS

2. Structures on which genes reside
5. Stage from eight weeks until birth
9. Stage where environmental damage is most likely to occur
10. Procedure involving collection of amniotic fluid
11. Constellation of problems caused by mother drinking alcohol
12. First twenty-two pairs of chromosomes
13. Trisomy 21
14. Baby's first picture!
16. The twenty-third pair of chromosomes
18. People who are heterozygous for a recessive disorder
20. The only gamete that carries an X or a Y
21. Number and spacing of children
22. From 46 chromosomes to 23

DOWN

1. "I felt it!"
2. Big word you'll need to know for the test...head to tail
3. Bigger word for egg
4. XXY
6. Gene not expressed in the presence of a dominant gene
7. Bb
8. Drug taken during pregnancy that caused malformations of arms or legs
15. XO
17. Implantation in the fallopian tube
19. Structures containing the code that provides the blueprint for development

Chapter 3 - Genetics and Prenatal

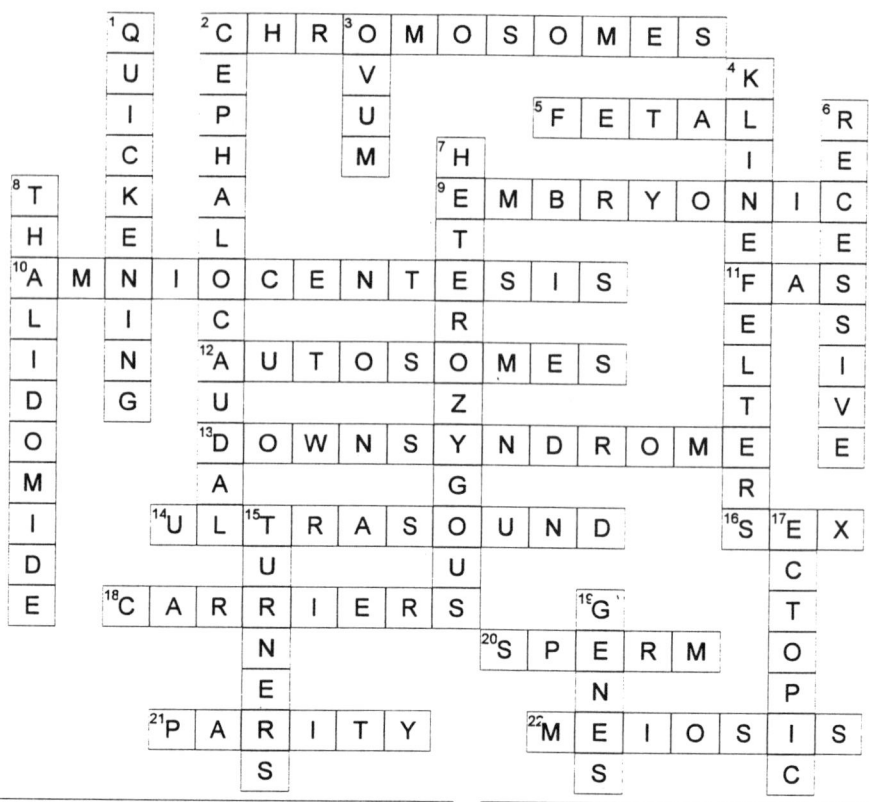

ACROSS

2. Structures on which genes reside
5. Stage from eight weeks until birth
9. Stage where environmental damage is most likely to occur
10. Procedure involving collection of amniotic fluid
11. Constellation of problems caused by mother drinking alcohol
12. First twenty-two pairs of chromosomes
13. Trisomy 21
14. Baby's first picture!
16. The twenty-third pair of chromosomes
18. People who are heterozygous for a recessive disorder
20. The only gamete that carries an X or a Y
21. Number and spacing of children
22. From 46 chromosomes to 23

DOWN

1. "I felt it!"
2. Big word you'll need to know for the test...head to tail
3. Bigger word for egg
4. XXY
6. Gene not expressed in the presence of a dominant gene
7. Bb
8. Drug taken during pregnancy that caused malformations of arms or legs
15. XO
17. Implantation in the fallopian tube
19. Structures containing the code that provides the blueprint for development

Chapter 4 - Birth and Neonatal

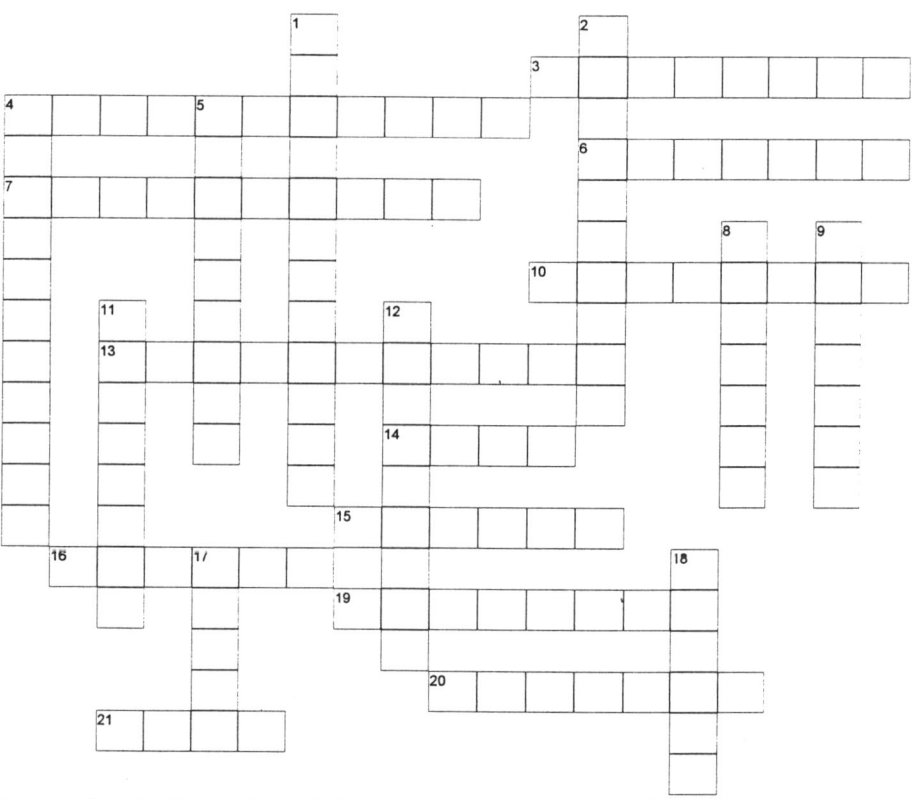

ACROSS

3. "I see its head!!"
4. Has previously given birth
6. Nerve cells that make up the communication system of the brain
7. Small incision to prevent tearing of vaginal tissues during birth
10. Simple, coordinated, unlearned responses
13. Having the first baby
14. Most common cause of unexpected death in infants
15. Upside down
16. Breathing and relaxation exercises to manage pain during childbirth
19. Toes spread and curl in response to stroking of sole
20. Medication given to start labor and delivery
21. Startle response

DOWN

1. Irregular contractions
2. Baby's shoulders and arms are leading the way
4. Smooth layers of fatty proteins cover the neurons
5. Babies are born with this ability for some facial expressions
8. Birth without violence
9. Another term for newborn
11. Feeling no pain
12. Fetus delivered through abdominal incision
17. Scale used to rate newborn in five areas
18. The least developed sense at birth

Chapter 4 - Birth and Neonatal

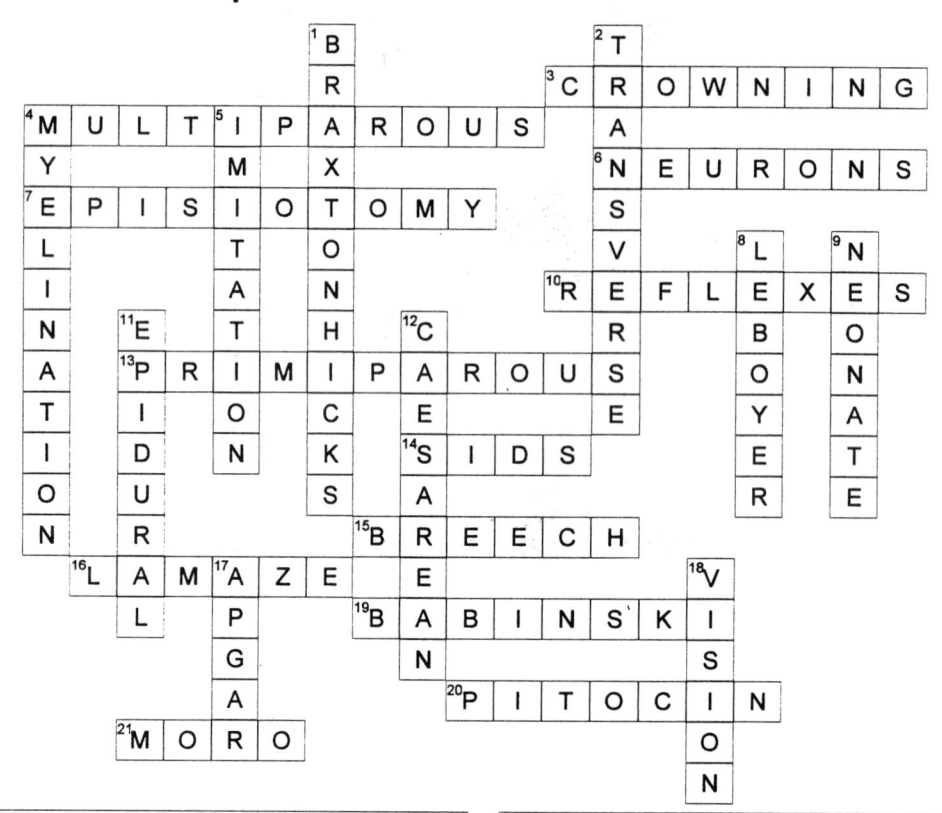

ACROSS
3. "I see its head!!"
4. Has previously given birth
6. Nerve cells that make up the communication system of the brain
7. Small incision to prevent tearing of vaginal tissues during birth
10. Simple, coordinated, unlearned responses
13. Having the first baby
14. Most common cause of unexpected death in infants
15. Upside down
16. Breathing and relaxation exercises to manage pain during childbirth
19. Toes spread and curl in response to stroking of sole
20. Medication given to start labor and delivery
21. Startle response

DOWN
1. Irregular contractions
2. Baby's shoulders and arms are leading the way
4. Smooth layers of fatty proteins cover the neurons
5. Babies are born with this ability for some facial expressions
8. Birth without violence
9. Another term for newborn
11. Feeling no pain
12. Fetus delivered through abdominal incision
17. Scale used to rate newborn in five areas
18. The least developed sense at birth

Chapter 5 - Infant and Toddler

Crossword Puzzles 275

ACROSS

2. "Mommy ball!"
7. Breast-fed babies are more likely to be this
8. Baby should see this person at least six times in the first year
9. Grammar or rules of language; word order
10. Informal teaching methods that guide children's participation in daily events
14. Best nutrition for baby
16. Moving around while holding onto things; Tom
17. "Look! Mikey is looking for the duck we hid. He has object _____!"
18. Children's understanding of language

DOWN

1. Piaget's first stage of cognitive development
3. Makes up 1/4 of baby's body size
4. Pre-milk substance containing antibodies to fight infection
5. An infant's favorite thing to look at
6. Decrease in attention to a stimulus that has been presented repeatedly
10. Word meaning
11. Practical rules guiding communication
12. Single words that mean entire sentences
13. Chomsky says we're born with this
15. Infants who do not grow at expected rates fail to _____

Chapter 5 - Infant and Toddler

276 Study Guide for Exploring Child Development

Crossword Solution Grid

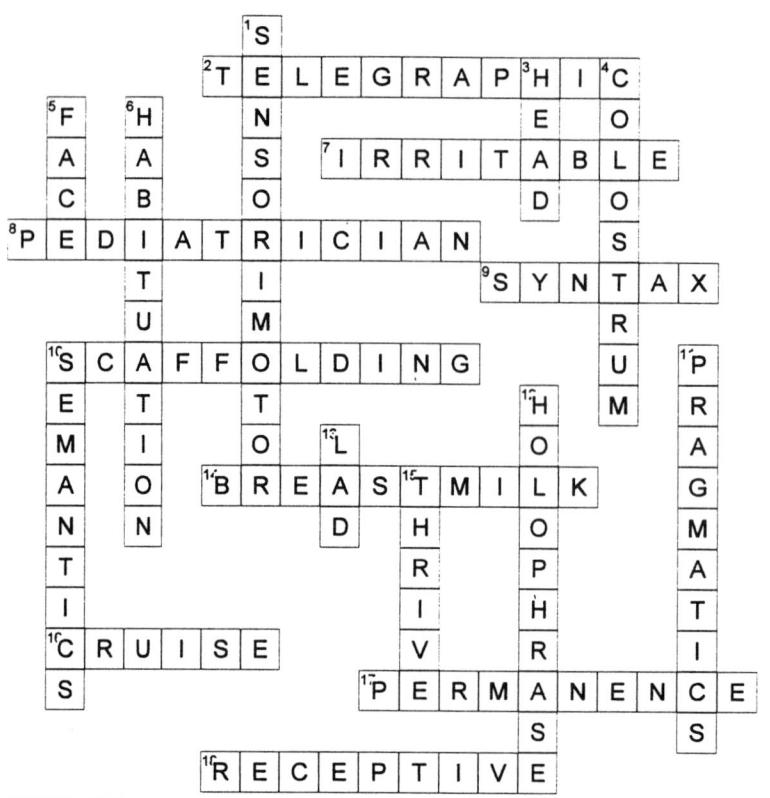

					¹S							
				²T	E	L	E	G	R	A	P	³H	I	⁴C
	⁵F		⁶H		N							E		O
	A		A		S		⁷I	R	R	I	T	A	B	L	E
	C		B		O							D		O
⁸P	E	D	I	A	T	R	I	C	I	A	N			S
			T		I					⁹S	Y	N	T	A	X
			U		M					R				
	¹⁰S	C	A	F	F	O	L	D	I	N	G		¹¹P
	E		T		T				¹²H		M		R
	M		I		O	¹³L		O				A
	A		O		¹⁴B	R	E	A	S	¹⁵T	M	I	L	K
	N		N			D		H		O			G
	T					R		O		P			M
	I					I		H				A
¹⁶C	R	U	I	S	E			V				T
	S					¹⁷P	E	R	M	A	N	E	N	C	E
								S				S
				¹⁸R	E	C	E	P	T	I	V	E

ACROSS

2. "Mommy ball!"
7. Breast-fed babies are more likely to be this
8. Baby should see this person at least six times in the first year
9. Grammar or rules of language; word order
10. Informal teaching methods that guide children's participation in daily events
14. Best nutrition for baby
16. Moving around while holding onto things; Tom _____
17. "Look! Mikey is looking for the duck we hid. He has object _____!"
18. Children's understanding of language

DOWN

1. Piaget's first stage of cognitive development
3. Makes up 1/4 of baby's body size
4. Pre-milk substance containing antibodies to fight infection
5. An infant's favorite thing to look at
6. Decrease in attention to a stimulus that has been presented repeatedly
10. Word meaning
11. Practical rules guiding communication
12. Single words that mean entire sentences
13. Chomsky says we're born with this
15. Infants who do not grow at expected rates fail to _____

Chapter 6 - Infant and Toddler

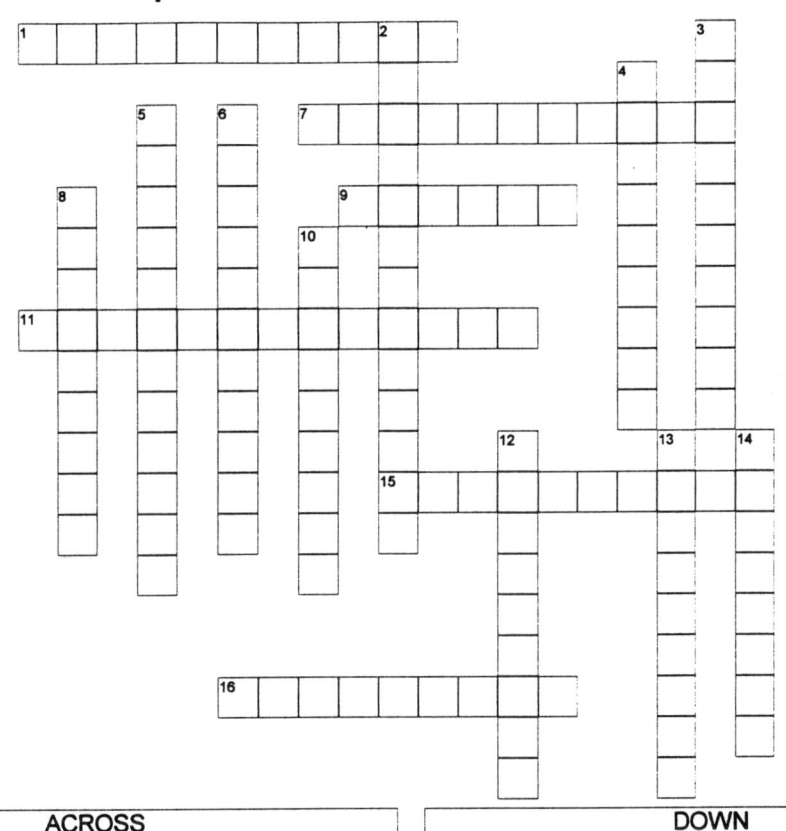

ACROSS

1. One component of temperament; regularity of basic functions
7. The predisposition to respond in certain enduring ways to the environment
9. Attachment pattern where child uses caregiver as secure base; happy when there, sad when not
11. Phase when infants do not discriminate in responses to caregivers
15. Attachment pattern characterized by inconsistent behavior toward caregiver
16. Smile triggered by external stimuli

DOWN

2. Type of tantrum
3. Enduring emotional tie to caregiver
4. What crying does after the first six weeks of life
5. One component of temperament; child adjusts to change
6. Caregivers need this to foster attachment
8. What crying does over the first six weeks of life
10. Prevention efforts that target high risk populations
12. Child with irregular schedule, slow to adapt, wary of people
13. The majority of infants with working mothers are cared for by these
14. Infant will be wary of this at around 7 months

Chapter 6 - Infant and Toddler

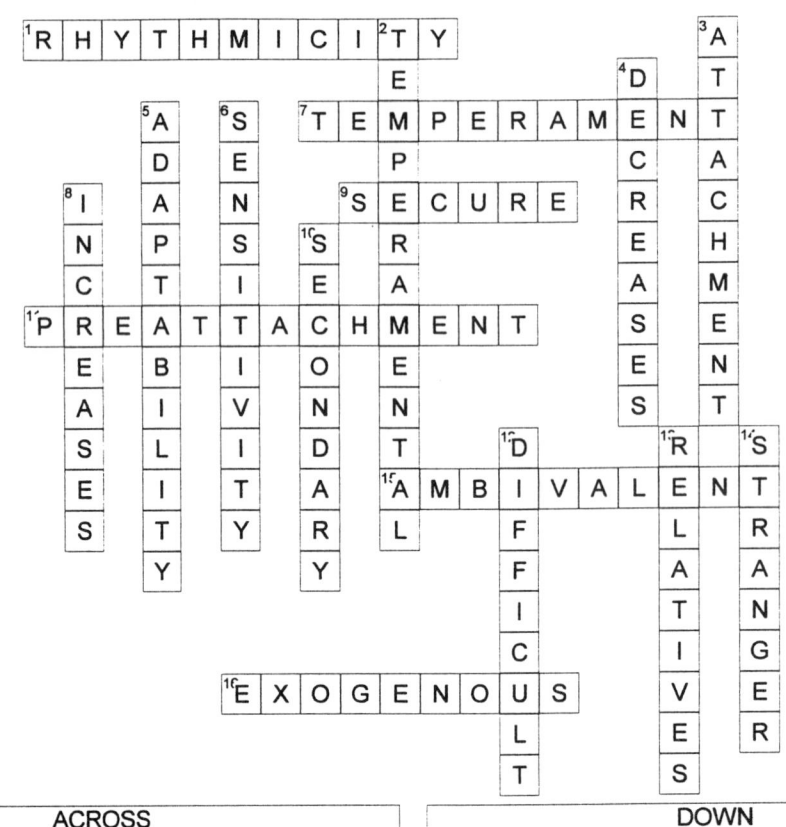

ACROSS

1. One component of temperament; regularity of basic functions
7. The predisposition to respond in certain enduring ways to the environment
9. Attachment pattern where child uses caregiver as secure base; happy when there, sad when not
11. Phase when infants do not discriminate in responses to caregivers
15. Attachment pattern characterized by inconsistent behavior toward caregiver
16. Smile triggered by external stimuli

DOWN

2. Type of tantrum
3. Enduring emotional tie to caregiver
4. What crying does after the first six weeks of life
5. One component of temperament; child adjusts to change
6. Caregivers need this to foster attachment
8. What crying does over the first six weeks of life
10. Prevention efforts that target high risk populations
12. Child with irregular schedule, slow to adapt, wary of people
13. The majority of infants with working mothers are cared for by these
14. Infant will be wary of this at around 7 months

Chapter 7 - Early Childhood

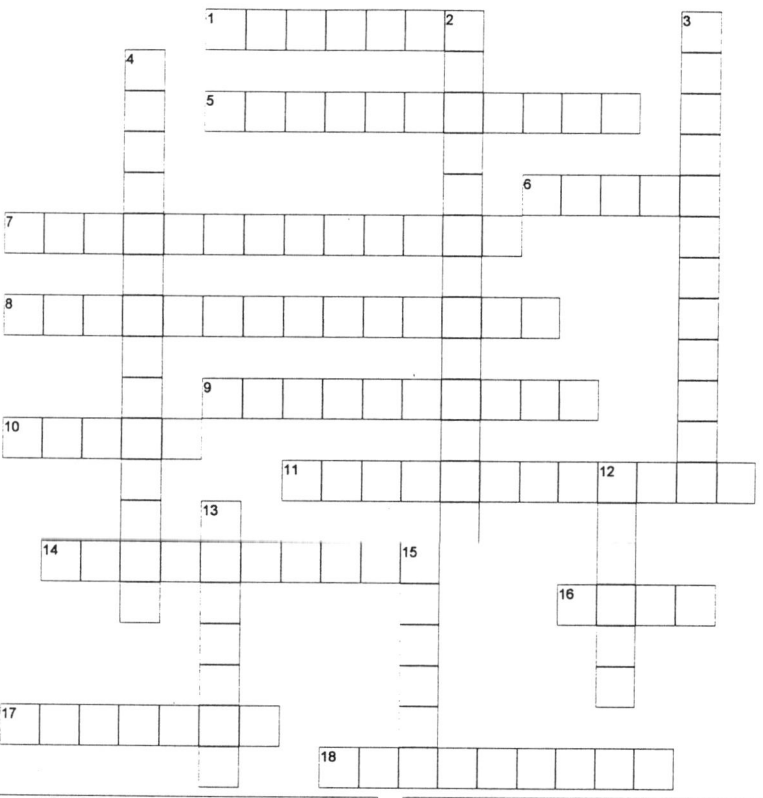

ACROSS

1. "Come on, car...you can make it!"
5. Assuming your perspective is shared by others
6. Motor skills that include skipping, running, and throwing
7. Using words to refer to things that are outside the bounds of the category named
8. Piaget's second stage of cognitive development
9. Tendency to focus attention on the most obvious characteristic of an object
10. Development of this reaches 75 to 90 percent adult size by age 5
11. Not receiving adequate proteins, vitamins, and minerals
14. Young children cannot apply these
16. Motor skills that include drawing, cutting, and buttoning
17. Vygotsky's term for speech used when solving problems
18. Leading cause of death in the preschool years

DOWN

2. Awareness of memory and monitoring of memory performance
3. Type of reasoning that infers causality because two events happened together
4. Not enough to eat
12. The context in which language learning occurs
13. Important teachers in children's lives
15. Thinking that focuses on the outcome, not changes that produced the outcome

Chapter 7 - Early Childhood

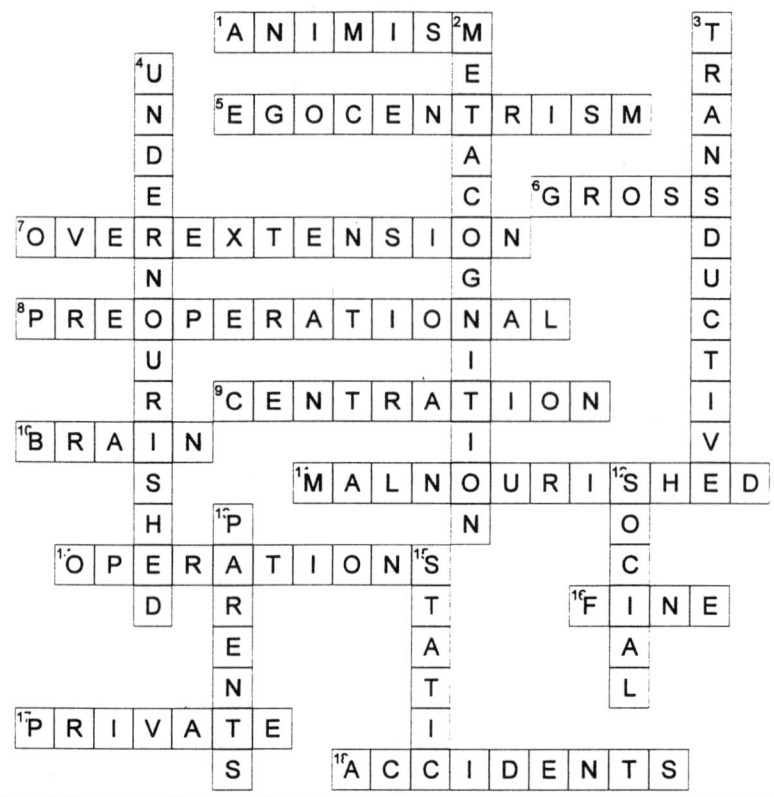

ACROSS

1. "Come on, car...you can make it!"
5. Assuming your perspective is shared by others
6. Motor skills that include skipping, running, and throwing
7. Using words to refer to things that are outside the bounds of the category named
8. Piaget's second stage of cognitive development
9. Tendency to focus attention on the most obvious characteristic of an object
10. Development of this reaches 75 to 90 percent adult size by age 5
11. Not receiving adequate proteins, vitamins, and minerals
14. Young children cannot apply these
16. Motor skills that include drawing, cutting, and buttoning
17. Vygotsky's term for speech used when solving problems
18. Leading cause of death in the preschool years

DOWN

2. Awareness of memory and monitoring of memory performance
3. Type of reasoning that infers causality because two events happened together
4. Not enough to eat
12. The context in which language learning occurs
13. Important teachers in children's lives
15. Thinking that focuses on the outcome, not changes that produced the outcome

Chapter 8 - Early Childhood

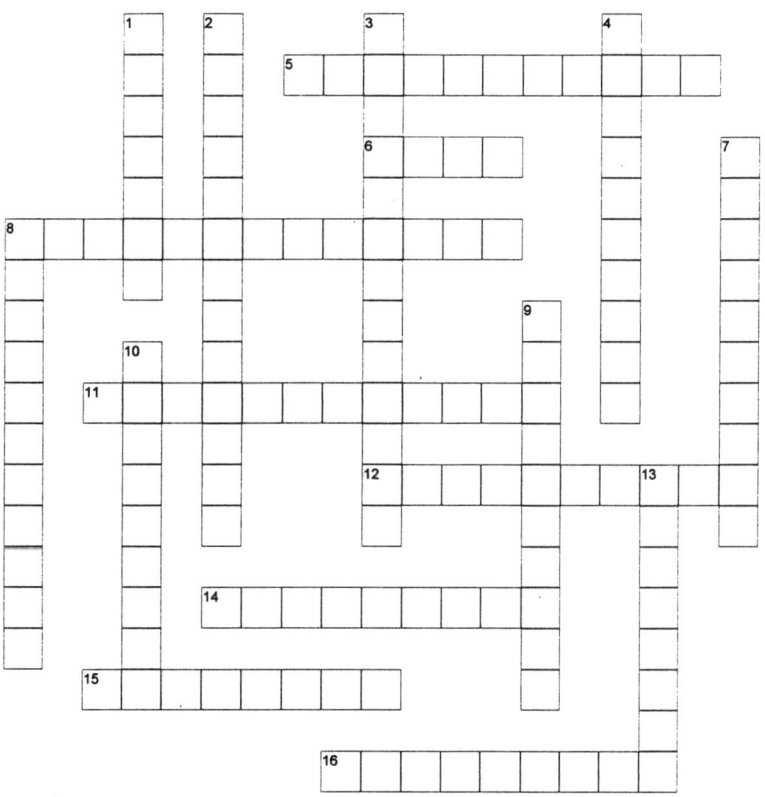

ACROSS

5. Beliefs people share about typical characteristics of certain groups
6. A girl would play with this
8. "If I say 'jump,' you ask, 'How high?'!!!"
11. Aggression used for a specific purpose
12. Research says television affects this
14. Type of self-esteem that occurs when there is a discrepancy between competence and worth
15. Play in which one child watches another but does not participate
16. Knowing that a boy grows up to be a man; gender _____

DOWN

1. An emotional state that matches another person's emotional state
2. These parents set limits but give reasons and listen to their kids
3. Mental representations about the sexes
4. Factor that predicts self-esteem
7. Attempts by parents to alter children's behaviors or attitudes
8. Play in which various children engage, but with different goals
9. The value an individual attaches to the mental picture of himself or herself
10. Discipline with reason
13. Understanding and accepting that one is a girl or a boy; gender _____

Chapter 8 - Early Childhood

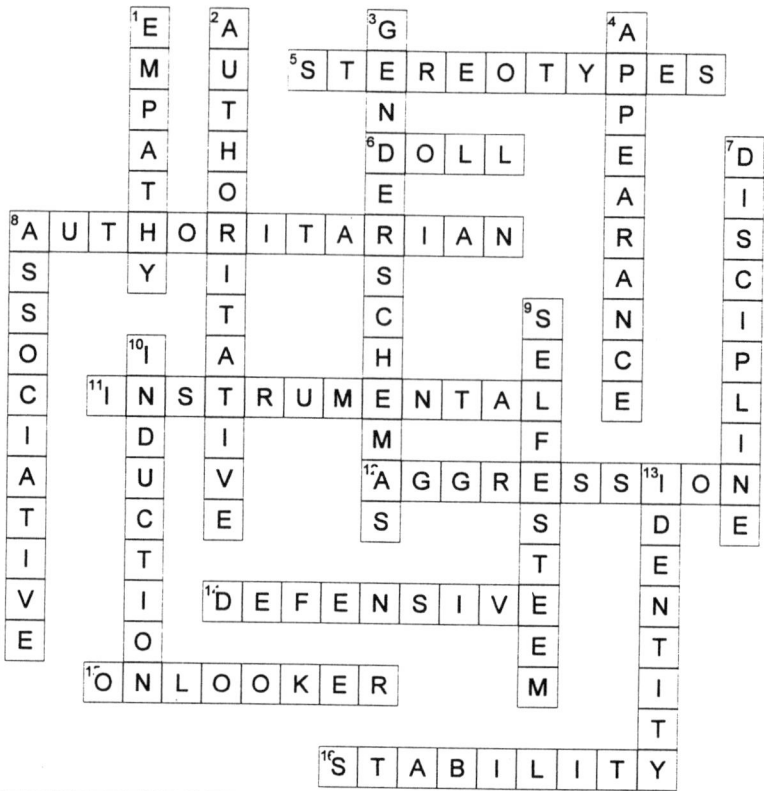

282 Study Guide for Exploring Child Development

ACROSS
5. Beliefs people share about typical characteristics of certain groups
6. A girl would play with this
8. "If I say 'jump,' you ask, 'How high?'!!!"
11. Aggression used for a specific purpose
12. Research says television affects this
14. Type of self-esteem that occurs when there is a discrepancy between competence and worth
15. Play in which one child watches another but does not participate
16. Knowing that a boy grows up to be a man; gender _____

DOWN
1. An emotional state that matches another person's emotional state
2. These parents set limits but give reasons and listen to their kids
3. Mental representations about the sexes
4. Factor that predicts self-esteem
7. Attempts by parents to alter children's behaviors or attitudes
8. Play in which various children engage, but with different goals
9. The value an individual attaches to the mental picture of himself or herself
10. Discipline with reason
13. Understanding and accepting that one is a girl or a boy; gender _____

Chapter 9 - Late Childhood

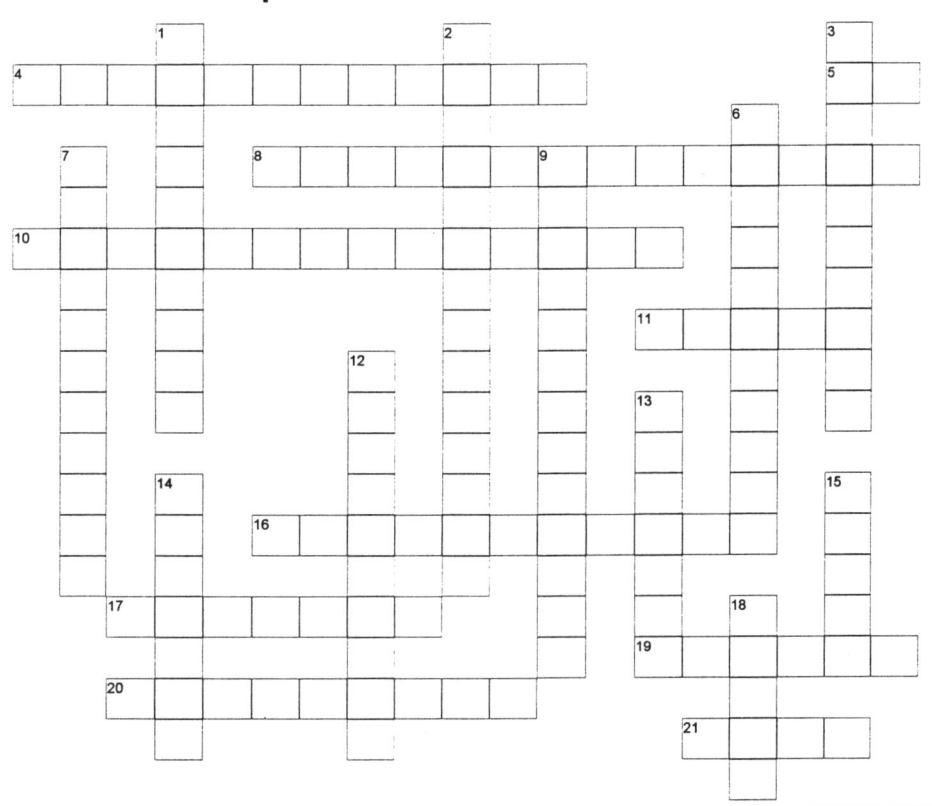

ACROSS

4. Programs that encourage children to move rapidly through coursework
5. Measure of intelligence
8. Component of intelligence that allows for monitoring task performance
10. Theories of learning in which students participate in their own education
11. Weighing more than 20 percent over one's ideal weight
16. Component of intelligence that involves encoding, interpreting, and retrieving info
17. People who show exceptional abilities in one area but are retarded in others
19. Growth rate compared to earlier childhood years
20. Learning where students discover principles for themselves
21. Popular test for measuring children's IQs

DOWN

1. Understanding that actions can be undone
2. Acting in an unfavorable manner toward people because of their group affiliation
3. Children have outstanding abilities and special needs to address those abilities
6. What older children are able to take from another
7. Learning occurs in groups
9. Putting children with special needs in a regular classroom
12. Learning where students are taught methods to integrate new info with pre-existing info
13. Children learn to read translating letters and groups of letters into sounds
14. Popular medication for hyperactive children
15. _____ language assumes that learning to read is natural
18. According to Piaget, school-aged kids can use this

Chapter 9 - Late Childhood

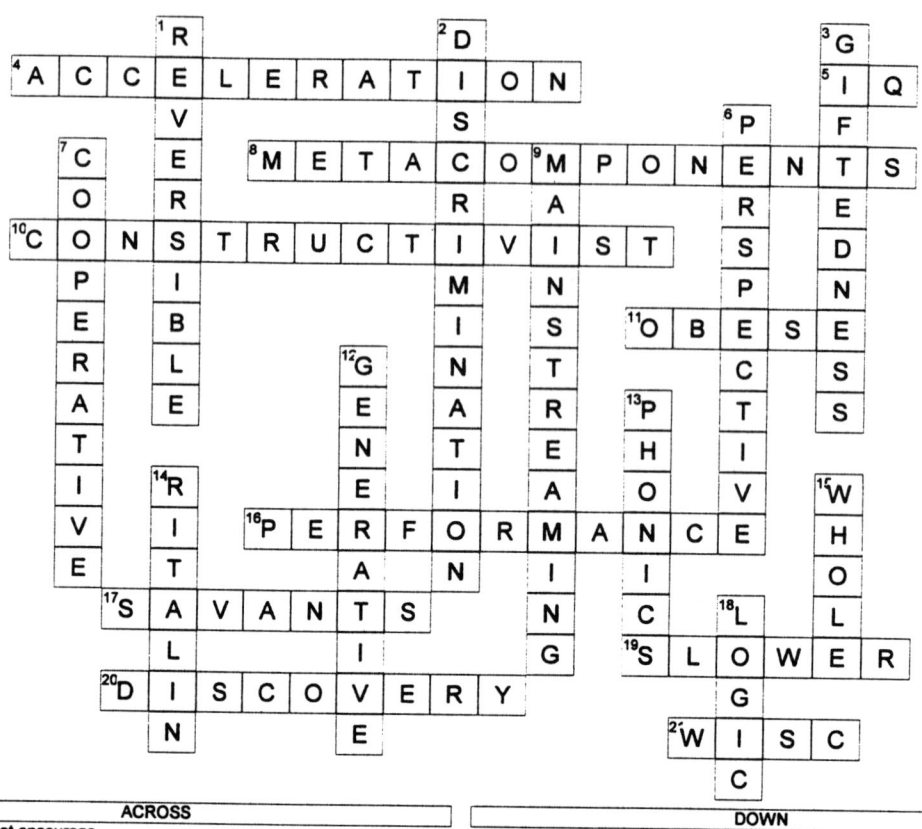

ACROSS
4. Programs that encourage children to move rapidly through coursework
5. Measure of intelligence
8. Component of intelligence that allows for monitoring task performance
10. Theories of learning in which students participate in their own education
11. Weighing more than 20 percent over one's ideal weight
16. Component of intelligence that involves encoding, interpreting, and retrieving info
17. People who show exceptional abilities in one area but are retarded in others
19. Growth rate compared to earlier childhood years
20. Learning where students discover principles for themselves
21. Popular test for measuring children's IQs

DOWN
1. Understanding that actions can be undone
2. Acting in an unfavorable manner toward people because of their group affiliation
3. Children have outstanding abilities and special needs to address those abilities
6. What older children are able to take from another
7. Learning occurs in groups
9. Putting children with special needs in a regular classroom
12. Learning where students are taught methods to integrate new info with pre-existing info
13. Children learn to read translating letters and groups of letters into sounds
14. Popular medication for hyperactive children
15. _____ language assumes that learning to read is natural
18. According to Piaget, school-aged kids can use this

Chapter 10 - Late Childhood

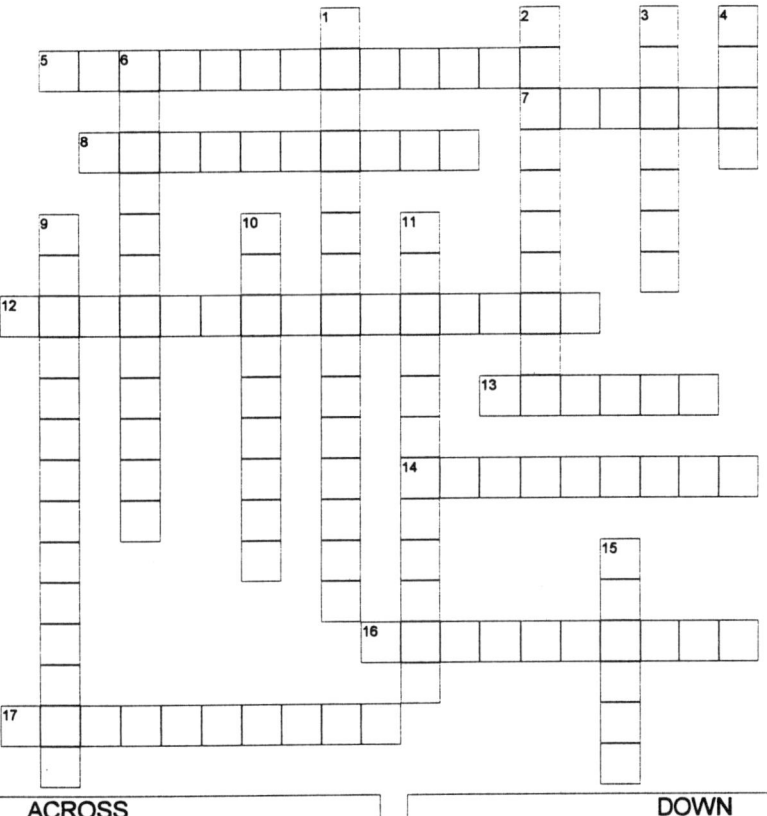

ACROSS

5. Stress that occurs when families move from one culture to another
7. One of the most common phobias of late childhood
8. Pattern of behavior that is aggressive, defiant, irresponsible, or dishonest
12. Moral stage where person is committed to set of principles that go beyond authority figures
13. Influences how much attention teacher gives student
14. Children who are reasonably well liked by peers but lack friends
16. Under the rule of self
17. Serious mental health problem that affects 1 in 6 children

DOWN

1. First level of moral development; morality based on external forces
2. Capacity to bounce back or recover from stressful situations
3. Persistent and irrational fears that significantly affect their social functioning
4. These children are not spoiled, insensitive, or socially awkward
6. Moral level where individuals strive for praise, recognition, and maintaining social order
9. Strategies used to manage or modify the source of a stressful situation
10. Socially competent children know how to manage these effectively
11. Under the rule of others
15. One factor that affects the development of antisocial behavior

Chapter 10 - Late Childhood

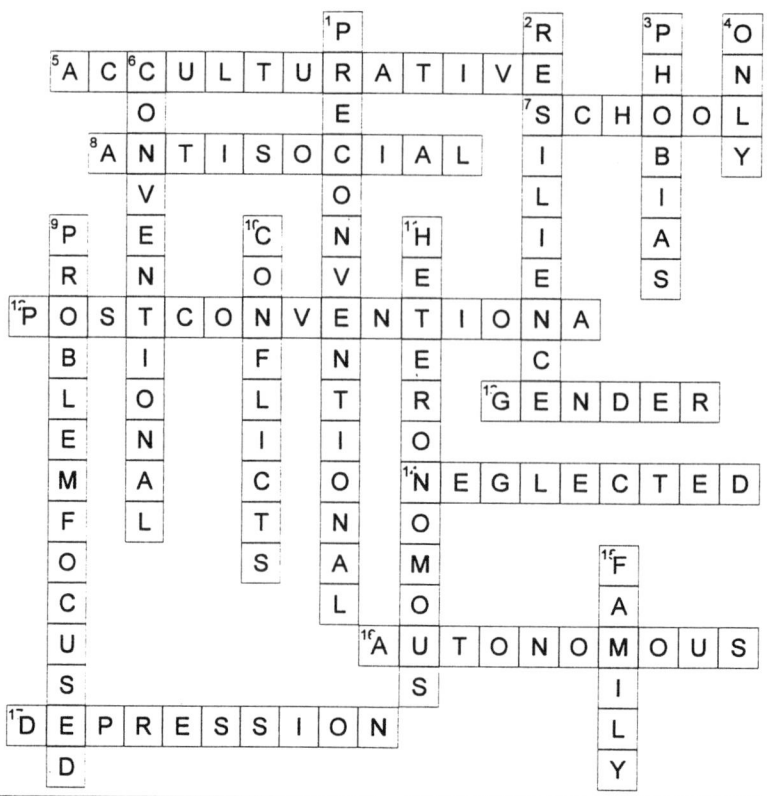

ACROSS

5. Stress that occurs when families move from one culture to another
7. One of the most common phobias of late childhood
8. Pattern of behavior that is aggressive, defiant, irresponsible, or dishonest
12. Moral stage where person is committed to set of principles that go beyond authority figures
13. Influences how much attention teacher gives student
14. Children who are reasonably well liked by peers but lack friends
16. Under the rule of self
17. Serious mental health problem that affects 1 in 6 children

DOWN

1. First level of moral development; morality based on external forces
2. Capacity to bounce back or recover from stressful situations
3. Persistent and irrational fears that significantly affect their social functioning
4. These children are not spoiled, insensitive, or socially awkward
6. Moral level where individuals strive for praise, recognition, and maintaining social order
9. Strategies used to manage or modify the source of a stressful situation
10. Socially competent children know how to manage these effectively
11. Under the rule of others
15. One factor that affects the development of antisocial behavior

Chapter 11 - Early Adolescence

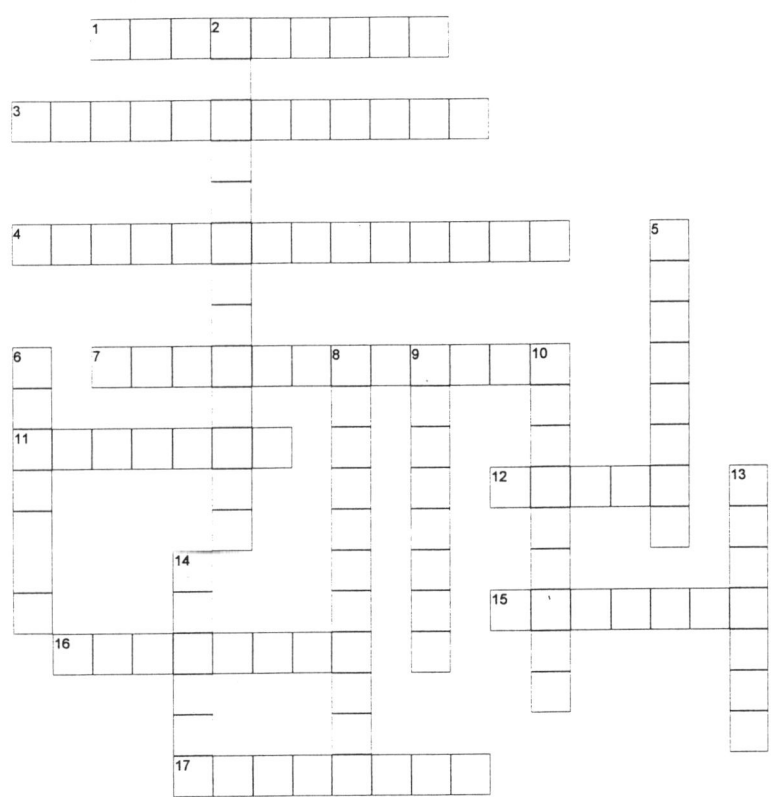

ACROSS

1. To the teen, this audience is very real
3. Menstrual cramps and discomfort
4. Initiations of adolescents
7. Part of the brain involved in onset of puberty
11. Eating disorder characterized by binging and purging
12. Broad term for the younger generation
15. Teens need more of this in their diet
16. "You can't arrest me! I'm under 18!"
17. Rare eating disorder where person eats too little

DOWN

2. Hormones secreted during sleep
5. Onset of the menstrual cycle
6. Developmental milestone when person becomes sexually mature
8. Developmental period between childhood and adulthood
9. Person with formal operational thought can deal with this
10. Sexual characteristics differentiating boys from girls but not involved with reproduction
13. Sexual characteristics related to reproduction
14. Caused by lack of iron

Chapter 11 - Early Adolescence

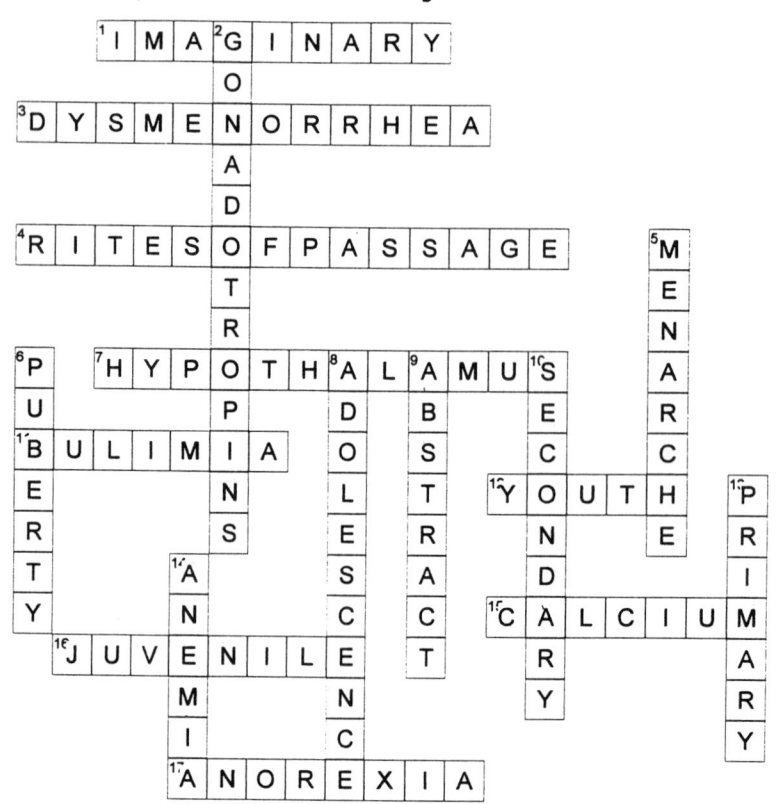

ACROSS

1. To the teen, this audience is very real
3. Menstrual cramps and discomfort
4. Initiations of adolescents
7. Part of the brain involved in onset of puberty
11. Eating disorder characterized by binging and purging
12. Broad term for the younger generation
15. Teens need more of this in their diet
16. "You can't arrest me! I'm under 18!"
17. Rare eating disorder where person eats too little

DOWN

2. Hormones secreted during sleep
5. Onset of the menstrual cycle
6. Developmental milestone when person becomes sexually mature
8. Developmental period between childhood and adulthood
9. Person with formal operational thought can deal with this
10. Sexual characteristics differentiating boys from girls but not involved with reproduction
13. Sexual characteristics related to reproduction
14. Caused by lack of iron

Chapter 12 - Early Adolescence

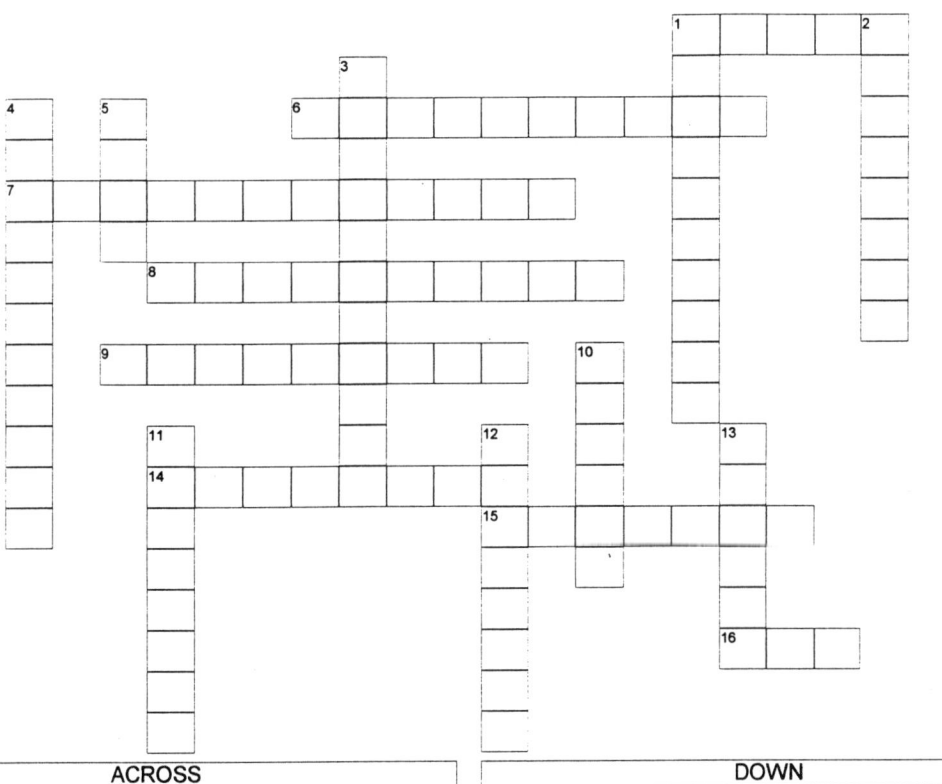

ACROSS

1. Central part of adolescent culture but not necessarily powerful one
6. One of Marcia's essential aspects for identity
7. Parenting behavior more likely to lead to less advanced moral values in adolescents
8. Adolescent identifies with majority and minority culture
9. Identity status in which adolescents experience self-doubt
14. Youths who have greater self-acceptance are identity _____
15. Theorist who coined the term "identity crisis"
16. Generally a sporadic and rare experience for young adolescents

DOWN

1. "When will you be home?"
2. Identity status in which adolescent appears aimless
3. ID status in which adolescent has committed but did not experience crisis
4. Process of considering options
5. Source of status and power for some young people
10. _____ identity that involves behaviors that reflect particular group membership
11. Individual lives within majority culture but feels alienated
12. One's sense of who one is and where one is going
13. Groups defined by members' activities and social standing

Chapter 12 - Early Adolescence

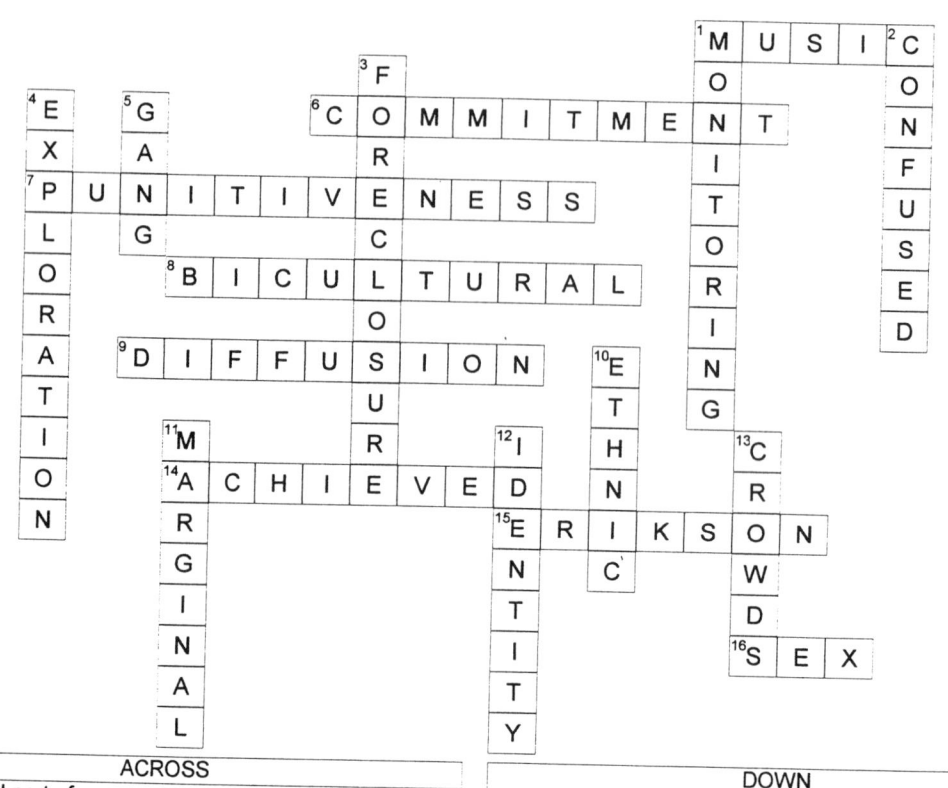

ACROSS

1. Central part of adolescent culture but not necessarily powerful one
6. One of Marcia's essential aspects for identity
7. Parenting behavior more likely to lead to less advanced moral values in adolescents
8. Adolescent identifies with majority and minority culture
9. Identity status in which adolescents experience self-doubt
14. Youths who have greater self-acceptance are identity _____
15. Theorist who coined the term "identity crisis"
16. Generally a sporadic and rare experience for young adolescents

DOWN

1. "When will you be home?"
2. Identity status in which adolescent appears aimless
3. ID status in which adolescent has committed but did not experience crisis
4. Process of considering options
5. Source of status and power for some young people
10. _____ identity that involves behaviors that reflect particular group membership
11. Individual lives within majority culture but feels alienated
12. One's sense of who one is and where one is going
13. Groups defined by members' activities and social standing

Chapter 13 - Late Adolescence

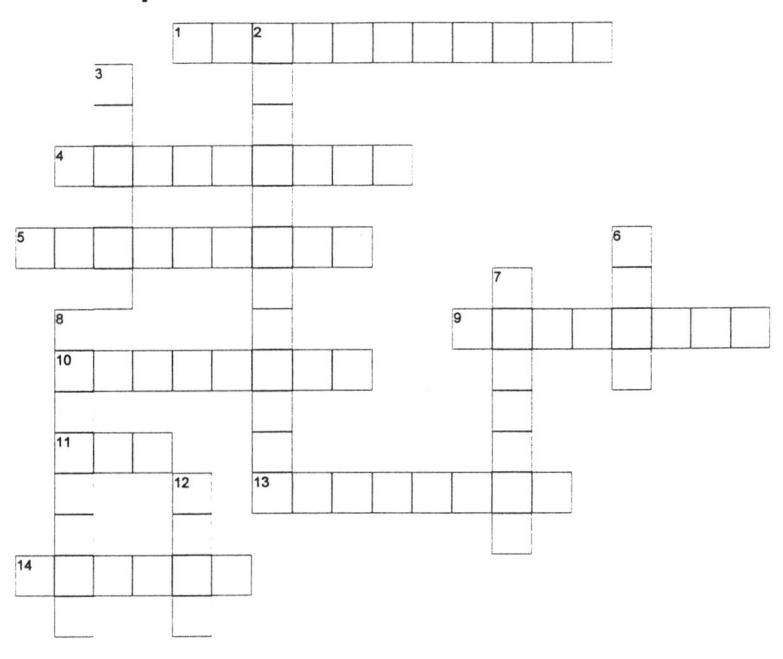

ACROSS

1. Part of physical fitness; girls have more
4. The leading cause of death among adolescents
5. Some educators believe this type of education should be taught in schools
9. Adolescents can think about this topic now (and vote)
10. Teens (and couch potatoes) seem to lack this
11. Disease most common during adolescence
13. Part of physical fitness; boys have more
14. Factor that influences boys' and girls' academic achievement

DOWN

2. These should be high if teachers want high academic achievement
3. Type of cognition involving thinking about people
6. Barbie finds this topic hard
7. Factor involved in dropping out of school
8. Domain of social knowledge related to issues of personal preference and taste
12. Gender more likely to be homicide or accident victim

Chapter 13 - Late Adolescence

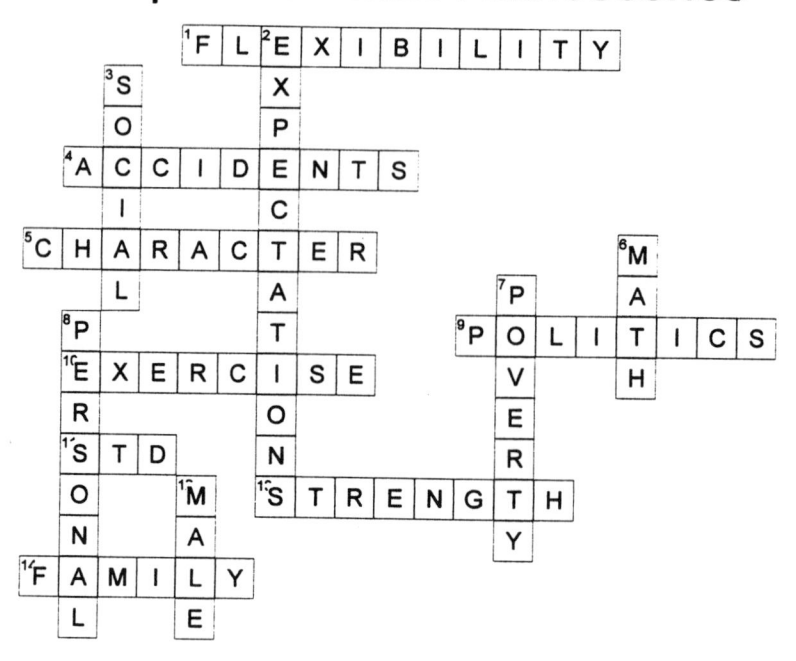

```
          ¹F  L  ²E  X  I  B  I  L  I  T  Y
              ³S      X
              O       P
          ⁴A  C  C  I  D  E  N  T  S
              I       C
          ⁵C  H  A  R  A  C  T  E  R           ⁶M
              L       A           ⁷P           A
          ⁸P          T           ⁹P  O  L  I  T  I  C  S
          ¹⁰E  X  E  R  C  I  S  E  V           H
              R       O           E
              ¹¹S  T  D   N           R
              O       ¹²M  ¹³S  T  R  E  N  G  T  H
              N       A           Y
          ¹⁴F  A  M  I  L  Y
              L       E
```

ACROSS
1. Part of physical fitness; girls have more
4. The leading cause of death among adolescents
5. Some educators believe this type of education should be taught in schools
9. Adolescents can think about this topic now (and vote)
10. Teens (and couch potatoes) seem to lack this
11. Disease most common during adolescence
13. Part of physical fitness; boys have more
14. Factor that influences boys' and girls' academic achievement

DOWN
2. These should be high if teachers want high academic achievement
3. Type of cognition involving thinking about people
6. Barbie finds this topic hard
7. Factor involved in dropping out of school
8. Domain of social knowledge related to issues of personal preference and taste
12. Gender more likely to be homicide or accident victim

Chapter 14 - Late Adolescence

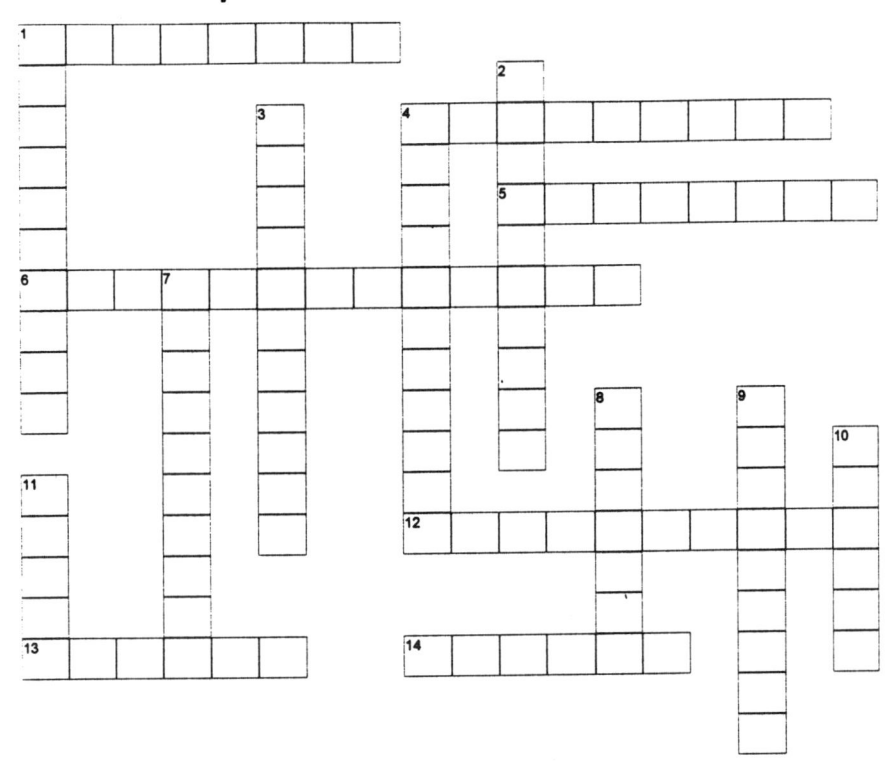

ACROSS

1. Pregnant teens rarely consider this
4. Babies born to teen mothers are more likely to be this
5. The ability to govern oneself and make independent decisions
6. Type of problem where individuals "act out" against society
12. Type of relationship with parents that protects adolescents when stressed
13. Type of offense only adolescents can do
14. One standard for boys and one for girls

DOWN

1. Form of contraception advocated for sex education
2. Type of autonomy where one has the capacity to make one's own decisions
3. Legal term for antisocial acts committed by juveniles
4. Most adolescents are not this
7. Has negative outcomes if over 20 hours per week
8. Most commonly used and abused drug
9. Use of this drug has increased among teens
10. Percent of adolescents with adjustment problems
11. Many adolescents take these

Chapter 14 - Late Adolescence

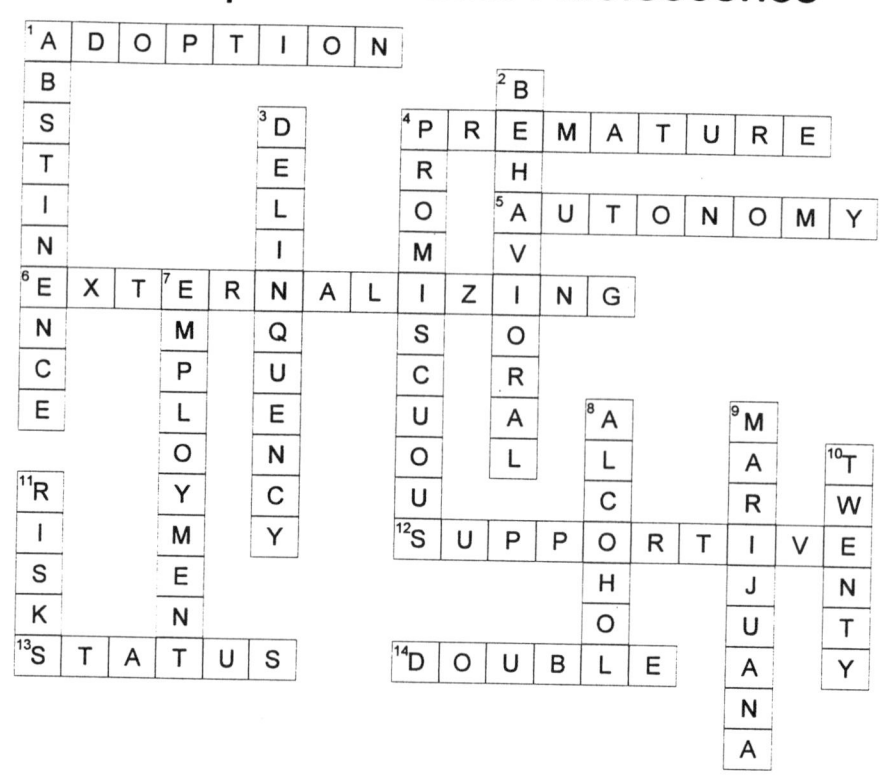

294 Study Guide for Exploring Child Development

ACROSS
1. Pregnant teens rarely consider this
4. Babies born to teen mothers are more likely to be this
5. The ability to govern oneself and make independent decisions
6. Type of problem where individuals "act out" against society
12. Type of relationship with parents that protects adolescents when stressed
13. Type of offense only adolescents can do
14. One standard for boys and one for girls

DOWN
1. Form of contraception advocated for sex education
2. Type of autonomy where one has the capacity to make one's own decisions
3. Legal term for antisocial acts committed by juveniles
4. Most adolescents are not this
7. Has negative outcomes if over 20 hours per week
8. Most commonly used and abused drug
9. Use of this drug has increased among teens
10. Percent of adolescents with adjustment problems
11. Many adolescents take these

Across answers: 1. ADOPTION, 4. PREMATURE, 5. AUTONOMY, 6. EXTERNALIZING, 12. SUPPORTIVE, 13. STATUS, 14. DOUBLE

Down answers: 1. ABSTINENCE, 2. BEHAVIORAL, 3. DELINQUENCY, 4. PROMISCUOUS, 7. EMPLOYMENT, 8. ALCOHOL, 9. MARIJUANA, 10. TWENTY, 11. RISKS

Appendix 2

Careers in Child Development

Careers in Child Development

It has been said that no person has ever stood so tall as when he or she stooped to help a child. Wonderful opportunities exist for anyone interested in working with children and thus are interested in shaping the future. Those people who major in child development will find that they have chosen a field that can be exciting, fun, challenging, interesting, gratifying, heart rending, and frustrating all at once. They also will discover that their knowledge will not only help them in their profession, but will be especially valuable in raising their own children well – probably the most important and satisfying job in the world.

The field of child development offers a wide array of job opportunities, from government employment to self-employment. Educational requirements to work with children also vary, from two-year degrees to graduate and professional degrees. Your opportunities in working with or for children are limited only by your own imagination. This, of course, is easy for me to say because I have been working with children for twenty-five years and have the benefit of hindsight. For those of you who are just starting out or even re-entering the job market, you may be confused about what exactly can be done with a background in child development. Perhaps the following information will assist you in finding "what you want to be when you grow up." Of course, the suggestions are not meant to be all-inclusive, but they may help point you in the right direction. Good luck in your future career!

High School Degree to Associate's Degree

Many career opportunities involving children are available to people with a high school diploma or two-year post-high school degree. These jobs include:

- Day care worker
- Teacher's Aide
- Nurse's Aide on a pediatric unit or in a pediatrician's office
- Camp counselor
- Bus driver
- YMCA/Boy's and Girl's Club Worker
- Group home worker
- Lifeguard and swim instructor
- Respite Care Worker
- Nanny
- After-School Care Program Counselor
- Police Officer in schools/youth programs
- Speech/Language Aide

Bachelor's Degree

As you probably know, each year of education offers a relative increase in salary and potential salary. A four-year degree will provide increased flexibility in terms of what you can do in the area of child development. Some positions may involve working with children directly (such as a teacher), while other positions may be related to children but not involve direct contact (such as toy designer or daycare lobbyist). Students who want to work right out of college (as opposed to going to graduate school) should consider taking an internship if available at their school. Internships can provide valuable on-the-job experience and many internship placements lead to direct hiring. In addition, consider doing volunteer work in an area of interest. This, too, leads to work experience and jobs. Positions often requiring a bachelor's degree include:

- Teacher
- Juvenile Probation Officer
- Group Home Supervisor
- Youth Program Coordinator (e.g., YMCA)
- Parent Educator
- County Extension Specialist
- Crisis Nursery Caregiver or Administrator
- Child Life Specialist
- Legislative Researcher
- Lobbyist
- Women's Shelter Administrator
- City or State Outreach Worker
- Consumer Researcher
- Learning Game Designer
- Case Manager for Child Protective Services
- Case Manager for Developmental Disabilities
- Recreation Specialist for Parks and Recreation
- Parent Interventionist
- Substance Abuse/Crisis Counselor
- Preschool Supervisor or Administrator
- Preschool Evaluator
- Physical/Occupational/Speech Therapy Assistant
- Legislative Aide
- Toy Designer (or copy writer)
- After-School Program Specialist
- Homeless Shelter Administrator
- Survey Researcher
- Advertiser for Children's Products

Graduate or Professional Degree

Many child development occupations require advanced education. These positions are often the highest paid. Students considering advanced degrees must make sure that they maintain a fairly high grade point average and take rigorous coursework that is valued by graduate programs. For example, students going to graduate school should consider taking a course in research practicum and a course in statistics. If you followed the path of many students and your grade point average for your first two years is not exactly "stellar," don't despair. Graduate schools are more likely to weigh your academic record for the last two years (so make sure you do your best during your last four semesters), along with letters of recommendation, volunteer experience, and Graduate Record Exam scores. Occupations requiring graduate or professional degrees include:

Marriage and Family Therapist	Family Law Attorney
Family Court Mediator	Pediatrician/Pediatric Specialist
University/College Professor	Researcher in Child Development
Child Psychologist	Speech and Language Pathologist
Pediatric Audiologist	Optometrist
Physical or Occupational Therapist	Pediatric Nurse
Pedodontist (dentist)	Business Manager

Miscellaneous Career Opportunities

Finally, don't forget specialized careers and self-employment. People have been very successful in areas such as magic shows, children's party planning, children's books, children's songs, swim schools, children's theater, and designing and marketing their own children's products. If you are good at something and see a need in your community, you might be the one to fill it!

The Internet offers a variety of websites dedicated to career opportunities and exploration. To get started, try visiting the following sites:

http://www.review.com	Princeton Review's Guide to Your Career
http://campus.monster.com	Job search, resources, Q&A about jobs, resumes, etc.

NOTES

NOTES

NOTES

NOTES

NOTES

NOTES

NOTES

NOTES

NOTES

NOTES

NOTES

NOTES

NOTES